MOVING PAST
MARRIAGE

MOVING PAST MARRIAGE

Why We Should Ditch Marital Privilege, End Relationship-Status Discrimination, and Embrace Non-marital History

JACLYN GELLER, PhD

CLEiS
PRESS

Published in the United States by Cleis Press, an imprint of Start Midnight, LLC, 221 River Street, Ninth Floor, Hoboken, New Jersey 07030.

Printed in the United States
Cover design: Jennifer Do
Cover image: Shutterstock
Text design: Frank Wiedemann

First Edition.
10 9 8 7 6 5 4 3 2 1

Trade paper ISBN: 978-1-62778-246-3
E-book ISBN: 978-1-62778-247-0

TABLE OF CONTENTS

For Alvin Geller,
who is never afraid to ask the obvious question,
and for Marcia Geller,
who believes that I can answer it.

Also, for nonmarital people everywhere,
who are making history as they live their lives.

Author's Note

People from Chapters 5 and 6 whose stories circulate in the public domain are identified by their real names. To protect others I have changed their monikers and the places where they grew up. Altered locales resemble original ones, with, for example, one mid-Atlantic city replacing another. Since divorce law varies by state, I do not change the states where interviewees terminated marriages or amounts of money demanded from those I call post-marital extortion victims. Ages and religions remain unchanged. The ages I mention are from the time of the interviews. Occupations have been altered. Changed professions are comparable to actual ones. Each narrative comes from a real interview with an actual person. There are no composite portraits.

Questioning language and trying to change it is an attempt to revise assumptions and ideals. Accordingly, the Glossary that follows Chapter 8 contains terms that challenge matrimony as a centering norm and the coupled nuclear family as superlatively timeless. Definitions are my own unless indicated. I use these terms throughout and invite readers to add their own words.

1

Through the Looking Glass:

Nonmarital Planning in a Marriage-centric World

---

*"The most powerful ideas are those which
are taken for granted."*

—DORIS LESSING,
*UNDER MY SKIN: VOLUME ONE OF
MY AUTOBIOGRAPHY, TO 1949*

I magine being a professor who's just earned tenure. You worked toward this goal for years, subsisting on abysmal wages while completing graduate coursework followed by doctoral examinations. Then came the real labor: researching and writing a 450-page dissertation. It was arduous, but eight years of weekends camped at various New York City libraries paid off. A doctorate in English Literature qualified you for the academic job market. A university in Connecticut made an offer; you accepted, relocated, and started up the next mountain: a six-year climb toward tenure. This meant publishing, serving on university committees, and proving yourself in the classroom. Again, diligence paid off, and you achieved tenure and promotion to the rank of associate professor.

This happened to me. The raise was modest, and the job remained demanding, but my satisfaction was palpable. Finally, I had a professional foothold and could stop thinking in twelve-month increments, from contract renewal to contract renewal. When the congratulatory phone calls stopped, reality began sinking in. I realized it was time to consider the future in a new way, putting financial plans in place for myself and my loved ones. Toward this end, I assumed there were choices. I was correct. But I learned that in the United States the central, and sometimes sole way to protect oneself and one's family involves marriage.

Looking down the road, I factored in Social Security. I anticipated one day receiving monies from a system into which I had long paid. Every paycheck I had ever earned withheld for Social Security. Hence, I should select a beneficiary. I decided on my sister. Incessant conversation, medical tests we'd seen each other through, and verbal pacts of commitment made her the right choice. Years of shared news—good, bad, irrelevant—had helped us both face the slings and arrows of outrageous fortune.

An hour of research derailed my plan. I learned that as a never-married professional, I can't leave Social Security benefits to a loved one. The support Frances and I give each other goes unrecognized in a culture that distinguishes sharply between marriages and all other partnerships. Because our bond does not fit the connubial model, American law treats us as strangers to one another.

It got worse: I discovered that my payments go back into the system. My situation is true of all never-married American wage earners; when they die, monies paid for their whole working lives are absorbed into Social Security's budget. So, whether they want to or not, all payers subsidize wedlock. If he married three times, a deceased worker's widow and both divorced spouses would get 100 percent of the sum he received while alive. None would have to demonstrate need or a history of financial dependence within the marriages. None would have had to pay anything toward Social Security. For a spouse, one year of matrimony is all it takes; ten years are required of an ex-spouse.[1]

Frances and I had been "together" for over ten years: no matter, but Social Security follows a "nonmarital relationships don't count" rubric. This, combined with a "matrimony is best for everyone, always" assumption, encourages Americans to wed, regardless of their beliefs. Since length of marriage determines one's ability to collect, the program goads each adult—happy or unhappy—to stay married.

Of course, a crux federal program that rewards only one relationship implicitly diminishes other styles of pair bonding that increase—no pun intended—social security. Case in point: Frances and I remain a constant in each other's lives. If I predecease her, a safety net would increase her peace of mind. It might encourage her to take chances and expand her work as a property manager. (Indeed, a nonmarital Social Security option would foster small entrepreneurship by giving millions of Americans such protection.) Social Security's lump-sum death imbursement could help her give me a proper funeral. All people in committed relationships deserve the opportunity to bury their loved ones respectfully, but Social Security reserves this benefit for spouses. This exclusion struck me as particularly disgraceful. We may not be married to each other, but neither Frances nor I would feel comfortable hurling the other's remains into a dumpster.

Social Security is a third-party benefit. Such entitlements don't come from a person but another entity such as the state or an employer. Since the federal government is Social Security's third party, I wondered how a national program could be so partial. If Social Security treated a particular ethnic or racial group preferentially, newspapers would publish exposés. Protestors would march; lawsuits would proliferate. But marriage-centric policies evoke little, if any, outrage.

A piece of related news caught my eye: actress Melanie Griffith's divorce from actor Antonio Banderas after eighteen years together. According to several magazines stacked in Central Connecticut University's Burritt Library reference area, Griffith and Banderas's union ended with a court mandate that he pay $65,000 per month in alimony.

What could explain this jaw-dropping amount? As I had heard it explained, alimony is compensatory. Spouses—so the rationale goes—deserve recompense for years when they put careers on hold to do matrimonial things. Griffith worked throughout her marriage to Banderas, appearing in films like Adrian Lynne's 1997 *Lolita*, Larry Clark's 1998 *Another Day in Paradise*, Woody Allen's *Celebrity* (made that same year), and Rob Minkoff's 2002 *Stuart Little 2*. The scion of actors, Griffith grew up in Acton, California on a 200-acre ranch. After enjoying a lifestyle undreamt of by most Americans, she launched her career in the late 1960s. Ironically, it peaked with Mike Nichols's 1988 film, *Working Girl*, the story of scrappy secretary Tess McGill, a Wall Street outsider who breaks into investment banking. Griffith, by contrast, is a Hollywood insider with an acting income buttressed by valuable assets. She split with Banderas proceeds from their Hancock Park, California estate ($15.9 million) and retains sole ownership of an Aspen, Colorado home. Her art collection includes an original Pablo Picasso work, "The Painter and His Model."[2] Clearly, no one needs to organize a bake sale for her.

Heading home, I thought of various gay celebrities fêting themselves with weddings: musician Elton John and filmmaker David Furnish, who married at Guildhall, Windsor, England in 2005; comedienne Ellen and actress Portia DeGeneres, who took 2008 vows in Los Angeles. I imagined these new matrimonial standard-bearers, years down the road, scanning divorce papers as they stammered, "But . . . no one told us about this part!"

Judith Plaskow, professor emeritus of religious studies at Manhattan College, might have warned them. In 2004, she and Smith College government professor Martha Ackelsberg, issued a public statement that they would not wed: "Were we to marry, we would be contributing to the perpetuation of a norm of coupledness . . . At this moment, when there is so much focus on celebrating the right to marry, we want to hold up a vision of a society in which basic rights are not tied to marriage, and in which there are many ways to organize one's intimate life."[3]

I had thanked Plaskow via email for taking such a morally coherent stance. Questioning wedlock—straight or gay—takes courage in a nation largely devoted to the marriage principle. Her reply caught me off guard; while their views hadn't changed, she and Ackelsberg were considering matrimony: "Unfortunately, there's only one way around the estate tax," she wrote ruefully.[4]

Estate tax? Recalling Plaskow's note, I decided to investigate.

My accountant, Mario, shared more disturbing information. Wedlock, he explained, is American inheritance's litmus test. In cases of intestacy, a spouse automatically receives all assets. Relationship length is irrelevant. At that point I had been with my boyfriend for four years. A man who married someone he barely knew in Las Vegas would have enjoyed stronger protections than Jim did if I had no will. This remains true. In most states—Georgia is an exception—disinheriting spouses who have not waived their rights with prenuptial agreements is illegal. Community property states consider everything accumulated during a marriage as belonging to both parties.

These laws aim to keep married people's focus exclusive. They can prevent a divorcing Californian from gifting cherished possessions to loved ones. Connecticut exempts husbands and wives from tariffs otherwise due when assets transfer from one person to another. Bequeathing one's residence to an unmarried partner is a "taxable event," so selling can be the only option for those in high-income brackets. "In estate tax the first two million dollars are tax-free," Mario explained. "After that, it changes. The next 1.6 million garners a 7.2 percent tax: that's just over $115,000. It goes up from there."

Hanging up the phone, I scrutinized my 1,600-square-foot house, which had been advertised with the phrase, "Needs TLC" After spending years in tiny apartments, refurbishing this Colonial had been a wonderful adventure. Jim insulated the attic, upgraded a flagging electrical system, and set up our Internet. Beneficiary of the house, he lives with me part-time—a setup common among academics, who require ample privacy to read and write.

I knew that the place would never appreciate to anything near two million dollars. So, my untimely demise would not produce a bill so steep that after losing me, Jim would also part with our home. But pricey estates are common in Connecticut. Many properties are worth at least two million dollars. If their occupants cannot write a $115,000 check, they will lose their homes when a co-owner dies. It can take less than a death for the state's approximately 5,500 farmers. Farming has become a growth field in Connecticut, especially among young people aware of the premium on organic food and eager to own land despite high real estate prices.[5] They qualify for "family farm" loans if applicants are linked by blood or marriage. Nonmarital farmers working cooperatively, who need money to sustain operations or handle emergencies, don't meet governmental criteria. They can lose property because of bad weather, broken equipment, or any shock that soil is heir to. Again, the law capriciously protects certain people—what does marriage have to do with farming?—and encourages everyone to follow a single model.[6]

"Curiouser and curiouser," Lewis Carroll's Alice says after tasting cake that elongates her neck. Like the naïf from *Alice's Adventures in Wonderland*, I felt as though I'd gone down a rabbit hole into someplace bizarre yet familiar. Like the world of *Through the Looking-Glass, and What Alice Found There*, this realm was laid out as a chess board, but promotion rested on betrothal rather than movement to the eighth row. A morning of Googling revealed data on nearby states. Massachusetts has a lower tax threshold than Connecticut: one million dollars. Danvers-based attorney David E. Peterson recommended splitting estates with assets of $1.5 million and opening two revocable trusts to keep each potential survivor under the million-dollar mark. This would prevent a $64,000 penalty: "Voila, no estate tax!"[7] No estate tax for married people, that is.

I had known that America incentivizes marriage. Just how powerfully it does so was coming into focus. This issue had not spurred my planning-for-the-future initiative. I set out to overcome a longstanding fear of money. Like many academics, I spent years without enough for essentials. This leaves vestigial anxiety. The mere prospect of getting organized and setting financial goals generates queasiness. In my effort to stop functioning like a nervous graduate student, I was discovering just how powerful the American marriage system was.

An investment advisor from my bank suggested opening a traditional IRA as an income shelter, explaining that I would get a deduction on my contributions, and taxes on the account's income would be deferred. I asked about opening an IRA for myself and one for Jim and learned that I couldn't. In spousal IRAs, one partner contributes to a tax-deferred retirement account. But, as its name suggests, this option is tailored to marrieds. Surely there were exceptions, I prodded. What if an unwed person is sick, unemployed . . . taking time from work to care for a dependent child or senior? No; spousal IRAs made no exceptions.

I could name Jim as a beneficiary, but even here, marital exceptionalism prevailed. Spouses who tap into an IRA early don't pay the 10 percent tax imposed on unwed people (if the expenses exceed the account-holder's adjusted gross income by 7.5 percent). Even a financially unsophisticated academic could grasp the ramifications; while it's generally unwise to draw on an IRA prematurely, never-married Americans who have no choice lose 10 percent of their withdrawals.[8]

I had entered the orbit of professionals paid to evaluate life's practical angles. They tend to operate in the here and now, withholding judgement and navigating a realm that simply does its business. Part of that business is legally gaming the tax system. Toward this end, financial advisors dispense advice that normalizes marital privilege. Matrimonial superiority is treated as an incontrovertible fact. Clients get the message. The message is passed on.

"Way leads onto way," Robert Frost wrote in his lyric, "The Road Not Taken."[9] I could see how one marriage-based benefit led to the next . . . and to the subsidy after that. All flowed from the belief that once married, spouses lose their separate identities. Each newlywed couple becomes a monad; accordingly, what belongs to one belongs to the other. A husband's health insurance must include his wife. Her employment at a college extends to her husband.

I'd knocked around universities long enough to observe the practice of spousal hiring, which gives married job candidates preferential treatment. Spouses are routinely interviewed for preexisting positions and job lines opened for people married to important scholars. In 1977 Harvard offered the titanic cognitive scientist, Amos Tversky, a tenured professorship. His biographer explains that "it took them a few weeks to throw in an assistant professorship for Barbara [Tversky]."[10] The phrase "to throw in" makes one of the world's most coveted academic jobs sound like a complimentary dessert given by a restaurant manager. In 1978 the Tverskys landed at Stanford University, whose psychology department accommodated them both. In 2014 Dartmouth appointed Carolyn Dever to a dual position: Professor of English and University Provost. "Dever will be joined in Hanover by her husband, Paul Young, who will be a professor of film and media studies at Dartmouth," the press release reads.[11]

The late Tversky built a career debunking assumptions: showing how people oblivious to their biases follow instinct with unwarranted optimism. Carolyn Dever studies Victorian fiction, focusing on representations of motherhood. Such policers of ideology become oddly complacent when receiving matrimonial benefits. I had yet to hear a professor whose wife found work at his home institution ask why their marriage positively influenced hiring, when a candidate's maleness or heterosexuality could not. I'd never heard a married academic question her husband's free access to university gyms, while nonmarital partners paid fees.

College orientations make strenuous efforts at sensitivity. I am regularly invited to events that encourage academics to unearth buried prejudice. Facilitators deploy now familiar terms: "otherness," "shaming," and what English professor Robert Boyers considers an overused noun: "privilege."[12] (Boyers notes that while no one could deny various forms of social advantage, to occasionally berate oneself for being privileged while making demonstrations of camaraderie with less privileged groups requires minimal emotional engagement.)[13] In my experience, academic professional development has expanded to include the words "diversity," "equity," and "inclusiveness." Yet it does not include diverse beliefs about family, relationship equity, or the inclusion of nonmarital people in benefit-conferring programs. Marriage as a privileging category and relationship-status discrimination are largely ignored. One must wonder why seminars designed to highlight power imbalances don't question an institution that unequally distributes hundreds of benefits. Perhaps the subject of relationship-status discrimination would disrupt proceedings by pushing academics to discuss how *they* live and which privileges *they* embrace, replacing perfunctory self-flagellation with dialogue.

A gift from our dean, Maike Ingrid Philipsen's book, *Challenges of the Faculty Career for Women: Success and Sacrifice*, had sat on my shelf for two years. I opened it, hoping to find something on women's concerns about marriage-centric hiring. Instead, I found a plea to give marrieds special treatment. Discussing an actual school assigned the pseudonym, "Flagship University," Philipsen describes a real couple. "Flagship" hired the wife for a permanent teaching job and generously gave the husband a postdoctoral fellowship. According to a (married) colleague, with whom the (married) author concurs, this was injurious: candidates married to people tracked for tenure should be foisted on departments: "In Dr. Ingerson-Noll's opinion, the university should . . . offer the spouse a teaching appointment . . . His research may not be completely what the department wants to do but 'it is more important to keep people happy than try to be very precise about what kind of science you want to have.'"[14] *More important for a university to "keep people happy" than set research standards?* I reread the sentence twice before grasping its claim: in academia, cheerfulness should trump intellectual rigor, but only where spouses are concerned. Philipsen advocates bending rules for married faculty—not unwed or never-married professors. She ignores academics who wish to put forth friends, lovers, or other long-term partners for consideration in package hiring deals. One must conclude that in her view, married scholars' feelings matter, and nonmarital professors' emotions don't.

Unfortunately, Philipsen's blind spot is common. Universities' overall message to students is, "repudiate bigotry and denounce nepotism—except for bigotry against the unwed and matrimonial nepotism. They're okay." Graduate and undergraduate students witness yet another example of special efforts on behalf of the married household made by those content to let other families fend for themselves. These reinforce larger cultural messages about marital exceptionalism.

Like Frost's narrator, I found myself wandering extemporaneously. Having entered marital privilege's deep undergrowth, I was stumbling on inequity after inequity, accumulating information faster than I could absorb its outrageousness. Researching real estate taxes in New York, where I grew up, I learned that the first $2,062,500 of an estate are nontaxable. After that, unwed residents pay. New York City swells with denizens who arrange their lives nonmaritally. In 2012 the *New York Times* featured three men and two women who shared an apartment "in the slowly gentrifying section of Bushwick, Brooklyn." This was no hodgepodge of tenants splitting bills until they found spouses. It was a friendship-based household consisting of "two architectural designers, two fashion designers, and one advertising executive—all in their twenties," who spruced up a 2,700-square-foot loft and agreed to live together for ten years.[15] Marriage fundamentalists denounce such setups as newfangled. Actually, friend-centered homes have a long history and support from thinkers like Aristotle (384–322 BCE), one of western philosophy's two most influential figures: "Those who welcome each other but do not live together would seem to have goodwill rather than friendship. For nothing is as proper to friends as living together."[16]

My homeowner's real estate appetite whetted, I checked

announcements of Bushwick open houses. A four-story town-house on Bleecker Street, "in the heart of trendy and upcoming Bushwick," had an asking price of $1,300,000. A similar Wilson Avenue property was listed at $2 million and a four-story Greene Street townhome at $3 million. Given the pace at which New York City real estate appreciates, a $2,062,500 exemption did not seem monumental. The discrepancy in treatment between married and unmarried New Yorkers looked punitive. Throughout neighbor-hoods like Bushwick, adults committing to each other in ways that flout marital norms were being penalized.

Philosopher Carrie Jenkins notes that the married family receives "the fullest and easiest access to social and legal benefits": it remains the model "we must choose to minimize the risk of potentially devastating social stigma and rejection."[17] Indeed, the notion that wedlock renders people special yokes to beliefs that spouses cannot lose their entitlements so easily. Singer Madonna's 2008 divorce from filmmaker Guy Ritchie, for example, entailed a $92 million settlement.[18] This high-profile case raises questions about spousal support. Many people who consider marriage civi-cally beneficial believe that those who stray must pay. Others less enamored of wedlock still tut-tut, arguing that lesser-earning spouses deserve compensation for abridged careers. (Ritchie slaving over a hot stove seems unlikely, but who knows?)

These claims have a wholesome sound. But they assume that marriage represents a singular form of caregiving. If curtailing one's career to care for a dependent (or dependents) justifies support, many people should qualify. Anyone who sustains a needy, injured, or aging companion over time ought to meet the criteria. When sociologist Ursula Henz asked interviewees, "Do you currently or have you ever regularly looked after someone, for at least three months, who is sick, disabled, or elderly?" more unmarried than married respondents said yes.[19] They include

London-based writer Kate Mulvey. "I moved into my parents' spare room in 2010—to help Dad when my late mother was diagnosed with dementia," she wrote in 2015. Mulvey quickly became the default caregiver for an elderly, grief-struck widower. "I just hope that one day my [married] sisters will see that a less-than-conventional life like mine is no less important than theirs," she reflects.[20] Everyone who makes such sacrifices should receive compensation, or no one should.

Mulvey's unwed friends have been her main support. This validates sociologists' Naomi R. Gerstel and Natalia Sarkisian's research on time allotment. Factoring in sex, resources, and scheduling demands, they found that marriage-free people devote more hours to communal exchanges than their wedded counterparts do. Gerstel and Sarkisian report that spouseless people socialize more. Unmarrieds come out ahead in helping friends and neighbors as well as giving more intergenerational assistance.[21] Apparently matrimony's formula for romantic oneness, according to which spouses have unrivaled claims on each other, does not benefit the public weal. Using sociologist Lewis A. Coser's definition, marriage is a "greedy" institution. Coser coined this term for social arrangements that make "total claims . . . and . . . attempt to encompass within their circle the whole personality."[22]

Yet marriage receives massive backing, including lavish communal celebrations that generate income for cadres of professionals. Jewelers, wedding consultants, event planners, gown designers, caterers, cake stylists, florists, photographers, dance instructors, and bridal beauticians benefit from our nation's addiction to romance with all the trappings. The American nuptial industry generates between $83 billion and $161 billion per year.[23] (The latter figure, from media company Condé Nast's bridal division, includes honeymoons and gifts heaped on couples through registries.) The *Huffington Report* appraises the global wedding business at $300 billion per annum.[24] Tax advantages are just one kind of bait offered would-be spouses with a promise: conform to the dominant conjugal model, and rewards will follow.

Why not conform? People do it every day. I recalled for myself reasons I had often shared aloud:

Marriage violates the ideal of governmental neutrality. A government that incentivizes one lifestyle with over 1,000 benefits penalizes other ways of living.

Having been blessed with several life partners, it seems wrong to elevate one relationship above all others. This does not mean obliterating every distinction between friendship and amorous relations. It means acknowledging that when genuine, both are powerful and life structuring. They should be placed on more equal footing. This is especially true since wedlock cannot be separated from the practical benefits it confers. Friendship is comparatively disinterested, which made it the relationship nonpareil for classical thinkers.[25] Today, philosopher Elizabeth Brake observes that "Friendship is perhaps a purer example than marriage of a relationship for its own sake, as it has no institutional form or associated enterprise."[26]

Matrimony has a blood-soaked history that originates in the state (Mesopotamia) owning each couple and the husband owning each wife's reproductive and sexual functions. The 1750 BCE Hammurabi Code and the Middle Assyrian Law Codes of the fifteenth through the eleventh centuries BCE sanctioned husbands' control of marital assets, including women's bodies. No misogynistic cabal shaped these policies. As they collaborated in developing early agricultural societies, men and women together produced patriarchal law.[27] (Female collusion is probably best understood in terms of women's separation from each other by categories of sexual respectability, with propriety granted wives.) Beginning in the Bronze Age, western law treated various forms of nonmarital sex as criminal. I cannot honor this legacy.

When bad times come, some people stay and others don't, regardless of what has been promised. Marriage entails especially problematic oaths. Conventionally, spouses pledge to love, honor, and cherish each other. These vows are unenforceable. How can a judge decide whether one person has been adequately honored? I could not keep a straight face if someone complained that I wasn't cherishing him enough.

Institutionalizing eroticism appears dubious at best. I believe that sex is a private activity, which should not be licensed. And I am not clairvoyant. I hope I will always love my boyfriend but cannot know that I will. The "commitment" lauded by marriage advocates comes into play if attraction ceases and affection evaporates; only a promise remains. This approach turns lovers into insurance policies.

Finally, wedlock touts lifelong monogamy, though primatologists tell us that no nonhuman primate group is monogamous.[28] Pre- and extramarital sex occur in every human society on record, including cultures that stone so-called "fornicators" to death. "Both genders face stonings . . . across fourteen Muslim countries, but women are more frequently the targets," explains journalist Terrence McCoy.[29] Perpetrators of honor killings murder their victims for having nonmarital sex (including being raped) and refusing arranged marriages. Nations that execute perceived miscreants include Iran, Pakistan, and Somalia.[30] If monogamy was intrinsic, would such measures exist?

Doctors David P. Barash and Judith Eve Lipton claim that erotic exclusivity is unnatural for every species, including human beings.[31] Perhaps they overstate their case; surely not everyone experiences monogamy as a straitjacket. However, these researchers reveal a flaw in the marriage principle. Monogamy

15

might work for some and not others, for people at one stage of life but not another. Making it a static norm is wrong. This happened in the 1940s, when American schools forced left-handed children to convert to right-handedness and the 1950s, when women were told they belonged at home. It occurred in the postwar years, when medical authorities instructed men, regardless of inclination, to sleep only with women. The insistence on monogamous coupling for all is equally extreme.

At one time mandatory right-handedness looked sensible. For numerous Americans, bundling Social Security and tax benefits with marriage feels similarly reasonable. That federal law protects only husbands and wives from testifying against each other when either is the defendant in a trial, seems fine to many people. But such policies pressure our entire population toward a style of relationship suitable only for some. They defy the egalitarian principle of accommodating differences between human beings.

As Plaskow and Ackelsberg wrote, nuptial ceremonies are prescriptive. They tell viewers, "Someday you may star in your own romantic show." Jim and I could do this, waving self-congratulatory "We're Together!" pom-poms. A sense of proportion tells me not to. Amorous compatibility is largely a matter of luck; luck should not entail triumphalism. I am a book-obsessed recluse who thrives on high-intensity friendships. Not every boyfriend would find these qualities charming. Jim seems to. When people ask if he'll propose, Jim says that he respects me too much. When I'm asked why we haven't set a date, I say that we're not sex-and-everything-else partners (SEEPs).

Dissenting beliefs usually incur penalties; anti marriage views are no exception. Some deprivations are small; while a marriage certificate would enable me to get a duplicate driver's license, Connecticut's Bureau of Motor Vehicles won't accept the medical proxy form I have with Frances. Some are not small. If Frances got sick I could not invoke the 1993 Medical Family Leave Act to take time from work and care for her. We are not blood relatives, and marriage is the only adult adoption this law recognizes.

I pay roughly $3,000 more in annual taxes than I would if filing jointly as part of a married couple, and every paycheck labels me as "single." It's bad enough to be categorized maritally when one doesn't perceive oneself in those terms; it's worse to be characterized negatively. "Single" denotes not being conventionally married; would African American professors like being called "not white" on their checks? But when I'd called our university bursar's department the previous fall, I learned there were no other options. I requested my preferred designation, "spinster," and was turned down. I suggested "interdependent," a term used in Canadian law.[32] This didn't fly, so I asked the woman fielding my query to leave a blank space. Again, no. Again, I encountered someone who presented romantic status as the determinant of human identity, sexual love as real love, and marriage as real love's culmination. If she didn't believe in matrimony as a centering norm, the concept didn't seem to bother her.

The American tax code situates adults within a hierarchy of relationships. Accordingly, its administrators deal with individuals in terms of imposed social personae. However, among my students I notice increasing skepticism about wedlock's categories. During the Spring 2016 semester, my best undergraduate, Annalise, commuted from Durham, Connecticut to our campus in New Britain, a town that draws large numbers of Polish immigrants. In my writing class she submitted essay after outstanding essay with a shrug, which implied, "That was fun." During our midterm conference she complimented me on a marriage-critical article that I had published in the *Connecticut Review*: "This piece cracked me up. I totally agree with it. But I probably will marry my boyfriend."

"How come?"

"I have no idea," she replied nonchalantly.

Annalise felt no need to give anyone, including herself, a rationale. The burden of proof falls on those who decline marriage in a culture that pressures people to follow commonly tread paths. Central Connecticut's Polish and Russian communities include myriad small entrepreneurs. They run successful house painting, landscaping, and contracting businesses; it's common for sons-in-law to inherit these operations. Gifting the down payment on a couple's home is standard—once they're engaged. For first-generation Americans, marriage has a you-come-first luster. No other style of relationship feels as authentic.

I wanted to tell Annalise that the road ahead would be sinuous. There would be time to explore careers and different ways of assembling a household; experimentation is how she would find her métier. Her romance ending or changing into another kind of relationship would not signify failure. I wanted to release her from marriage ideology's grip, which demands utter certitude. Most importantly, I wanted to discourage her from making decisions fueled by anxiety about what other people think.

I couldn't. Giving students unsolicited advice is inappropriate. Anyway, Annalise wouldn't have heard me. At age nineteen, she knew her generation was thwarted by bad economic policies, sent into a world of constricting opportunity. Understandably, such people crave security or its facsimile. And second-generation Americans usually want to fit in. This means dismissing living arrangements that seem outré. It means grasping familiarity in the form of a roadmap: college, betrothal, bridal shower, wedding, marriage license, house, job.

Millennials like Annalise cultivate an unflappable style, but those poker faces conceal vulnerability. They may roll their eyes at "wedding porn" like *Brides* and *Martha Stewart Weddings*.

But that dismissiveness doesn't stop many from donning the white gowns worn by glazed-looking models in bridal photo spreads. If anything proves marriage ideology's power, it may be young people's willingness to embrace what they consider risible.

Of course, images of coupling inundate them through social media. It doesn't help that women like Annalise grew up under the influence of a highflying wife: Michelle Obama, who appeared in magazine after magazine, striking exalted poses. She operated in a tradition of presidential consorts who become instant celebrities. Martha Washington (1731–1802), Abigail Adams (1744–1818), and Dolley Madison (1768–1849), who presented themselves as a new nation's moral guides, knew that their prominence came from being married. They "stood at the center of America's political world through their husbands."[33] Hosting dinners, maintaining correspondence, and dressing appropriately called for finely honed domestic abilities. Ironically, though, the term "first lady," seems to have first been applied to Harriet Lane, biological niece of America's sole never-married president, James Buchanan (1791–1868), with whom she hosted social functions. That Buchanan's best friend (and housemate), Alabama Senator William Rufus King (1786–1853), could not have done so shows the marriage principle working in tandem with gender norms. Antebellum America demanded a woman at Buchanan's side. If he lacked a wife, her stand-in would do.

Early first couples occupied a precarious space between the rock of European custom and the hard place of Republicanism. Journalists faulted Martha Washington for greeting guests from a raised seat that resembled a queen's throne. Her formal interior decorating also drew criticism.[34] This was not, after all, Versailles. By the time Jacqueline Kennedy became a 1960s media sensation, the noun, "queen," repeatedly applied to her, had become romantic. Besotted reporters and eager fashionistas enshrined

Kennedy as a monarch holding court at Camelot. She engineered this iconography by shrewdly evoking Arthurian legend during a *Life Magazine* interview.[35]

Times have changed and stayed the same; the Obama watchwords were "role model" and "power." Journalists continue to present this former first lady as an exemplar despite (or because of) conventionally feminine choices: marrying, relinquishing her name, bearing children that got her husband's name, vacating her job to support his career, and putting her law license on inactive status. When she beamed from *Newsweek's* March 22, 2010 cover, exhorting, "Feed your children well" or told television viewers that kids must be forced to play competitive sports, Obama was acting the part of America's authoritarian married mom.[36]

Incongruous rhetoric characterizes Obama; she's a wife who radiates wifeliness; she's a powerhouse. The contradiction points to a deeper question: Why are first ladies there? Do we need an arbiter of national taste and decorum? Should teenagers be encouraged to forge illusory filial bonds with such figures? Any first lady's critics—and they all have them—avoid this question. Acolytes and detractors alike present the role of first spouse as inevitable. This tells girls that betrothal is the great drama of a woman's life and marrying is *de rigueur* for those who want access to corridors of power. And American taxpayers fund a figurehead's entourage, which includes a chief of staff, a press secretary, an assistant press secretary, a director of correspondence, and a makeup artist.

To his credit, President Obama chose Janet Napolitano as United-States secretary of Homeland Security in 2009. At a Philadelphia meeting of governors, Ed Rendell, then Governor of Pennsylvania, pronounced the never-married Napolitano "perfect" for this position. With a University of Virginia law degree and experience as Governor of Arizona from 2003 to 2009, she seemed qualified to me, but Rendell wasn't instancing qualifications. "For that job, you have to have no life," he explained helpfully. "Janet has no family."[37] Napolitano hosted travelers from Atlanta, Los Angeles, Philadelphia, San Francisco, Seattle, and Washington, DC to her 1983 gubernatorial swearing in. They attended a post-inauguration party at Phoenix's Science Museum.[38] Surely, some of these people formed her inner circle, but Ed Rendell didn't care. In his view, spouseless adults live emotionally sterile lives. With nothing else to do, they may as well enter public service.

Millennial females get the idea: even an accomplished never-wed woman has no chartable existence. Young men, too, take mental notes. They may not know that Theodore Roosevelt was a boxer, Dwight D. Eisenhower a five-star general, and John F. Kennedy a war hero. Few are familiar with the name "Adlai Stevenson," that presidential hopeful whom postwar reporters labelled "a genteel spinster."[39] But they sense that Americans like married leaders with macho vocations. Former actor, Ronald Reagan didn't have one, so he compensated by presenting himself as the ultimate husband.

Vague on Reagan's policies, my students know him in terms of what reporters call a "Great American Love Story."[40] In the Ron-and-Nancy saga, passion reaches pitches of hysteria with notes reading, "I won't be able to let you out of my sight for more than five minutes at a time," and, "I really can't even remember a life before you."[41] Their feverish symbiosis has furthered Reagan's posthumous canonization.

Not all politicians assert masculinity through marriage, and not all companions play the helpmeet card. I thought of Diana Taylor, former New York City mayor Michael Bloomberg's girl-friend, who spent four years as New York's Superintendent of Banking and proceeded to a managing directorship at the private equity firm, Wolfensohn Fund Management. When journalists asked if she would marry Bloomberg, Taylor replied, "What's the point?"[42] "You should never quit your day job," she told *Forbes Magazine*. "And never, ever depend on anyone else for money."[43]

Marriage aversion earns Taylor few plaudits. She's unlikely to achieve Jackie Kennedy, Nancy Reagan, or Michelle Obama's media-darling status. Considering these women, I could see how history entombs certain people and vivifies others. But Diana Taylor seemed credible as a role model. Her coresidence with Bloomberg in his Manhattan townhouse confirmed what I already knew; wedlock is not a synonym for love. Large segments of the population now avoid city hall and the bridal registry. Our laws, customs, and language need to catch up. Even in a culture of sexting, hookups, and studied insouciance about relationships, wedlock retains mythopoeic appeal. Students like Annalise learn that life without it would be amorphous.

In the twenty-first century one still imagines the challenges an uncoupled politician running for president would face. "Why isn't he married?" people would ask. "Why couldn't she find a husband?" This question's variants don't fly. My linguist colleague, Leyla, would be stunned if I asked why she hasn't converted from Islam to Christianity. I know from experience that married couples don't enjoy the query, "So, when are you kids getting divorced?" But "When are you tying the knot?" and "Why not?" are still acceptable questions. Regularly, I field them both.

Midway through my planning adventures, I took a break and flew to Colorado. The Aspen Music Festival was underway; one of its performers, Blake, was a fellow guest at the Snow Queen Lodge, which has charmingly cramped quarters and, for Aspen, reasonable prices. We talked over coffee some mornings. I learned that while wedlock holds little appeal for Blake, he may marry his American boyfriend. Blake is a Canadian citizen who lives in Los

Angeles. This means paying taxes in two countries; matrimony would grant him eligibility for American citizenship, ultimately making life financially manageable.

When Blake travels home he's often stopped at the border and interrogated as a noncitizen. With terrorism on the rise, security procedures everywhere are justifiably tighter. A wedding band, however, should not make someone seem less like a terrorist. This kind of magical thinking pervades matrimony.

At age twenty-two Blake is part of a new generation of gay people facing an old, straight dilemma: conform or suffer. Because he was not my student I could speak frankly. I pointed out that marriage demands cast-iron certainty about every year to come for the rest of one's life. If recent research in behavioral economics is correct, the mind can "lead its owner to a feeling of certainty about uncertain things."[44] While this confidence makes people mediocre predictors, I imagine that it's sometimes necessary. Simplifying pictures of the future stave off anxiety about life's myriad uncontrollable aspects.

However, I've found that people between eighteen and twenty-five can be alarmingly certain. Teaching undergraduates means witnessing numerous false starts: goals embraced and, before long, abandoned. I've watched students seize belief systems (evangelical Protestantism, separatist feminism, veganism) and eschew them in disenchantment. Those tattoos affirming life philosophies turn out to be . . . not such a great idea.

Changes in religion, politics, or diet are generally forgiven as experimentation that helps young adults learn who they are, what they want, and where they can make their best contributions. Frequently, the decision to undo a marriage is not absolved in this way. I told Blake that matrimony rewards people for coupling, but when they decouple, it punishes. Los Angeles is located in a joint property state. If he marries his guy, everything, from that moment on, belongs to both of them. Author Glenn Campbell explains: "You may think you still have your own checking account, credit cards, clothing and possessions, but under the law, this separate ownership is fiction. The only things you still own by yourself are those you acquired before the wedding."[45] If they divorced, Blake could end up relinquishing half of what he owns and paying alimony.

"Alimony? Does that still exist?"

"Yes, and the longer people stay married, the lengthier the payments are. Marrying young seems practical now. In twenty years it could look very different. If you've grown apart, you'll feel like separate entities, but the law won't view you that way."

"Prenuptial agreements?"

"Notoriously hard to enforce."

I said that regardless of age, no one should have to order their personal life a certain way to gain tax relief or avoid interrogation. Also, frankly, one cannot use a 5,000 year-old institution without being used back by it. An unenthusiastic groom who mutters, "I do," still represents marriage. He participates in a ritual of status elevation, advancing himself above nonmarrieds. As a scholar of Restoration and eighteenth-century studies, I knew that early modern Britons heard sex outside marriage denounced at weddings. Ministers intoned that marriage "was ordained for a remedy against sin and to avoid fornication."[46] These ceremonies did not just celebrate brides and grooms. They punitively contrasted married couples with those in nonmarital relationships.

Remarkably little has changed in terms of weddings' symbolic conveyance of their subjects from lower to higher positions within an arrangement of such stations. But demographics have shifted. In 2012 the Census Bureau reported that less than half of American homes were headed by married pairs.[47] Five years later it revealed that the percentage of adults living without a spouse had increased from 39 percent in 2007 to 42 percent in 2017.[48] A 2015 Gallup report on Americans between the ages of eighteen and twenty-nine showed a related trend: avoiding romantic cohabitation altogether. The percentage of millennials who defined themselves as single and not living with someone had increased over ten years, from 52 percent in 2004 to 64 percent in 2014.[49] Journalist Rebecca Traister reports that 40 percent of first births in the United States were to unwed women in 2013. Approximately 60 percent of American women who give birth before turning thirty do so out of wedlock. And "Forty-one percent of all births are to unmarried women, a number that is four times what it was in 1970.[50]

Surely this means that fewer Americans condone wedlock, rejecting the shibboleths of unmarried men as emotionally stunted man-children and unwed women as ireful man-haters or desperate man-hunters. But, I told Blake, those who disdained such caricatures, eschewing blockbuster weddings and marrying austerely, for practical reasons, still reinforced the marriage system. I asked him to research California marriage law before deciding and suggested that he read my favorite conjugally critical tome: *Singled Out: How Singles Are Stereotyped, Stigmatized, and Ignored, and Still Live Happily Ever After,* by Dr. Bella DePaulo. I couldn't help mentioning my own book, *Here Comes the Bride: Women, Weddings, and the Marriage Mystique.*

Our conversations reminded me that wedlock looms like an enormous Janus, with romance on one face and pragmatism on the other. Americans who opt out can't escape the prejudices but rarely complain. Discussions about what matrimony "means" generally occur at dinner tables or in therapists' offices, with the assumption that a spousal relationship is private, involving two distinctive personalities. Actually, every marriage is a sociopolitical relationship—a contract between two people and the state. Spousal conflicts are intrinsically historical and political, taking shape, as they do, within a culture that has long nurtured pro-marriage biases. Neither Republican nor Democratic politicians acknowledge these partialities; no lobbying group pressures them to do so.

Returning home, I learned of another draconian judgment against an ex-spouse: actress Morena Baccarin. Untying the knot with director Austen Chick was going to cost her $20,349 per month, with an additional $2,693 in monthly child support. While the first sum was excessive, the latter was inexplicable, since these two agreed to share child custody. And why wouldn't the presiding judge let Baccarin deduct money she paid for Chick's New York City rental, from her alimony bill?[51] Once again, an Internet search supplied the answer, turning up photos of a pregnant Baccarin and her then boyfriend, actor Ben Mackenzie. Baccarin slept with someone other than her husband. A Los Angeles court could not festoon her with a scarlet "A," but it could extract blood. Clearly, our government's immersion in marriage means that private choices—taking a sexual partner or selecting one relationship over another—can have grave repercussions. Baccarin's celebrity did not prevent her sacrifice to the gods of Comstockian morality.

I recalled that period in 2010, when Bill Clinton took time from his postpresidential career to do some wedding planning. Anticipating Chelsea Clinton's Rhinebeck, New York, nuptial (to investment banker Marc Mezvinsky), he shared his trepidation with interviewer Jenna Bush: "I just hope I can keep it together [until] I walk her down the aisle and do the handoff. Like your dad was telling me when he did it with you . . . it proves you've done what you were supposed to do."[52]

While it makes wedding guests blubber, "the handoff" has

roots in classical Greece. Weddings were transactional; a woman's *kyrios* ("lord" or "controller") gave her away. If her biological father was deceased, the nearest male relation was called upon.[53] Contemporary wedding protocol mimics this tradition. Eliding history and stating that he and Hillary excelled by raising a successful husband magnet, Clinton showed Democrats and Republicans' shared values where wedlock is concerned. Neither party acknowledges marriage's sexist origins. Neither recognizes matrimonial privilege. At a period decried by pundits as dangerously polarized, wedlock offers many politicians what looks like neutral territory.

But matrimony is hardly impartial, as Jim saw when he opened a Flexible Spending Account (FSA). This involves agreeing on an amount to be taken from one's salary before payroll taxes are applied. The sum is put on a debit card. It can go toward a deductible, cover medication, or pay for doctor's visits. A 2015 adjustment letting holders roll monies over to the following year made these accounts especially attractive.

While applying for his FSA, Jim tried to establish one for me, aware that many employers now give "significant others" benefits. Companies like the ice-cream manufacturer, Ben & Jerry's; newspapers such as the *Village Voice*; and corporations as established as IBM provide insurance to domestic partners. My alma mater, Oberlin College, offers campus housing and insurance to cohabiting partners with "long term emotional commitment, and financial interdependence."[54] These practices assume that employees should not have to live their personal lives according to one (conventional) script in exchange for a roof over their heads and health care. While neither "significant other" nor "domestic partner" is our designation of choice, Jim was ready to check the requisite box.

He received the following communiqué: "If you enroll in a

medical FSA you would not be able to use the funds to pay for a domestic partner's medical expenses . . . the FSA only allows you to pay for qualified medical expenses for yourself, a spouse, or any dependent claimed on your tax returns."[55] The Benefits and Wellness Administrator explained that this was not a company decision but an Internal Revenue Service regulation.

"What a rip-off," Jim grumbled over dinner the next night. "Who are these bean-counters to judge my relationship?"

It was a keen question. Historians, ethicists, and jurists struggle to qualify the word "family." A phalanx of accountants seems especially unsuited to the task.

This news coincided with my triennial eye exam. My optometrist told me that I needed a new eyeglass prescription and recommended custom lenses, which reduce eye strain. Minus frames, the lenses cost $570. Given my intense regimen of reading, writing, and grading I decided not to be penny-wise and pound foolish. I would take the upgrade. But FSAs cover eye glasses.

Mine are reading glasses, but I thought about unwed Americans with truly bad vision. Should their choice be, marry or walk into walls?

Antireflective film that covers lenses originates in the work of scientist Katherine Burr Blodgett, who codeveloped a method for using single-molecule coatings of barium stearate (a water-insoluble solid) to intensify the light passing through glass. In 1938 she expanded this process with a technique that entailed layering the coating forty-four times to create 99 percent transmissive, low-reflective glass. She patented the method, which subsequent researchers perfected, creating antireflective eyeglass coating.

Hired in 1918, Blodgett was the first female research scientist to work at General Electric. In 1926 she became the first woman to earn a doctorate in physics from Cambridge University.[56] Like many never-married people, she had deep community ties, setting down roots in Schenectady, New York, where she bought a house. Schenectady's married couples had no moral edge on Blodgett, who shopped for homebound neighbors every week. For a time, she cohabited with girls school director, Elsie Farrington.[57] Documentary evidence of their relationship is scant; it's unclear if they were lovers or close friends. Really, it doesn't matter. If they were alive today, Blodgett would not quality for a relationship-based FSA. Millions of people benefit from technology she invented. Elsie Farrington would not be one of them.

This upset me more than my inability to get an FSA through Jim. The exclusion was not, after all, injurious for a health nut whose job provides good insurance. Given the circumstances, did it matter that my colleagues' spouses were covered?

Yes, because I couldn't add another adult to my plan. The university wouldn't—won't—include Frances or Jim. Funds for my coworkers' spousal policies come from somewhere . . . Again I saw myself augmenting benefits reserved for married couples. Gratitude I felt for good health coverage was dampened by awareness of my workplace's wage gap: unequal pay for the same job. As someone who donates 1 percent of her gross annual salary to the school union, I wondered about its stance. Hunting online, I found that the Connecticut State University American Association of University Professors takes no position on wed/unwed wage imbalances.

I phoned the union office and reached our Director of Member Services: "Michelle, it's Professor Geller from English. I have a question. Has our union ever dealt with the wage gap between married and unmarried university employees?"

"Oh, you're interested in unmarried women . . . women's issues. In New Haven there was a committee . . . "

"Actually, this isn't a gender question. It's a question of relationship status, or, rather, lack of status for unmarried people. We pay the same Social Security but can't name beneficiaries. And here, we can't put another adult on our plan. So, effectively, we earn a different salary."

She paused before replying: "I've been here for twenty-three years, and to my knowledge you're the first person to ask that question. In my experience it's never come up. Not at a single meeting or bargaining session."

"That's very telling."

"Now that I think about it, you're right. But you know, I've had a career in faculty advocacy. Before that I worked in real estate."

"Lots of imbalances there."

"I bet. But honestly, I've never thought about this."

I realized that this was one of those rare, humbling interactions with someone who is willing to listen, reflect—perhaps change her mind. "That's pretty common" was all I could muster.

"My best friends are four women between their fifties and seventies. Tonight we're celebrating a fifty-eighth birthday. Some of us have husbands; some don't. We talk books, politics . . . gossip. But this subject, as you're framing it, has never come up."

"It doesn't make headlines."

"I don't think that's why. I have to admit, I've been married for a long time, and that's made me take certain things for granted."

"I think married people learn to feel justified in claiming certain benefits. Conversely, unmarried people are taught that we don't deserve those benefits."

"And it's not like you don't have relationships."

"Close ones, like yours. But spinsters like me, and bachelors, aren't exultant about our relationships. We don't assume that they entitle us to legal privileges. I'm thinking it's time for a change of mind."

"When they're institutionalized, economic imbalances boil down to one group receiving the fruits of another group's labor.

As a union professional I've thought about this from many angles . . . but not married/unmarried. Will you come by my office some time? I want to talk more."

"Absolutely."[58]

This exchange showed me that just mentioning marital privilege can raise awareness and pique curiosity. It also reminded me that while some people are nondefensively inquisitive, entire organizations dedicated to work equity turn a blind eye. The National Organization for Women (NOW), for instance, broadcasts its dedication to economic justice, with a focus on equal work for equal pay.[59] So does the American Association of University Women (AAUW), which sponsors salary-negotiation workshops.[60] Neither group's agenda includes eliminating marriage as a brightline monetary distinction, despite international precedent. In Tasmania, for instance, a "caring relationship" category has long recognized nonmarital partners and nonmarriage-based family members, qualifying them for various work-related benefits.[61]

It could be argued that NOW and NAAUW exist to advocate for women. This makes its leaders' silence on relationship-status discrimination especially puzzling; of America's 107 million unmarried citizens, 53 percent are women. The remaining 47 percent of men earn less than their married counterparts for performing the same jobs. The discrepancy is roughly 26 percent. Sociologist Steven Nock explains this imbalance as evidence that employers value matrimony; he calls it the "marriage premium."[62] I call it bigotry.

The halo effect probably factors in. Psychologist Edward Thorndike coined this term after studying the United States Army in 1915 and noting that officers who identified a key strength in any given soldier tended to imagine that he possessed other unrelated abilities. They projected a "halo" of excellence onto such candidates.[63] Business professor Phil Rosenzweig claims that this process occurs frequently during job interviews.[64] The American belief that married people are better at having relationships remains pervasive. One can see how it might influence employers' judgments about who deserves the better position or higher salary.

Whatever the case, any employee undercompensated because of relationship status deserves consideration by nonprofits dedicated to workplace parity. Accepting the marital status quo seems odd for female-centered groups, since marriage critique has fueled feminist analysis like that of philosopher Simone de Beauvoir, whose stringent interrogations of wedlock dovetailed with her discussions of gender. She argued that matrimony produced or ratified most strictures imposed on women. De Beauvoir focused on women's socialization for marriage in lieu of career. She decried a vicious cycle through which girls were told to place romance before work and failed to develop their professional capacities, resulting in dependence, which created greater desperation to find husbands.[65]

Pondering the married/unmarried wage difference led me to a larger question; with matrimony subvented in so many areas, is the often quoted figure of women earning seventy-nine cents to the male dollar accurate?[66] Can a sex-based analysis that does not consider relationship status yield accurate results?

Among northeastern professionals who pivot suddenly toward marriage, one often hears that it is "just a piece of paper." Couples are quick to make this assertion and state that marrying won't change them. I think many believe it but fall prey to unintended consequences: lapsing into coupled behavior patterns, demoting friends from positions of centrality, and feeling increasingly entitled in various domains. For others, the claim is probably easier than admitting one's willingness to compromise with pragmatism. Whatever the case, wedded Americans lead lives unlike those of their nonmarital counterparts, receiving entirely different kinds of support. It's a nonzero sum game in which spouses start ahead when they get household essentials in the form of wedding presents. Each gift is a matrimonial subsidy. Post-honeymoon, the real backing, including employment-related privileges, kicks in.[67] The issue is one for statisticians, but looking around, I found no studies. As far as I could see, no scholar or think tank was pursuing the issue of relationship-status discrimination as it pertains to pay for both sexes. As of this writing, there seems to be a paucity of data on the subject. Perhaps the seventy-nine-cent to the male dollar figure should not be too stridently affirmed.

No organization or hotline exists for those who experience relationship-status discrimination. The family court system preserves matrimonial privilege. It is, among other things, a venue through which erstwhile spouses are persecuted. HR offices are conduits for promarriage policies. In general, the nonmarital adult has nowhere to bring legitimate complaints.

An employee-assistance organization called the Lexington Group, for example, exists to help professors. The last Lexington newsletter I received features a young white couple photographed at a laptop. "The Challenge of Step Parenting," its byline reads. "It is important to remember that you and your new spouse are creating a new family," the anonymous writer intones: "Sit down with your spouse and work it out." Then, a warning: "You might have to take your wife or husband's ex into consideration when making decisions about how much authority you will have as a parental figure."[68] An attractive black duo beams from the newsletter's second page. "Better Communication for Couples," the heading reads. Edifying tidbits follow. Readers are advised to "Make 'I' Statements" and bask in togetherness: "Experience has shown that people, particularly men, are more likely so share their feelings when they are doing something together that both can enjoy."[69]

The Lexington Group addresses a wedded professoriate. Its writers assume that families coalesce around matrimony, marriages are the relationships worth "working on," and togetherness is a psychic bromide. A bulletin this condescendingly obvious seems harmless, and I cannot imagine my coworkers taking it too seriously. But its circulation through our university's human-resources department is disturbing. One cannot imagine turning to this office with incidents of relationship-status discrimination and expecting support or, for that matter, comprehension.

I know something about nonmarital Americans' frustration over such matters. Nature really does abhor a vacuum, and since my book's appearance I've been a de facto contact person for never-wed Americans as well as those who married and lived to regret it. I've lost track of how many letters and emails have come my way. Correspondents tend to describe three experiences: alienation as intimates jump on the marriage bandwagon; irritation at being asked to subsidize nuptial festivities, thereby reifying an institution they disavow; and a sense that the philosophical space they occupy is so narrow that few others will join them there.

Ann, a Brooklyn-based academic administrator, wrote to me of her childhood in Utah, where Mormon elders taught that unwed women can't enter heaven. She detailed her experience as a student at Brigham Young University—"more of a marriage factory than a school"—where her roommate feigned betrothal, complete with a fictitious fiancé and fake diamond displayed throughout their dormitory: "Honestly, I started to think that she had really lost her grip on reality, so thoroughly did she seem to believe that she was engaged."[70]

"This pressure to couple and live happily ever after is no less noxious than sexism or homophobia in terms of the psychological destruction it imposes, but unlike those isms, it goes largely unchecked," wrote Bill, a Washington, DC policy consultant.[71] Stella, a thirty-two-year-old Texan who cohabits with her boyfriend and works in university development described the estrangement she felt watching each friend get engaged "to some dude she barely knew." Her alienation was poignant: "I look up, look around, and find that I no longer recognize my friends . . . I am somewhat unmoored . . . I go to weddings reluctantly (I refuse to attend showers or bachelorette parties), and I feel literally sick when faced with the absurdity of it all."[72]

Others wrote in solidarity. Marc, a Manhattan-based attorney, admitted, "My girlfriend and I got into at least a few fights when I would talk about your book . . . I'm glad to let you know I enjoyed it and found it was a major conversation (and in most cases, argument) starter."[73] Marshall Miller and Dorian Solot wrote, "Since there are so stunningly few public voices who are willing to question marriage, we thought it made sense for us to be in touch and maybe even get together for coffee some time when we next make it to New York."[74] When we met, these authors shared their story. College sweethearts, they moved to San Francisco after graduating from Brown University. It was the mid 1990s, and their application to rent an apartment was rejected because they weren't married.

Miller and Solot parlayed their experience into a guidebook for marriage-free twosomes encountering similar obstacles: *Unmarried to Each Other: The Essential Guide to Living Together as an Unmarried Couple* (2002). Thirteen years later, not much had changed according to Bella DePaulo, America's premiere expert on nonmarital life. In 2015 she conducted a study with two other social scientists. They gathered fifty-four real estate agents from the Charlottesville, Virginia area. The realtors read applications from a married couple, a cohabiting pair, and two opposite-sex friends, finally listing their preferences. Subjects favored the married duo 61 percent, the cohabiters 24 percent, and the friends

15 percent of the time. DePaulo's team then ran an expanded version of the study, with 107 nonagent participants. Its respondents preferred married tenants 80 percent of the time, and most said so unselfconsciously.

DePaulo's study shows clear bias against nonmarital people where housing is concerned. Just as importantly, it shows willingness to admit this prejudice. It is hard to imagine a landlord blatantly stating that he prefers non-Hispanic tenants to Hispanics, even if this is the case.[75] Yet lessors comfortably admit relationship-status bigotry.[76]

On November 29, 2016, the Twenty-First Century Cures Act went into effect, sending ripples of excitement through the healthcare world. The world's largest biomedical research institution, the National Institutes of Health, would receive $4.8 million in funding. As a clinical informaticist who works with medical data, Jim was pleased. I was somewhat less excited—aware that this hospital, which sets worldwide standards, favors the married. Earlier that month I had travelled to its Bethesda, Maryland campus with a friend who was being evaluated for surgery. I planned to stay if the operation took place but learned that the NIH only subsidizes travel and hotel costs for spouses of patients undergoing procedures. Our relationship predates this individual's tie to his wife, but longevity doesn't matter in our nation's marriage-centric ambit.

Actually, this policy doesn't even treat marrieds fairly. It denies those undergoing serious, invasive procedures the opportunity to choose their companions. Not everyone would select a spouse. Someone might prefer the childhood friend who finishes his sentences and knows to leave certain sentences unfinished. Someone else could favor her sister, who has a nursing degree.

Our visit did not lead to surgery. Had it, I would have paid the tab and stayed at my friend's side. But I found it appalling that a hard science environment, where policymakers should strive for neutrality, rolls out the red carpet for marrieds. Again, wedlock is prescribed and sponsored. Again, never-married taxpayers foot the bill.

When presented with such facts, marriage fans usually don't say what law and social practice imply: spouses are better than marriage-free people. They don't warn that without wedlock our nation will degenerate into moral turpitude as adults fall prey to their base appetites or morph into disturbed loners. This argument no longer stands in a nation that includes 14 million male and 18 million female solo dwellers, whom sociologist Eric Klinenberg describes as productive people with strong community ties.[77] Marriage advocates tend to cite sexual partnership as the quality that makes wedlock exceptional. It's not licensure but romance and eros that distinguish marriage.

Pointing out that most people, at most times, in most places, would have disagreed leaves the zealous coupler unmoved. Telling marriage advocates that the amorous valuation of wedlock is relatively new doesn't work either. They answer that westerners have progressed to a place where romance-based matrimony earns its due. A better response occurred to me: if sexual relationships are the ones that count—if sex distinguishes marriage—marriage should entail sex. According to journalists Bob Berkowitz and Susan Yager-Berkowitz, 40 million Americans live in marriages with little to no sex: "A sexless marriage is defined by experts as making love ten times a year or less."[78] Fifteen to twenty percent of America's married couples meet this criterion.

If marrieds expect to maintain their benefits, they should undergo relationship assessments similar to the sexennial reviews required of professors and license renewals mandated for drivers. Every six years, spouses should submit signed documents that certify an ongoing sex life. I could hear friends telling me that this would never happen. I wondered why and found no reason—only the standard, "Marriage is too venerably enmeshed with citizenship, inheritance, and employment law. You can't shake all that up."

I decided the issue was historical consciousness. No one has yet pieced together an account that corrals the values nonmarital people often share and connects it to some larger picture of the world. Whether they're never-married, contentedly divorced, partnered, unpartnered, friend-centered, asexual, nonmonogamous, or celibate, most people lack the time and inclination to comb through history searching for nonmarital experience. So, a dominant narrative remains entrenched. It goes like this: traditional Europe sanctioned arranged marriages. These were cold, utilitarian, and loveless. They curtailed wives' rights and basically functioned to produce male heirs. Then humanity evolved, and wedlock followed suit. Western women mobilized as a force, demanding suffrage, educational inclusion, and professional opportunity. Their strides levelled the conjugal playing field, and matrimony became a personal choice. Amorous compatibility, attention to psychological dimensions of relationships, and fairer laws differentiate today's unions from those of the past. Now, when spouses reach to each other beyond the boundaries of self, they find exquisite intimacy; sharing or hyphenating names expresses this closeness. Married couples are best friends, lifelong lovers, and optimal childrearing partners. Progress continues, with the inclusion of gay men and lesbians. There have been—still are—people who don't marry, but they're outliers. Matrimony doesn't affect them, and they don't really count.

Not coincidentally, this tale of evolution from primitive to mature marriage celebrates modern beliefs and rituals. The narrative shows companionate marriage as a repressed yearning that fought its way free of antiquated models. It emerged in the eighteenth century, gained momentum in the nineteenth, and culminated in twentieth-century pairings like those of Ronald and Nancy Reagan or Barack and Michelle Obama. Twenty-first century couples, like fashion designer Tom Ford and editor Richard Buckley, complete the happy story.

Philosopher Alfred North Whitehead cautions against such triumphalist thinking. "The progress of civilization is not wholly a uniform drift towards better things," he writes. "It may perhaps wear this aspect if we map it on a scale which is large enough. But such broad views obscure the details on which rests our whole understanding of the process."[79] My recent reading had revealed details of another history: that of nonmarital people. Such individuals kept showing up as achievers, community builders, and thought leaders. I discovered never-married forbearers whose numbers were substantial; they were neither a tiny minority nor a lunatic fringe. Their impact on culture was incalculable. Yet these people, along with those born out of wedlock, lacked a language for articulating shared experiences.

This has not changed; there is no unifying nomenclature to capture nonmarital experience. Is it any wonder then, that such people endured—and still tolerate—overriding disadvantages? I wondered if nonmarital history might not be the key to generating nonmarital consciousness.

The writing on the wall was getting bolder: someone had to highlight a set of inequities, help repoliticize conversations about wedlock, and provide more precise terms than now exist for nonmarital experience. Someone needed to adumbrate a partial history of the never-married, the nonmaritally born, and the renegades who have left marriage. Someone had to suggest options.

I did not expect to be that person. But no one else seemed to be putting the unmarried experience in historical perspective while contesting marital privilege and exposing prejudices that masquerade as facts. There was no avoiding it: the study on eighteenth-century satire I was starting would move to a back burner. I had other work to do.

(Endnotes)

1   For a straightforward explanation of how Social Security works, see Nancy D. Polikoff, *Beyond (Straight and Gay) Marriage: Valuing All Families Under the Law* (Boston: Beacon Press, 2008), 202–7.

2   Rachel McGrath, "Melanie Griffith 'Got the House in Aspen, the Picasso Painting and $65,000-a-month' in Divorce from Antonio Banderas," DailyMail.com, December 9, 2015, https://www.dailymail.co.uk/tvshowbiz/article-3351620/Melanie-Griffith-got-house-Aspen-Picasso-painting-65-000-month-divorce-Antonio-Banderas.

3   Martha Ackelsberg and Judith Plaskow, "Why We're Not Getting Married," *Lilith*, Fall 2004, http://lilith.org/articles/why-we're-not-getting-married.

4   Judith Plaskow, email message to author, April 26, 2012.

5   Gregory B. Hladky, "A New Era in Farming: Connecticut's Agricultural Landscape Continues to Evolve," *Hartford Magazine*, June 20, 2019, https://www.courant.com/hartford-magazine/hc-hm-farming-overview-20190630-20190625-z4ifvny2izhylaab3jeyinurr4-story.

6   Lisa Arnold and Christina Campbell, "Does Federal Law Favor Married People? Let Us Count the Ways," *Singlism: What it is, Why it Matters, and How to Stop it*, ed. Bella DePaulo (DoubleDoor Books, 2011), 43.

7   "Estate Planning," The Law Office of David E. Peterson, accessed January 22, 2018. http://www.deplawfirm.com .

8   See Lisa Arnold and Christina Campbell, "The High Price of Being Single in America," *The Atlantic*, January 14, 2013, http://www.theatlantic.com/sexes/archive/2013/01/the-high-price-of-being-single-in-america.

9   *The Poetry of Robert Frost*, ed. Edward Connery Lathem (New York: Henry Holt, 1969), 105.

10 Michael Lewis, *The Undoing Project: A Friendship That Changed Our Minds* (New York: W. W. Norton & Company, 2017), 296.

11 "Dartmouth Appoints Carolyn Dever as Provost," *Dartmouth News*, Office of Communications, January 9, 2014, https://news.dartmouth.edu/news/2014/01/dartmouth-appoints-carolyn-dever-provost.

12 *The Tyranny of Virtue: Identity, the Academy, and the Hunt for Political Heresies* (New York: Scribner, 2019), 11.

13 Ibid., 16-17. Conor Friedersdorf, "A Columbia Professor's Critique of Campus Politics," *The Atlantic*, June 30, 2017, https://www.theatlantic.com/politics/archive/2017/06/a-columbia-professors-critique-of-campus-politics.

14 Maike Ingrid Philipsen with Timothy Bostic, *Challenges of the Faculty*

Career for Women: Success and Sacrifice (San Francisco: Jossey-Bass, 2008), 55.

15 Elaine Louie, "Making Family Out of Friends," *New York Times*, September 26, 2012, http://www.nytimes.com/2012/09/27/greathome-sanddestinations/friends-become-family-in-a-bushwick-loft.

16 Aristotle, Nicomachean, *Nicomachean Ethics*, trans. Terence Irwin (Indianapolis: Hackett Publishing Company, Inc., 2019), 147.

17 Carrie Jenkins, *What Love Is and What It Could Be* (New York: Basic Books, 2017), 98–9.

18 Dave Goldiner, "Madonna Forks Over $92 Million for Divorce Settlement from Guy Ritchie," *New York Daily News*, December 15, 2008, https://www.nydailynews.com/entertainment/gossip/madonna-forks-92-million-divorce-settlement-guy-ritchie-article.

19 "Informal Caregiving at Working Age: Effects of Job Characteristics and Family Configuration," *Journal of Marriage and Family* 68 (2006): 411–29.

20 "Why is One Sibling Always Left to Care for Elderly Parents?", *Daily Mail*, July 2015, https://www.dailymail.co.uk/femail/article-3162892/Why-one-sibling-left-care-elderly-parents-asks-KATE-MULVEY-did-me.

21 "Marriage: The Good, the Bad, and the Greedy," *Contexts* 5, no. 16 (2006): 16–21.

22 *Greedy Institutions: Patterns of Undivided Commitment* (New York: The Free Press, 1974), 4.

23 Rebecca Mead, *One Perfect Day: The Selling of the American Wedding* (New York: Penguin: 2007), 26.

24 Andre Bourque, "Technology, Profit, and Pivots in the $300 Billion Wedding Space" (blog), May 1, 2016, http://www.huffingtonpost.com/andre-bourque/technology-profit-and-piv_b_7193112.

25 Aristotle, *Nicomachean Ethics*, 142–5.

26 "Equality and Non-hierarchy in Marriage: What Do Feminists Really Want?", *After Marriage: Rethinking Marital Relationships*, ed. Elizabeth Brake (New York: Oxford University Press, 2016), 112.

27 Gerda Lerner, *The Creation of Patriarchy* (New York: Oxford University Press, 1986), 217.

28 Christopher Ryan and Cacilda Jethá, *Sex at Dawn: How We Mate, Why We Stray, and What It Means for Modern Relationships* (New York: Harper Perennial, 2010), 98.

29 "In Pakistan, 1,000 Women Die in 'Honor Killing" Annually. Why is This Happening?" *Washington Post*, May 28, 2014: https://www.washingtonpost.com/news/morning-mix/wp/2014/05/28/in-paki-

stan-honor-killings-claim-1000-womens-lives-annually-why-is-this-still-happening.

30   In 2008 Somali authorities ordered the execution of thirteen-year-old Aisha Ibrahim Duhulow, who reported that she had been raped. She was stoned to death in a southern Somalia stadium before 1,000 spectators. Rhiannon Redpath, "Women Around the World Are Being Stoned to Death. Do You Know the Facts?", *Mic*, October 16, 2013, https://mic.com/articles/68431/women-around-the-world-are-being-stoned-to-death-do-you-know-the-facts.

31   *The Myth of Monogamy: Fidelity and Infidelity in Animals and People* (New York: W. H. Freeman and Company, 2001).

32   Polikoff, *Beyond (Straight and Gay)*, 114–15.

33   Jeanne E. Abrams, *First Ladies of the Republic: Martha Washington, Abigail Adams, Dolley Madison, and the Creation of an Iconic American Role* (New York: New York University Press, 2018), 7.

34   Ibid., 79.

35   Lily Rothman, "This is the Real Life *Jackie* Interview with Life Magazine," *Time*, December 2, 2016, https://time.com/4581380/jackie-movie-life-magazine. For an analysis of the Jackie Kennedy obsession see Jaclyn Geller, *Here Comes the Bride: Women, Weddings, and the Marriage Mystique* (New York: Four Walls Eight Windows, 2001), 247-50.

36   Obama gave David Letterman childrearing instructions on *The Late Show with David Letterman*, CBS, New York City, August 2012.

37   Gail Collins, "One Singular Sensation," *New York Times*, December 4, 2008, http://www.nytimes.com/2008/12/04/opinion/04iht-edcollins.

38   "Friends See Napolitano '83 Sworn in as Governor of Arizona," *UVA Lawyer*, Spring 2003, http://www.law.virginia.edu/html/alumni/uvalawyer/s03/napolitano.

39   *New York Daily News* quoted in Richard Hofstadter, *Anti-Intellectualism in American Life* (New York: Vintage Books, 1963), 227.

40   *People*, March 2016, cover.

41   Sandra Sobieraj Westfall and Champ Clark, "'Thank God We Found Each Other:' Together, Nancy Reagan and her Husband, 'Ronnie,' Wrote a White House Love Story Worthy of Old Hollywood," *People*, March 2016, 52.

42   Ruth LaFerla, "Her Term is Up as Well: Mayor Michael Bloomberg's Companion, Diana Taylor, Gives a Rare Interview," *New York Times*, December 27, 2013, http://www.nytimes.com/2013/12/29/fashion/Mayor-Michael-Bloomberg-Diana-Taylor-New-York-City.

43   Mary Ellen Egan, "Diana Taylor: Success at Every Age," *Forbes* (blog), November 9, 2009, http://www.forbes.com/2009/11/09/diana-taylor-success-at-every-age-forbes-woman-power-women-charity.

44   Lewis, *The Undoing Project*, 42.

45   *The Case Against Marriage* (Geoaktif Publications, 2013), 10.

46   *The Proposed Book of Common Prayer*, http://justus.anglican.org/resources/bcp/1689/Marriage_1689.

47   Elizabeth Harrington, "Less Than 50% of U.S. Households Now Led by Married Couples, Says Census Bureau," CNSNews.com, April 25, 2012, http://www.cnsnews.com/news/article/less-50-us-households-now-led-married-couples-says-census-bureau.

48   Richard Fry, "The Share of Adults Living Without a Partner Has Increased, Especially Among Young People," Pew Research Center, October 11, 2017, https://www.pewresearch.org/fact-tank/2017/10/11/the-share-of-americans-living-without-a-partner-has-increased-especially-among-young-adults.

49   Lydia Saad, "Fewer Young People Say I Do—to Any Relationship," Gallup, June 8, 2015, http://www.gallup.com/poll/183515/fewer-young-people-say-relationship.

50   *All the Single Ladies: Unmarried Women and the Rise of an Independent Nation* (New York: Simon & Schuster, 2016), 189.

51   Michele Corriston, "Morena Baccarin to pay Ex Austin Chick $23K per Month in Child and Spousal Support," *People*, November 20, 2015, http://people.com/tv/morena-baccarin-gotham-star-to-pay-austin-chick-child-and-spousal-support.

52   *The Today Show*, NBC, New York City, April 19, 2010. Tim Nudd, "How Bill Clinton is Helping Chelsea Clinton with Her Wedding Plans," *People*, September 23, 2016, http://people.com/celebrity/how-bill-clinton-is-helping-chelsea-with-her-wedding-plans.

53   See Jaclyn Geller, "Why the History of Marriage Matters," *Singlisim*, 35–8.

54   Polikoff, *Beyond (Straight and Gay)*, 49 50.

55   Kristen Flint, Employee Benefits and Wellness Coordinator, Capital District Physicians' Health Plan, email message to James O'Connor, December 1, 2016.

56   "This Month in Physics History. March 16, 1938: Katharine Blodgett Patents Anti-Reflective Coating," *APS News* 16, no. 3 (March 2007), https://www.aps.org/publications/apsnews/200703/history.

57   Susan Ware, ed., "Blodgett, Katharine Burr," *Notable American Women: A Biographical Dictionary Completing the Twentieth Century* (Cambridge: Belknap Press of Harvard University, 2004), 66–7.

58 Michelle M. Malinowski, conversation with author, December 9, 2016.

59 National Organization for Women, http://now.org/about (December 28, 2016).

60 American Association of University Women, http://www.aauw.org/what-we-do (December 28, 2016).

61 Polikoff, *Beyond (Straight and Gay)*, 117.

62 DePaulo, *Singled Out*, 215. For an analysis of work-condition disparities between married and unmarried people, see DePaulo, "The Workplace, the Marketplace, and the Price of Single Life," *Singlism*, 78-83.

63 Britta Neugaard, "Halo Effect," in *Encyclopedia of Epidemiology*, ed. Sarah Boslaugh (Los Angeles: Sage Publications, 2008), 449.

64 *The Halo Effect . . . and the Eight Other Business Delusions That Deceive Managers* (New York: Free Press, 2007), 52–3.

65 *The Second Sex*, trans. H. M. Parshley (Toronto: Bantam, 1961), 126-7.

66 According to sociologist Stephanie Coontz the accepted figure is now 81 percent. Email message to author, January 3, 2017.

67 See DePaulo, "21 Ways Single People Are Taxed More Than Married People on Tax Day and Every Other Day," Psych Central, *Single at Heart* (blog), April 21, 2016, http://blogs.psychcentral.com/single-at-heart/2016/04/21-ways-single-people-are-taxed-more-than-married-people-on-tax-day-and-every-other-day.

68 "The Challenge of Step Parenting," *The LexLine*, Summer 2016, https://outlook.office.com.

69 "Better Communication for Couples," *The LexLine*, Summer 2016, https://outlook.office.com.

70 Email message to author, February 27, 2003.

71 Email message to author, September 7, 2001.

72 Email message to author, December 19, 2011.

73 Email message to author, January 3, 2002.

74 Email message to author, October 9, 2001.

75 Conversation with author, November 1, 2016.

76 Traister, *All the Single Ladies*, 188.

77 *Going Solo: The Extraordinary Rise and Surprising Appeal of Living Alone* (New York: Penguin, 2012).

78 *He's Just Not Up for it Anymore: Why Men Stop Having Sex and What You Can Do About It* (New York: William Morrow, 2008), 13.

79 *Science and the Modern World* (New York: The Free Press, 1925), 1.

2

Kin to Nobody:
Nonmarital Children

---

*"Most people cannot quite rid themselves of the sense that
controlling the sex of others, far from being unethical, is where
morality begins."*

—MICHAEL WARNER,

*THE TROUBLE WITH NORMAL:
SEX, POLITICS, AND THE ETHICS OF QUEER LIFE*

Not Designated Natural

Long before there was a war on drugs, a war on crime, or a war on terrorism, there was a war on nonmarriage. The practice of disenfranchising children born out of wedlock—so-called "illegitimates"—proves this. Marriage advocates frequently hallow wedlock as civilization's inaugurating structure. They construct the distant past as "a sort of permanent disaster area"[1] where lust, greed, and violence ran unchecked. By imposing a scheme of bounded, particularistic family units centered on the couple matrimony tamped down chaos, they insist. It channeled human energies constructively and elevated humanity from antediluvian barbarism to social coherence. This myth elides vilifications of and hardships imposed upon nonmarital children: customs embedded in European history.

To have any sense of what marriage means historically, one must understand the uncivilized treatment such children have received. Westerners have traditionally used wedlock as a yardstick for measuring human worth, deeming those born outside matrimony undesirable, shameful—even criminal. In the Hebrew Bible's Book of Genesis, Abraham, a wealthy patriarch, has two biological sons: Ishmael, born to Hagar, his wife Sarah's servant; and Isaac, born to Sarah. At Sarah's insistence, Abraham banishes Hagar and Ishmael to the desert, where divine intervention saves their lives.[2] Determined to preserve Abraham's estate for Isaac, Sarah operates from maternal self-interest. For later interpreters, though, this story exemplifies the Bible's ranking of marital children above those born to concubines or from sex considered illicit: incest or intercourse between a man and a married woman. In Hebrew, the second type of child is called a *mamzer*.

Prophets' Book of Zechariah bans nonmarital sons from political leadership.[3] The Wisdom of Solomon, an apocryphal biblical book, states that adulterers' progeny will die, and "the offspring of an unlawful union will perish. Even if they live long they will be held of no account, and finally their old age will be without honor . . . "[4] So, nature will eliminate most nonmarital children. Those who escape early death will creep innocuously, shamefully toward senescence.

In classical Greece, producing marital offspring was wedlock's stated function, at least for propertied citizens. Marital youth were said to respect ancestors, honor elders, and keep assets within the wedlock-based family: responsibilities "illegitimates" could not be trusted with.[5] A contract between the groom and the bride's male guardian legalized Greek marriages. "The father [or his surrogate] declared, 'I give you this woman for the procreation of legitimate children.'"[6]

St. Paul, a Jewish convert to Christianity who heavily influenced the early church's development, did not admire wedlock but conceded that it was "better to marry than to be aflame with passion."[7] Paul's writing instructs virgins to remain chaste; he tells widows and widowers to avoid remarriage. Paul describes conjugality as a distraction from Christ, since, "he that is married cares for things that are of this world, how he may please his wife."[8]

Octavian (63 BCE–14 CE) ruled as Rome's first emperor from 29 BCE to his death. Initially called "First Citizen," he assumed the name Augustus ("Revered One") after 27 BCE. These monikers demonstrate his Janus-faced persona as an austere Roman living simply on the Palatine Hill with his wife and a leader nonpareil. From both roles, Augustus launched a campaign to bolster marriage. It disempowered men and brought women under increased surveillance. In 17 BCE new laws made wedlock mandatory for twenty-five to sixty-year-old males and twenty to fifty-year-old females. Unwed marrying-age Romans could not attend public games. Their inheritance rights were restricted to blood relatives with whom they shared six or less degrees of relation.[9] Divorce had long been accessible to Romans, but a new requirement of seven witnesses made it harder to obtain.[10]

Augustus's *Lex Julia De Adulteriis* (18 BCE) moved jurisdiction over sexual matters from family to state. A standing court would adjudicate cases against wives and their lovers. Any man who condoned his spouse's extramarital liaisons became a criminal accessory. Extramarital sex was punishable by banishment; children born from such relationships could not receive birth certificates.

Myriad Romans continued to legally support themselves

as prostitutes. As historian Nils Johan Ringdal explains, "The Roman Empire distinguished itself from the rest of antiquity by treating male and female prostitution the same way. In large bordellos, male and female prostitutes worked side by side."[11] Augustus discouraged prostitution with laws that withheld licensure from upper-class sex workers and penalized men who patronized those without licenses.[12] He encouraged marriage by releasing freeborn wives who had birthed at least three children from the requirement of obtaining a male custodian's approval in property transactions.[13]

As countless marriage fundamentalists would, Augustus claimed that he was returning a wayward culture to erstwhile decency. Over the next 300 years, emperors reshaped and shored up his laws. Constantine (232–337), Rome's first Christian emperor, made adultery a crime punishable by death.[14]

Between the first and sixth centuries, Christian authorities denounced extramarital sex, forbidding encounters with prostitutes, concubines, divorced people, Jews, and heretics. Roman law absorbed these views after the fourth century. As Christianity spread, religious admonitions against nonmarital sex melded with public policy. The law considered children born to or adopted by legally married heterosexual couples "legitimate." "Illegitimates" came from sex between unwed lovers, adultery (i.e., relations between a wife and a man other than her husband), concubinage, or incest. Such children could be legally abandoned.

"Illegitimates" also included children born from rape, free Romans' intercourse with slaves, and group sex.[15] These youngsters' plight worsened over time. Taking an increasingly religious view of eroticism, sovereigns denounced such people as execrable. The Eastern Roman emperor Justinian (482–565) designated them unnatural. Accordingly, they could not receive support, "whether by gifts given during the parents' lifetime or legacies left for them after the parents' death."[16] Here Justinian reversed a longstanding rule allowing biomothers to sustain their nonmarital offspring. He assigned such children one function: suffering, while evincing the previous generation's perceived transgressions.

Constantine's 313 Edict of Milan gave Roman Christians the right to openly practice their religion. Constantine also enforced class divisions by forbidding government officials to marry slaves, actresses, barkeepers, merchandizers, or gladiators. Accordingly, "Children of all such unions were . . . branded as irredeemable bastards and foreclosed from any support . . . "[17]

Nonmarital Spaces

As Rome Christianized, matrimony became the sole acceptable outlet for erotic expression, with monogamy imposed on men as well as women. Simultaneously church esteem for celibacy intensified. The learned convert Athenogoras of Athens (133–190) argued that wedlock drew people from God. He interpreted Christ's statement, "there are eunuchs who have made themselves eunuchs for the sake of the kingdom of heaven" as an endorsement of sexual abstention.[18] The fourth through the six centuries witnessed an outpouring of writing that extols erotic self-denial as a means of redemption.[19]

Christian monasticism began in Egypt, spreading to the Judean Desert, North Africa, and Rome. Legend names Anthony the Great (251–356) as monasticism's architect. Born to wealthy denizens of an Egyptian village called Coma, Anthony crossed the Nile, settled in the desert, and lived there for twenty years. Saint Pachomius (292–348) emulated him, dwelling eremitically in the wilderness until a voice allegedly instructed him to create homes for like-minded Christians. Pachomius's first monastery, established in Tabennisi, Egypt was followed by larger ones in Fauo, Tismenae, and the Latopolis region. He built a convent for nuns, located across the Nile from Tismenae. Each collective made celibacy a condition for membership.[20]

The Galatian monk, Palladius of Aspuna (363–c. 431), travelled through Alexandria and the Nitrian desert, meeting ascetics who sometimes lived as cenobites, sometimes as hermits. He described them in biographical sketches anthologized as *The Lausiac History*. This early account of monasteries depicts them as populous; the Tabennisi collective included more than 5,000 monks. Palladius memorializes a highborn virgin named Olympia, fiancé to Nebridius, sometime prefect of Constantinople. Olympia ends the engagement, eschews her possessions, and becomes a religious teacher: "She is said to have died a spinster but a spouse to the word of truth."[21]

Scholar Peter Brown explains that for early Christians, Adam and Eve's error made propagating the species a duty. Seen in this light, sexual intercourse was obligatory and abstinence liberating. Sexual attachments were also synecdochical for involvement in social and commercial life. Eremitic existence signaled noble disengagement from these domains. From France to the Zagros Mountains, celibacy became a sacrosanct ideal.[22]

Historian Jo Ann McNamara pinpoints chastity's power for distaff Christians: "Women found two things in Christianity that they found nowhere else. First of all, they found their own selfhood. Second, they found one another."[23] Asceticism also authorized a woman's role other than genitor of "legitimate" children. Through abstemiousness, women became men's companions in pursuit of spiritual perfection. Some female cenobites claimed to have transcended biological sex. Stereotyping rendered women conceited, lubricious, and passionate, with men seen as comparatively rational. The fifth-century hermit, Amma Sarah, struggled with sexual urges for sixty years. Accused of vanity by two anchorites, she allegedly replied, "According to nature I am a woman, but not according to my thoughts." Several desert mothers were called female men of God—a compliment suggesting that they had subdued their eroticism.[24]

Religion scholar Rosemary Rader's study, *Breaking Boundaries: Male/Female Friendship in Early Christian Communities* (1983) shows that celibacy engendered mixed-sex Christian friendship during the fourth, fifth, and sixth centuries. This period witnessed partnerships in which purportedly chaste men and women—*agapatae* in Greek—cohabited, sharing religious observance, household duties, and sometimes, beds.[25] The 206 Council of Antioch castigated a bishop, Paul of Samasota, for living with several women he called his sisters. How common these mixed-sex households were in late antiquity remains unclear. My guess would be, more common than is generally thought, with occupants observing discretion—the easiest way to do anything verboten. The Council of Nicaea (325) forbade such arrangements.[26] Church authorities ultimately eradicated them. But male celibates and their *agapatae* represent a telling chapter in nonmarital history. They show people unmotivated to produce "legitimate" children finding each other, despite official censure.

The theologian St. Jerome (c. 347–420) expressed scathing hostility to wedlock: "To marry for the sake of children, so that our name may not perish . . . is the height of stupidity," he observed. "For what is it to us when we are leaving the world if another bears our name, when . . . there are countless others who are called by the same name."[27] Jerome ridicules distinctions between "legitimates" and "illegitimates:" "Children are not born one way of adultery and prostitution, in another of pure marriage."[28]

The life of Saint Augustine (354–430), late antiquity's preeminent Christian writer, problematizes views of marriage as a timeless good. Born in Thagaste, Augustine relocated to Carthage for the education subsidized by a nonrelative. From his late teenage years, Augustine lived with someone whose name has fallen between nonmarital history's cracks. The *Confessions* (400), Western Europe's first complete autobiography, describes their separation (after some fifteen years) with imagery from Genesis: "The woman with whom I had been living was torn from my side . . . and this was a blow which crushed my heart to bleeding . . . "[29] His inferior in class terms, she stepped aside to avoid impeding Augustine's ambitions, leaving with him their nonmarital child, Adeodatus.[30] Augustine conceded to an arranged nuptial, agreeing to wait until his rich fiancée turned twelve, the legal age for Roman female marriage. He would have been thirty one.

His conversion prevented the wedding: he was baptized with a lawyer friend, Alypius, and Adeodatus (who would die at age seventeen). The Catholic Augustine perceived matrimony, secular advancement, and wealth, as hollow, status-conferring inducements. Accordingly, he left a prestigious teaching position. Earlier, he had hoped to establish a communal home with nine friends; several of their marriages obstructed the plan. But when he returned to Thagaste, Augustine achieved a version of it, turning his childhood home into a pseudomonastery whose occupants prayed and discussed theology together. During these dialogues Augustine reconciled the never-married philosopher, Plato, with biblical sources, concluding that universal properties come from God's mind. Effectively, this collective was Latin Africa's first monastery.[31]

Augustine's writing allegorizes continence as a benevolent matriarch shepherding "great numbers of the young people of all ages . . . and women still virgins in old age."[32] She nurtures a transgenerational community of celibates. When he became a priest,

Augustine instructed parishioners "to love the sexuality of their wives and the physical bonds of their families only as a Christian must love his enemies."[33] Subsequent promotions brought him to Hippo (today a Northern Algerian port city), where he created a proper monastery comprising laymen and clergy who relinquished private property. (Augustine cashed in his inheritance and distributed it among the local poor.) "Men and women are differentiated in body, not in soul or powers of mind," he insisted. Soon, a corollary facility for nuns was built.[34] When the local Roman slave trade burgeoned, Augustine opposed it, pressing Alypius to locate antislavery laws, and organizing rescue missions, one of which liberated 120 people.[35]

His hostility to sex and enshrinement of elderly virgins alienate Augustine from contemporary audiences. But he brings readers back to a time when body and soul were said to occupy discrete worlds, and pietists renounced marriage. Reading his prose, moderns can bracket mental habits that privilege sexual coupling, "try on" Augustine's viewpoint, and gain a clearer understanding of the past.

As a young man, St. Benedict of Nursia (c. 480–544) fled his aristocratic Roman household to found several monasteries, which he organized into units whose members dressed uniformly, studied, copied manuscripts, taught, and farmed under the direction of elected abbots. The most famous sits atop Monte Cassino in Italy's Latin Valley. These nonmarital spaces preserved important manuscripts and ran schools that kept literacy alive. According to historian C. Warren Hollister, "Benedictine monasticism became the supreme civilizing influence in the early Christian west."[36] Clearly, myriad Europeans found nonmarriage amenable. Thriving monasteries and convents gave such people livelihoods and camaraderie. They also sheltered marriage refugees. Sociologist Stephanie Coontz explains that "A friendly monastery could

provide refuge for a wife who was divorced or left her husband
. . . ." Monasteries could shelter widows uninterested in remarriage, who sought religious backup.[37] Foundling children were a
particular object of monastic care.

While it encouraged a flourishing nonmarriage culture, the
church accepted Justinian's birth status categories. Coming from
concubinage, premarital sex, or fornication, natural "illegitimates" could sometimes be legitimized.[38] The products of adultery,
rape, incest, intercourse with prostitutes, the seduction of virgins,
sex with clergy, or orgies, spurious "illegitimates" were irredeemable. Natural "illegitimates" could take financial assistance from
their biomothers; spurious bastards could not.[39] Canon lawyers
justified these policies with Sarah's condemnation of Hagar and
Ishmael in Genesis: "Cast out this slave woman with her son; for
the son of this slave woman shall not be heir with my son Isaac."[40]

Conjugal Hierarchies

During the fourth and fifth centuries, Rome's strained boundaries
became indefensible, and its empire lost cohesiveness. Migrating
Germanic tribes filled the vacuum, building a patchwork of kingdoms and fiefdoms. Groups like the Ostrogoths, Alani, Vandals,
and Visigoths largely used marriage to secure political alliances.
Men arranged engagements and paid a bride price; women had
little say. Betrothal involved a pledge followed by the groom and
brides' clans dining together.[41] Anglo Saxon literature's greatest
poem, *Beowulf*, opens with the image of an abandoned (and
presumably nonmarital) child, Shield Sheafson, who founds a
Danish line of kings.[42] *Beowulf* features an indefatigable, never-
married warrior who becomes a successful king. Its lauded social
unit—perhaps reality, perhaps literary ideal—is the *comitatus*

(warband) in which loyal soldiers repay a leader's generosity by following him unhesitatingly into battle.[43]

Vague definitions like that of the 752 Council of Ver circumscribed marriage: "Let all lay-people make public marriages, both noble and non-noble."[44] Witnesses were optimal, but vows uttered with no priest or onlookers sufficed. Not only was the medieval wedding a less formal event that its modern iteration: the nuptial pledge was one among several interpersonal oaths. Within feudalism's socioeconomic framework kings gave nobles land in exchange for military aid. Property holders bestowed lands on lesser nobility and peasants. The latter worked as tenant farmers, giving their lords a portion of annual crops. Large land grants were formalized by the recipient kneeling with his hands on those of the monarch or lord to demonstrate vassalage. A vassal might pledge, "To this end I shall devote and consecrate myself with all the intelligence that God has given me for the remainder of my life."[45] Until the eighteenth century, poets would celebrate vassalage as a mystically intense bond.

During the Carolingian era (800–900) clerics urged Christians to leave their natal families in pursuance of a God-centered life. A longstanding conflict between this mandate and the obligation to produce "legitimate" heirs intensified. Simultaneously, church authorities moved toward clearer definitions of matrimony. In 829 Frankish church leaders crafted a set of propositions that can be distilled to three dictates: monogamy, wedlock outside one's kin group only, and intercourse for procreation, not pleasure.[46] Jonas, Bishop of Orléans, codified these rules in a treatise written to help monarchs model conjugal standards, *On the Institution of the Laity*.[47]

Seeking secular partners, the church found one in King Charlemagne (748–814). He offered Pope Leo III military aid and sweetened the deal by issuing a 789 decree prohibiting remarriage among divorced subjects. In 799 Charlemagne wed Luitgard, his companion of five years—just in time for a papal visit. And on Christmas, 800, the pope crowned him Holy Roman Emperor, a role in which he would reunite much of Europe, support the expansion of abbeys, and sponsor the construction of architecturally innovative churches such as Aachen Cathedral, where he is interred.[48]

For a defender of the faith, Charlemagne had rather laissez-faire sexual practices. At least four nonmarital lovers followed Luitgard's 800 demise. He sired eleven girls and promoted their education. Charlemagne encouraged them to live at court, where several conducted nonmarital relationships that produced children. Royal lineage protected princesses like Rotrude (c. 775–810) and Bertha (c. 780–after 824) from the dishonor associated with birthing bastards.[49] One wonders if these literate, sexually unfettered women enjoyed a life that many of their female contemporaries would have chosen if they could.

The "father of Europe" backed his pope against Church enemies like the Germanic Lombards. Charlemagne did what was expected by marrying and then lived as he liked. Exceptional power and wealth made this possible. The king's quid pro quo papal dealings left his subjects in a very different position: vulnerable to a clergy increasingly bent on enforcing its conception of marriage. Perhaps bishops were learning that the ability to validate certain relationships and condemn others, to endorse some children and negate others, was the power to control populations.

Stigmas against nonmarital birth dovetailed with concerns about female sexual conduct. A wife with extramarital lovers might carry "illegitimate" children who would inherit family fortunes. Rumors swirled that Charlemagne's daughter-in-law, Judith (797–843), was doing just this by sleeping with her chamberlain. In 830 she swore an oath affirming her bioson

Charles the Bald's birth within marriage.[50] This enabled his eventual kingship and reminded Carolingians that wedlock was largely about bearing "legitimate" offspring.

Ninth- and tenth-century France ritualized this process. Upper-echelon wedding processions paraded a bride into her new home's marriage chamber. Optimally, a boisterous crowd gathered and encouraged the newlyweds to consummate their relationship. To signal their absorption into marriage, some wives took new first names: "Mathilde might thus become Blanche or Rose—a mark of her complete break with the past."[51]

The Danish prince, Cnut (c. 990–1035), took England's throne in 1016 after more than two centuries of Viking raids. He became King of Denmark in 1018, temporarily united the two nations, and instituted a legal code. According to the Laws of Cnut (1021), a wife convicted of sex outside marriage lost her property and possessions. She then lost her nose and ears. Widows had to refrain from remarriage for twelve months to ensure children's clear paternity.[52]

Church authorities were coming to define matrimony as instrumental (God's way of authorizing procreation), contractual (a joint compact), and sacred (a symbol of unity between Christ and His Church). The church did not extend this hallowed status to significant nonmarital relationships. I am continually surprised by how few experts note this omission.

But even in the High Middle Ages, marriage was not considered humanity's loftiest state. Ecclesiastics still occupied that plateau. They had been admonished not to marry since the fourth century. But the Second Lateran Council (1139) forbade clerical marriage.[53] Whether it did so to protect church assets from priests' "legitimate" oldest sons, whom primogeniture had recently granted inheritance privileges, or to distinguish clerics from laypeople, the council issued a benchmark edict. Permissible sex only occurred within wedlock, so proscribing clerical marriage imposed lifelong celibacy on priests, monks, and nuns. Women who slept with priests would be classified as whores whose offspring was spuriously "illegitimate."

The thirteenth-century church increased its regulation of wedlock, probably in an attempt to standardize Christianity and center its authority in Rome. In a papal monarchy, outliers had to be identifiable. Jews settled peacefully in England, France, Germany, and Italy were required to wear identifying badges.[54] Tagging them probably helped authorities clarify their notions of what Christians were and how they should look. Similarly, pathologizing nonmarital children made it easier to accentuate the alleged virtues of birth within wedlock.

Outliers, Dissidents, and the Most Rightless Citizens of Christendom

Héloïse (1098–1164) may be medieval Europe's most renowned woman. She may also have been nonmaritally born. After an education at the abbey in Argenteuil near Paris, she lived with her natal uncle, Fulbert, a Notre Dame canon. Years later, when recording biographical information in church records, she omitted paternity. This lacuna and the fact that an uncle—perhaps not an uncle?—supported Héloïse raises questions.[55] Nonmarital birth may provide a context for her razor-sharp antimarriage writing.

Héloïse's reputation is linked to Peter Abelard, a charismatic Bible and Aristotle scholar approximately ten years her senior. Abelard (1079–1142) moved into Fulbert's Paris home to tutor this intellectual wunderkind. They commenced a relationship that Abelard described in his (c.1132) memoir: "We left no stage of love untried in our passion, and if love could find something novel or strange, we tried that too."[56]

After several months Fulbert discovered these goings-on and ejected Abelard from his house. Pregnant, Héloïse fled to Brittany disguised as a nun. When she gave birth to a boy Abelard suggested marriage; Héloïse demurred. She argued that their relationship defied matrimonial norms and insisted that they live apart. Drawing on St. Jerome, she stressed the incompatibility of conjugality and scholarship. She claimed to prefer life as Abelard's whore over an empress's existence. The words "husband" and "wife" implied specific privileges offset by obligations. It was these she seemed determined to reject.

Ultimately, however, Héloïse succumbed, wedding Abelard clandestinely, returning to Fulbert's home, and publicly denying her marriage. Outraged, Fulbert ordered a group of servants to finagle their way into Abelard's rooms, attack, and castrate him. Abelard then elected to become a monk, residing first at the monastery of St. Denis near Paris. He insisted that Héloïse become a nun. Again she capitulated, entering the convent in Argenteuil. Héloïse eventually became its prioress and finally, abbess at the Oratory of the Paraclete, where she left vague records of her lineage. The child, Astrolabe, fell into nonmarital history's interstices; his story remains unknown.[57] Abelard and Héloïse maintained a correspondence to which she contributed indignant letters. Reading them, one feels their author virtually tearing herself apart on the page. She details her abiding passion for Abelard and doubles her attack on matrimony, denouncing women who cagily wed rich men: "Reward such greed with cash and not devotion/for she is after property alone/and is prepared to prostitute herself/to an even richer man given the chance."[58]

When Héloïse died she was buried beside Abelard at the Paraclete. Her example proves that a medieval woman could consider wedlock undesirable without automatically recurring to religious orders. I like to think that for every Héloïse there were ten similar people. This is a fantasy. Then again, who knows? Medieval attitudes reach us through sources mainly crafted by an elite. At some level, extant writing reveals little about what most Europeans thought.

Marriage's indissolubility was receiving great emphasis. Under such circumstances, relationships that allowed egress may have held appeal. At a period when matrimony entailed property transactions, landless Europeans could have made discreet nonmarital arrangements. Violating antifornication laws and producing bastards might have been worthwhile risks given wedlock's enforced permanence.

Thirteenth-century peasants in Lincoln, England created a way to sidestep Church doctrine. They legitimized children by kneeling at an altar and stretching a cloth over them. This ceremony had no Catholic or common-law basis. Lincoln's poorest citizens did not care. They considered wedlock unnecessary and thought legitimacy deserved a mere ritual nod.[59]

Microhistorical analysis of Church records reveals some nonstandard relationships. In late fifteenth and early sixteenth-century Paris, for instance, a number of long-term lovers cohabited. Neighbors seem to have turned a blind eye.[60] It would be anachronistic to see these nonconformists as practitioners of civil disobedience. This is not so with Héloïse, who argued for erotic relationships other than wedlock. She is a tantalizing example of what might be known if history included a fuller range of opinions from medieval society's different strata.

Héloïse's writing suggests that premodern relationships were more multidimensional than many histories indicate. Simplification often occurs when scholars work backwards from contemporary models. The medieval same-sex marriages that some describe are, for instance, dubious. Historical fishing expeditions in search of gay matrimony yield scant evidence.[61] Building mythologies upon such evidence does not clarify how our gay forbearers lived. If, however, the word "marriage" is replaced with "meaningful relationship" or "pair bond," gay and lesbian history opens up. Evidence abounds. Myriad declarations of same-sex love express homosocial passion. Others don't mention sex but drip with eroticism. In the late eleventh century, Anselm of Canterbury (1033–1109) wrote to another Benedictine monk, "Our separation from one another has shown me how much I love you . . . Not having experienced your absences, I did not realize how sweet it was to be with you and how bitter it was to be without you."[62] Their nonmarital framework does not cheapen Anselm's words.

Between the late twelfth and the early fifteenth centuries, mass contained a ritual for men to jointly take Holy Communion. Such "sworn brothers" were sometimes buried together. Cambridge University's Merton College Chapel contains the tomb of John Bloxham and John Whytton, who met around 1364, when Bloxham was a college fellow. A brass plaque shows them standing side by side in prayer. Their names appear at the monument's base with "Johannes" written on a banner depicting John the Baptist. Fourteenth-century Catholics commonly took first names from godparents and surnames from natal parents, suggesting dual ancestry: one religious, the other familial. This iconography seems to depict John the Baptist as a spiritual godfather of two partners united in faith.[63]

In a decretal of 1234, Pope Gregory IX attempted to streamline laws of birth outside marriage. Using Justinian's vocabulary, he named conditions that rendered bastards ripe for legitimation. Two unwed people could retroactively legitimate their offspring by marrying. Witnesses' declarations confirming a child's birthstatus trumped gossip. The Pope could legitimize bastards.

Irreligious spouses produced "illegitimate" progeny, but if both parties converted, the children became "legitimate."[64]

Seemingly shaped to widen avenues of legitimation, Gregory's decretal shows how marriage-centric laws can backfire onto nonmarital populations. The High Middle Ages made bastardy a legal handicap, a mark of disgrace, and an obstacle to inheritance. Its penalties deterred nonmarital sex by impoverishing and humiliating nonmaritally born children. The decretal also suggests that birth status must have generated local controversies, since Gregory mentions witnesses' statements in contrast to rumormongering.

In addition to lacking inheritance rights, spurious "illegitimates" could not testify in court, hold public office, or occupy clerical positions. The Church offered one viable option: joining a religious community. Some monasteries took "illegitimate" foundlings in, ultimately letting them choose between departure and self-oblation. Even here, priests, nuns, and monks' offspring required papal consent to achieve higher ecclesiastical positions.[65] Legal historian, John Witte, Jr., writes that spurious illegitimates "were regarded as the most 'rightless' citizens of Christendom."[66]

These policies epitomize what literary theorist Michael Warner calls "hierarchies of shame and stigma."[67] Such schema, which inhere in wedlock, delineate permissible and deviant sex. Perpetuating shame hierarchies usually involves pretending they don't exist. Indeed, with their theatricality, elaborate weddings camouflage the divisions they enforce. So does advice literature that characterizes marriage as civically beneficial, maturity inducing, and, sexy.

The medieval canonist's illegitimacy pyramid penalized children for behavior that occurred before its victims were born. Best on its spectrum was birth to unwed Christians who later married. Worst was birth to a priest and his lover. This scale shows what happens when a culture deems marriage salvific and nonmarriage iniquitous. A thirteenth-century Englishwoman unfamiliar with canon law's arcana surely understood that pregnancy within wedlock put her on the right side of the dividing line. This was not because medieval canon lawyers accepted the current mythology of wedlock as a beneficial childrearing enterprise (i.e., a way to model exemplary relationships, the guarantor of stable homes). It was not because clerics sermonized against a narcissistic "singles" culture or pundits offered recipes for revivifying marriages. Such language would have baffled people living at a time when wedlock required consent, not consummation. It was because matrimony had become a religious mandate, a social habit, and a shield against nonmarriage's opprobrium. This means that at some level, medieval Europeans married because living unwed was frightening.

"To act on a fear is always the wrong, the insufficient move," Vivian Gornick observes in her stunning essay, "Against Marriage." "To secure against fear one must move into it, face it down, live with it."[68] This standard cannot be retroactively imposed, but contemporary Americans can learn from medieval culture while considering Gornick's question: Is living unmarried hazardous, or has it been made to seem that way? This query is crucial because marrying is not a stand-alone act devoid of social consequence. Prejudice against people born outside wedlock remains widespread. As Chapter 7 shows, it has recently been repurposed in the name of social justice.

Medieval "illegitimates" were defined by their relationship to wedlock rather than as persons in their own right. Spurious bastards were differentiated from "natural" children. The Church recorded these distinctions on birth and death certificates. Applying Warner's idea of shame hierarchies, one can speculate that medieval schemas of illegitimacy strengthened marriage by stigmatizing noncompliers. Really, these functions cannot be separated. Elevating marital people means demoting nonmarital people.

Sacrament and Satire

The 1439 Council of Florence made marriage a sacrament: a sacred act—or its physical sign—in which the Holy Spirit operates. The decision to include matrimony among Catholicism's sacraments was finalized in 1547. Wedlock now signified Christ and the Church's union.[69] Like baptism, it gave the soul a singular, definitive impression.

Church authorities maintained draconian anti-adultery and fornication laws. Female servants who brought sexual partners into their employers' homes could be whipped or branded. A Jewish man marrying a Christian woman could be executed; the technical crime was adultery. Couples who dissolved betrothals required clerical permission and even then received fines. Fourteenth-century Germany punished sexually active unwed women with a *leirwite* ("fee for lying down"). Each nonmarital child generated a separate charge.[70]

Literature presents a woolier picture. Geoffrey Chaucer's "The Reeve's Tale," from his fourteenth-century estate satire, *The Canterbury Tales*, features a Cambridge-based miller named Symkyn. A foul-tempered swindler, Symkyn has an obnoxious wife, who takes pride in having been sired by a priest.

"The Reeve's Tale" is a fabliau: a raucous story that uses sex to get laughs. Chaucer shows two Oxford students trying to outwit Symkyn and cuckolding him before they all come to fisticuffs. Given the genre, interpreting Chaucer's characterization of Mrs. Symkyn is difficult. Her high self-regard may evince detachment from reality so total that it makes her ridiculous. Or, Chaucer could be observing that laws regarding "spurious" illegitimates were one thing and reality another; perhaps medievals didn't care about birth distinctions as much as they were supposed to.

The Canterbury Tales satirize Church hypocrisy by showing

clergy and religious officials expressing attitudes antipodal to their roles. In this vein, Chaucer provides a telling glimpse of the "father" who fathered Mrs. Symkyn. He hoards a dowry for her biological daughter, Malyne, so she can marry well: "In purpos was to maken hire his heir,/Bothe of his catel and his mesuage" (3978–9).[71] The cleric's goal ("purpos") of making Malyne his beneficiary betrays shallow worldliness. Having sworn vows of poverty, he should possess neither social ambition nor property. His understanding of birth status is equally incongruous. He believes that the priestly blood in Malyne's veins elevates her: "Therefore he wolde his hooly blood/honoure." (3984–5).[72] This is how priests were not supposed to think. Spurious "illegitimates" had no honor, only shame; their blood was said to be polluted.

Enjoying sex with one of the Oxonians as Symkyn snores peacefully nearby, Malyne reminds readers of Europe's nonfictional, nonmarital daughters. Between 1449 and 1533, 19,558 papal dispensations for illegitimacy were issued to progeny of men in religious orders.[73] "The Reeve's Tale" comically represents this chasm between theological ideals and lived reality.

The western Church brought Catholic theology and Roman law into alignment. Wedlock required mutual consent and provided an arena in which Christians could have sex. The sacrament justified their intercourse and validated their offspring. Terminating a union with the right to remarry was illegal. Separations were valid on grounds of adultery, extreme cruelty, or heresy.[74] Consanguinity, prior marriage, or impotence justified annulment: the retroactive invalidation of a union. In proof of the latter, husbands sometimes underwent an ordeal designed to catch conspiring annulment-seekers. A couple would stay in bed, surrounded by several women who watched for an erection, sometimes taking matters into their own hands.[75]

The Autonomous Marital Household

Martin Luther's 1517 denunciation of Church simony sparked a theological inferno that led to his 1520 excommunication and the emergence of another Christianity. During the Reformation, Protestantism quickly ramified into numerous denominations that spread throughout Europe.[76] By the mid-sixteenth century, Saxony (now East Germany), Denmark, Norway, and Sweden had adopted Lutheranism as their state religions.

Luther (1483–1586) did not merely condemn the sale of Church indulgences.[77] He treated Catholicism as a corporate religion marred by obsessive ritualism. Luther considered confession impossible because sin's etiology lay beyond human cognizance. Acts of contrition, alms-giving, and pilgrimages were at best distractions, at worst performances. Only self-scrutiny that produced acute humility beckoned salvation.[78]

A former Augustinian brother, he considered monastic oaths incompatible with New Testament religion. This perspective crystallized preexisting disapproval of monasticism, which, in one viewpoint, sucked disproportionate wealth into its institutions. Luther's disdain for communally practiced Christianity, however, went further. It rendered chastity impracticable and the sequestered meditative life pointless.

Despite his suspicion of public rites, Luther endorsed the marriage ceremony. He blamed Catholic anti-marriage writing for keeping many eligible spouses unwed. In tones reminiscent of Augustus, he fretted about Europe's myriad "single" adults.[79] Perhaps no other marriage evangelist has made such strange claims. Luther preached that people and animals were physically designed for wedlock. He claimed that plants married other plants and trees married other trees. He said that rocks and stones married each other.[80]

As a soldier in the war on nonmarriage, Luther famously smuggled twelve nuns from their Cistercian convent to Wittenberg. (He stashed them in a cart used for the transport of herring.) In 1525 one of these sisters, Katherine von Bora, became his wife. Fittingly, they made their home in a former Wittenberg monastery. Six children attested to an active sex life, which meshed with Luther's belief that while marital intercourse diverted people from holy thoughts, it beat the alternatives. Luther's 1522, "The Estate of Marriage," treats wedlock as a divine fiat, amplifying Genesis's commandment to "be fruitful and multiply."[81] Men, Luther opines, should marry no later than age twenty, women between fifteen and eighteen. A handicap that hinders intercourse, unmet conjugal duties, or extramarital sex justify divorce.[82]

Myriad histories detail the Reformation's dismantlement of traditions around which Christian communities cohered: "mandatory fasting; auricular confession; the veneration of saints, relics, and images . . . wakes and processions for the dead and dying."[83] The movement's blow to nonmarital life often receives short shrift. Ultimately, the Reformation made marriage more compulsory. Intellectual historian John Farrell writes, "The sense of the dignity of married life in the modern era is due in part to Luther's teaching."[84] Whenever a culture grants marriage dignity, nonmarriage suffers.

Early Protestant thinkers, however, preserved longstanding ideas about bastardy. At a period of sweeping religious change, the stigmatization of nonmaritally born people remained entrenched. And by the sixteenth century matrimony generated minimal equivocation. It was largely affirmed rather than tolerated as a requisite evil. Between 1536 and 1640, King Henry VIII (1491–1547), who had broken with Rome, closed England's monasteries, convents, and priories, dissolving nonmarital collectives whose centrality to English culture extended back centuries.[85] Dismantling institutions that harbored nonmarital youth left each parish to manage its abandoned "illegitimates," a practice sanctioned by the 1576 Poor Law. Two justices of the peace per parish would decide its bastards' fates. A 1610 law enjoined justices to imprison "every lewd woman which shall have any bastard which shall be chargeable to the parish." Men could be jailed as their lovers' accessories.[86] Anglican church canons of 1604 instructed churchwardens (laypersons invested with special authority) to identify "fornicators," whom ecclesiastical courts could try. The courts could order them to marry if they had subsequent intercourse.[87] After marriage, legal pressure did not abate. Spouses seeking privacy, who took discrete lodgings, could be prosecuted for living apart.

Wedlock validated peasants, tradespeople, and monarchs alike. Henry learned this in the 1520s when he tried to situate a nonmarital child for the throne. Sired with his companion, Elizabeth Blount, Henry FitzRoy ("Son of the King"), grew up in London and received an earldom at age six. The immensely powerful Cardinal Wolsey was his godfather. Henry and his queen, Catherine of Aragon, had no male heir. Prejudice against female monarchs created pressure to keep their "legitimate" scion, Mary Tudor (1516–1558) off the throne. England clamored for a male alternative. FitzRoy would not do, the king's advisors insisted; his birth circumstances created intractable problems. A special act of Parliament would legitimate him, but no erstwhile bastard could rule as monarch.[88] So, Henry began a futile six-year attempt to have his marriage annulled—an effort that led to England's Reformation.[89] After his death, the zealously Catholic Mary Tudor (aka Bloody Mary) did rule for five years, ordering the execution of almost 300 Protestants, who became popular martyrs. These Tudors provide an example of relationship-status discrimination outweighing gender bias. Born within marriage, Mary and Elizabeth Tudor would occupy the throne. Henry FitzRoy could not.

A gifted politician, Queen Elizabeth (1533–1603) turned her key vulnerability—being never-married—into a strength. She fashioned herself as a multipart being: virgin and mother (of her subjects), male and female, divinity and mortal.[90] From 1558 to 1603 she brought stability to England by maintaining a broad religious settlement—requiring adherence to Protestantism without too closely scrutinizing any one group's religious observance.

Elizabeth's relationship status, however, did not ameliorate nonmarital people's situation. Early modern Britain made wedlock a marker of adulthood. In parts of England, never-married peasants of all ages were referred to as "lads" and "maids." Married people, called "masters" and "dames," expected their deference.[91] Early Protestantism's worldview naturalized a series of imbalances: highborn and lowborn, rich and poor, old and young. Designating never-married people children and spouses adults had great significance. Where does the American belief that matrimony signals maturity come from? Perhaps it originates in Europe's post-Reformation.

Trade guilds banned "illegitimate" businesspeople, denying them key benefits: commercial-partnership opportunities, the ability to impose boycotts, and payment of members' funeral expenses, to name a few.[92] In 1581 the Tailor's Guild of Münster barred any "illegitimate," "so that a proper citizen who has to earn a hard living . . . might better provide for his legitimate children."[93]

Matrimony granted a husband personal and economic authority over his wife. But patriarchal cultures, by which I mean cultures that institutionalize male authority, cannot suppress wives' ability to influence—even dominate—husbands through persuasion, emotional manipulation, and the undercutting of nonmarital attachments. Wedlock also gave women overt power over children, servants, apprentices, and never-married relatives.

Matrimony made a woman a "mistress."[94] The title "Mrs.," popular since the late seventeenth century, is a shortened version of "Mistress."[95]

Even a brief marriage raised an Englishwoman's status. To stretch the term, it "legitimated" her. Having inherited her husband's jointure (at least one-third of his estate), a widow of means controlled resources. Widows could reside independently and function as heads of households. They could work in cloth manufacture, operate boarding houses, and borrow money commercially. A never-married woman's prescribed role was that of daughter. As such, she belonged in a household headed by someone else. Throughout much of Tudor England it was illegal for never-married women to live alone. Coventry and Southampton enforced this rule through public edicts. Norwich made solo distaff living punishable by imprisonment.[96]

Historian Silvia Frederici believes that restricting female sexuality to marriage supported enclosure: the privatizing of public lands on which farmers had long grazed animals. Turning communal fields into couples' property impoverished small farmers, forcing many to seek work in cities. Frederici notes that the large-scale uprooting of Europe's rural underclass coincided with witch trials in which female defendants were accused of debauchery and fornication with Satan.[97] The witch craze lasted from 1450 to 1750 and left most women untouched. But the one typically accused "was a woman of 'ill repute' . . . She often had children out of wedlock . . ."[98] As well, "Female friendships were one of the targets of the witch hunts, as . . . accused women were forced under torture to denounce each other, friends turning in friends."[99] Many of the women most vulnerable to witchcraft accusations had wandered afield of matrimonial norms. Elderly females living outside the marital family's border were especially vulnerable.[100]

So were never-wed men. In February 1615 a pauper named

Peter Kleikamp, from the North German town, Ahlen, was jailed on sodomy charges. At some point the accusation changed to witchcraft. Under interrogation (during which his limbs were crushed) Kleikamp confessed to having copulated with a demon and become a werewolf. He was executed by public burning in July 1615.[101]

England's common law streamlined legitimacy protocols. The jurist Edward Coke (1552–1634) wrote that everyone born outside marriage should receive similar treatment. For Coke, canon law's gradations and after-the-fact ceremonies smacked of Catholic pettifogging.[102] Drawing a bright-line distinction between "legitimates" and "illegitimates," he and his cohorts simplified inheritance rules, making any nonmarital child a permanent bastard, tout court. Common law discarded the belief in marriage as a sacrament, thereby rendering children born of mixed religious unions "legitimate." The 1603 legalization of clerical marriage made clergymen's marital offspring "legitimate." So, canon law ranked nonmarital children by parental behavior. English common law upheld wedlock as a tent that covered maritally-born people and left everyone else out. Now any child born before the wedding—even one that appeared two hours early—was "illegitimate" for life.[103]

French theologian John Calvin (1509–1564) influenced this jurisprudence. Like Luther he dismissed good works, positing that God predestined individuals to salvation or damnation. Like Luther, he promoted matrimony. Issued in Geneva, Calvin's 1546 Marriage Ordinance made engagement contracts hard to dissolve. Calvin imposed protocols: a witnessed proposal, parental consent, and registration with the presiding magistrate. These requirements inserted a courtship element into marriage by encouraging prospective spouses to spend time together. One can see modern matrimony taking shape as a tripartite process: courting, engagement, ceremony. Although he disliked interfaith marriages, Calvin conceded that since wedlock had no sacramental dimension, they stood legally and produced "legitimate" children.[104]

Amendments that denuded matrimony's sacramental status introduced the possibility of divorce. In England divorce was expensive and inaccessible to the general populace until 1857. Couples found other ways to separate, such as *divortium a mensa et thoro*: ecclesiastical permission to live apart. Such "bed and board" separations required proof of bigamy or cruel treatment; those who obtained them could not remarry, and, theoretically, have sex, while the other spouse remained alive. So, rural and small town dwellers sometimes employed the ritual of wife sale. A husband led his haltered wife into town and, before witnesses, sold her, often to her lover, with whom the couple had planned events beforehand.[105] These two methods of separation show the English Church's authority in policing Britons' personal lives and the powerful, if not official influence of neighbors in monitoring sexual relations. Technically illegal, wife sales were advertised through broadsides and word of mouth. They remind us that one of wedlock's original purposes was yoking each woman to a man empowered as her legal superior.

At some point the sixteenth-century Londoners Griffin and Marion Jones became noticeably miserable. Their St. Alban's Parish minister tried "to set them at unity."[106] Two neighbors—a cordwainer and a mercer—joined him. Marion argued unsuccessfully to William Rowe, Lord Mayor of London, that she should be able to leave Griffin, who had turned violent. This couple next took its grievances to the Clothworker's Guild, where leaders again urged reconciliation. The Jones' then appeared at a meeting of London aldermen; despite Griffin's testimony that Marion had tried to murder him, magistrates urged marital unity. Finally, the Jones' simply decided to live apart, with Marion paying Griffin alimony. When she ceased to make payments due to failing health, he sued her. The case was dismissed.

Historian Tim Stretton notes the chasm between legal theory and lived reality that this incident shows. The Jones' took separate lodgings without permission. Griffin then sued Marion for money that was technically his, since she was his economic subordinate, and the case went to court.[107] I am struck by the number of individuals and organizations involved and their unanimous stand; clearly, each marriage was viewed as community property, with individual contentment rated lower than togetherness. Griffin Jones's harassment of a sick woman attests to his sense of entitlement: the still prevalent belief that spousal privileges should not end when marital relations sour. At the very least, this example shows marriage history as a confusing flux, with numerous sordid elements, rather than a clean inspirational story.

During England's Interregnum (1649–1660), when no king occupied the throne, local authorities doled out retribution. Justices of the peace empowered to "punish bastard-bearers" handled individual cases.[108] The Act of 1650 mandated execution for women found guilty of adultery and their male partners. While this sentence was rarely carried out, its severity affected England's psychological landscape. As well, neighbors practiced sexual vigilantism. A ritual called the Skimmington Ride humiliated conjugal transgressors. A Skimmington might punish lovers with nonmarital children or wives who slept around. Villagers would encircle the culprit's home, singing and banging pots. They would force the accused man to ride backward on a donkey as spectators jeered. Offending women were led through villages astride mules as onlookers hurled garbage.[109]

Throughout the seventeenth-century, French Jesuits arrived in North America to establish a Gallic presence and convert indigenous populations. They encountered peoples like the

Montagnais-Naskapi, whose culture did not monitor female sexuality. One Father Paul Le Jeune warned a Montagnais man that his tribe's practices confused bloodlines; no man could identify his children. The Montagnais's reply is illuminating: "You French people love only your children; but we love all the children of our tribe."[110]

Fictitious Ailments, Bachelorphobic Purges, and Marriage Primers

British medical literature of the 1550s describes greensickness, a "disease" that afflicted unwed women. Historians suspect that its name came from early modern England's attribution of greenness (i.e., jealousy) to unmarried virgins.[111] Alleged symptoms included heart palpitations and headaches. Somehow, marriage alleviated them. While its lore originated in Europe, greensickness—also called chlorosis—"spread" to North America, where it remained a diagnosis for husbandless women until 1930.

The never-married French philosopher Jean de La Bruyère (1645–1690) considered conjugal love rare. In 1687 he wrote that most husbands envied men without wives.[112] But as La Bruyère composed a caustic character book, attitudes were shifting. Citizens of Protestant countries found careers as priests, nuns, or monks increasingly unattainable. In England celibacy became associated with popishness, as it was derisively called. A general suspicion of never-married people began to set in.[113] Puritan cleric William Gouge's influential 1622 tract, *Of Domesticall Duties*, mandates matrimony for everyone but the crippled, the impotent, and the contagiously ill.[114] As wedlock became a general dictate, it was often mentioned in the same breath as love. Sermons, poetry, and letters started to mention—even recommend—amorous feeling between spouses.

The romantic-marriage ideal had linguistic consequences. Traditionally a respectful word for any self-supporting female who spun yarn, "spinster" took on unfavorable connotations. Wives were now love objects, so never-married women were depicted as unlovable throwaways. In 1673 Richard Allestree, Provost of Eton College, encapsulated the stereotype: "An Old Maid is now looked on as the most calamitous creature in nature."[115] An anonymous twelve-page poem, "A Satyr Against Old Maids" (1713), circulated throughout London. It characterized never-married women as "nasty, rank, rammy, filthy sluts" who should wed any available candidates to avoid being "piss'd on with Contempt."[116]

Nonmarital men also suffered. In February 1726 constables raided a London molly house (gathering place for gay men) on Field Lane. (I anachronistically use "gay" and "homosexual" in lieu of malevolent eighteenth-century descriptors.) The approximately forty people arrested included a milkman named Gabriel Lawrence and an upholsterer named William Griffin. Two months later, Lawrence and Griffin were tried for sodomy alongside Thomas Wright, proprietor of a Beech Lane molly house. All were found guilty. Lawrence, Griffin, and Wright hung at Tyburn in May 1726.[117] Their executions epitomize anti gay hatred and bachelorphobia—feelings that contemporaries would not have separated. In the same breath, broadsides like the 1707 "Woman-Hater's Lamentation" condemned homosexuals for same-sex eroticism and apathy toward marriage.[118]

In 1739, naval captain Thomas Coram established the London Foundling Hospital to care for abandoned children. Nonmaritally born charges got new names, as if monikers could blot out their origins.[119] Every day they said prayers apologizing for their births. One girl memorized and performed on cue the following song:

Wash off my foul offence,
And cleanse me from my Sin;
For I confess my crime, and see
How great my Guilt has been.

In Guilt Each part was form'd
Of all this sinful frame;
In Guilt I was conceiv'd and born
The Heir of Sin and Shame.[120]

In this spirit, Britain produced a stream of conduct literature for the bourgeoisie that stressed matrimony's importance,
especially for women. In her 1675 advice book, teacher Hannah
Wooley (1622–c. 1675) declares it a wife's duty to admire her
husband more than any other person.[121] She provides a remedy
for greensickness that combines claret, currants, rosemary, and
mace.[122] Scottish minister James Fordyce's *Sermons for Young
Women* (1766) discourages female wit because it could engender
negativity toward marriage. (Fordyce [1720–1796] may have been
onto something.) The ultimate feminine joy, he writes, is making
a husband happy.[123]

In 1753, Britain's Parliament passed legislation that shows how
thoroughly marriage-centrism had come to permeate Anglophone
culture. The Parliamentary Act for the Better Preventing of Clan-
destine Marriage—usually shortened to Hardwicke's Marriage
Act—set requirements that remain nuptial staples: a ceremony, a
cleric, vows uttered before witnesses, and legal paperwork. From
1753 on, marriages required at least two witnesses, announcements read three Sundays prior to each wedding, an Anglican
cleric, and both parties' signature in a parish register. Unless it was
Quaker or Jewish, a valid wedding had to occur in an Anglican
church.

For 800 years, countless Europeans had married by exchanging pledges. Now British law nullified this practice, making nonmarital children more starkly "illegitimate." Nonmaritally born Englishmen were barred from high political office, upper-level military posts, jobs as prison superintendents, positions as church wardens, and jury service. Even without competing heirs, bastards could not inherit.[124]

Marital Supremacism Sweeps North America

North American colonies basically assimilated British common law. Nonmarital sex was illegal in the Jamestown settlement, which tasked churchwardens with ferreting out transgressors.[125] A 1657 act stated that manservants who had nonmarital sex with maidservants had to compensate the latter's employers financially or serve them for one year.[126] Virginia's Act of 1727 charged "any lewd woman . . . delivered of a bastard child" with a fee: 500 pounds of tobacco or fifty shillings. Failure to pay meant twenty-five lashes. Virginia lawmakers sought to isolate unwed pregnant females; anyone who harbored such women received identical penalties.[127]

A Virginia edict targeted unwed white women impregnated by black men. (I avoid the modifier, "African American," since black people did not become United States citizens until 1868.) The former had one month after giving birth to pay their respective parishes fifteen pounds. Churchwardens could place the children into indentured servitude until age thirty-one.[128]

Set in seventeenth-century Boston, Nathaniel Hawthorne's *The Scarlet Letter* (1850) realistically describes seamstress Hester Prynne clasping her nonmarital infant as she emerges from a dungeon. Onlooking women murmur that the "A" Prynne wears as a badge of shame should have been seared into her skin—an actual punishment.[129] Standing on a scaffold for three hours, Prynne endures her community's punitive gaze. Some of her nonfictional counterparts found themselves defenseless against physical assaults when they were locked in pillories.[130]

Puritan theology held that marital families were divinely ordained; when they wed, husband and wife became one flesh. Effectively, the married household replaced the universal church as a locus of godlinesss. This made solitude aberrant. Massachusetts mandated that any colonist with a spouse in Britain return "by the next sailing."[131] Never-married people could not legally reside alone. Town officials had to install "all single persons" into marital homes as boarders subject to heads of household.[132] This in itself provided a potent incentive to marry.

The Puritan marriage obsession had a counterweight: an obligation to reserve one's strongest feelings for God. Spouses who adored each other too much effectively committed idolatry.[133] The Westfield, Connecticut minister Edward Taylor (1642–1729) wrote his desideratum, "I send you not my heart, for . . . it hath not taken up any one's bosom on this side of the Royal City of the Great King."[134]

Historian Carol F. Karlsen writes that late seventeenth-century legal records in counties like Essex, Massachusetts "show a new focus on illicit conception and, especially, illegitimate births, rather than on sexual misbehavior *per se*."[135] Law required that a nonmarital child's father pay for its upkeep. To determine paternal identity, officials questioned women in labor, whose blurted-out names were deemed accurate. Until he turned twenty-one, an indentured servant's nonmarital child had to serve the former's master.

Benjamin Franklin's nonmarital son, William, was no secret, though Franklin hid the woman in question's identity. But a

Declaration of Independence signatory harboring his nonmarital child had little effect on the populous. Most "illegitimate" children were nailed to their origins. Birth certificates, tax rolls, property registrations, and death certificates recorded their status. Authorities regularly placed foundling children in homes that needed servants, with an indenture legalizing the barter of work for room and board. This contract lasted until the child reached their majority. When the Constitution's Thirteenth Amendment abolished involuntary servitude, current adoption practices emerged.[136]

Financial concern underscored antibastardy laws. Shifting monetary obligations to individuals shielded communities from the costs of nonmarital children's upkeep. Meanwhile, the marriage-propaganda machine hummed—albeit not as powerfully as it does today. British author William Hayley's 1785 poem, *A Philosophical Essay on Old Maids*, became popular in England, France, and Germany. It caricatures never-wed females as deluded misfits. Certain that men adore them, they react angrily when suitors do not materialize. Lacking husbands and babies, these women were, according to Hayley (who strikingly anticipates Sigmund Freud), "maimed."[137]

Marriage bias infiltrated university curricula. English clergyman William Paley's popular textbook, *The Principles of Moral and Political Philosophy* (1785), argues for wedlock as a conduit to happiness and a guarantor of societal stability. Paley depicts nonmarital sex as a slippery slope to "lewdness," "desperate villainies," and "dissolution of principles."[138]

Wedlock was no longer simply a dynastic alliance, contract, or sacrament. It was a love affair. That love does not sit comfortably alongside coercion was the new model's paradox. And since love requires no ceremonies or licensure, why did the modern ideal not reach its logical endpoint with matrimony evaporating?

Coontz, who directs research and publication for the Council on Contemporary Families, argues that "harsh penalties for illegitimacy" preserved wedlock as a crux institution.[139] Stigmas around nonmarital birth remained so powerful that intercourse had to be contained within wedlock.

So, why didn't people drubbed by bastardy laws object? Feverish political discourse raged throughout the late eighteenth century. For one hundred years, philosophers had challenged monarchs' divine rights. In 1689 the never-married political theorist John Locke argued that government boils down to a mutually consensual contract between ruler and ruled. If a monarch abused their power, the compact was nullified and popular rebellion justified.[140] As Lockean notions of social contract took hold, royal privilege became less palatable. American and French revolutionary soldiers tested Lockean tenets in the fire of armed conflict.

France's ruling revolutionary body overturned laws against homosexuality in 1791, guided by the principle that government should steer clear of people's intimate lives. After taking control of France, Napoleon confirmed this decision in 1811, when the Dutch legal code was similarly amended.[141] Bavaria expunged antisodomy laws in 1813. In 1811 English philosopher Jeremy Bentham criticized such prohibitions because they brought government into consenting adults' beds.[142]

The period also produced an international *querelle des femmes*. In 1776 Abigail Adams famously wrote her husband, future American president John Adams, that if legislators did not oppose women's legal disadvantaging, the latter were "determined to foment a rebellion."[143]

It seems that during such an era, nonmaritally born people and nonmarital adults would talk among themselves and forge coalitions. I think this did not happen for the same reason it has not occurred today; nonmarital people occupy discrete categories that prevent them from seeing their own common ground. They—we—have had trouble perceiving ourselves as what feminist Hilda Smith calls, "a distinct sociological group for which there are established patterns of behavior, special legal and legislative restrictions, and customarily defined roles."[144]

In 1779 Thomas Jefferson successfully pushed for a change that enabled Virginia's "illegitimate" children to be retroactively legitimated if the parental culprits married. Jefferson did not touch wedlock as a legal rights vector. He made a "rights of man" argument, claiming that all people deserved the ability to inherit. Lifting nonmarital inheritance bans would remove "feudal and unnatural distinctions."[145]

Dismantling marriage, with its punitive pecking orders, would have achieved Jefferson's end. Avoiding this route, he made his ideas palatable. By 1870 over half the states had enacted laws allowing retroactive legitimation by marriage. None had clauses that protected bioparents who wished to embrace nonmarital life. Nonmarriage seemed not to have been among the rights of man. And nonmarital children's vilification continued. In 1870 bestselling physician/author George H. Napheys explained that biology, not social disadvantaging, deterred "illegitimates:" "Generally they have a taint of viciousness or of monomania running in their blood, which spoils their lives."[146]

By 1830 thirteen states were allowing biomothers to grant nonmarital children legacies. By 1930 this was the rule in all states but one. American courts admitted only women as benefactors. In the words of one jurist, these rules reified "the relation of mother and child . . . in all its native and binding force."[147] Children could be legitimated by a biofather's pronouncement, epistle, or will, but until 1950 most states prohibited nonmarital kids from receiving paternal inheritances.

In 1927 the Supreme Court's *Buck v. Bell* decision protected a state's right to sterilize its citizens, so "generations of imbeciles" would not duplicate themselves. The "imbeciles" instanced were Emma Buck, a former prostitute; Carrie Buck, whom Emma bore out of wedlock; and Vivian, whom Carrie bore outside marriage. Evaluators designated Carrie a "moron" despite an acceptable academic record, achieved before the foster parents she lived with removed her from school to do their housework. Untrained observers pronounced Vivian mentally impaired, a conclusion presumably based on sleeping and crying, since she was seven months old. Carrie was forcibly sterilized and sent to live at the Virginia State Colony for Epileptics and Feebleminded. In a cruelly ironic touch, her foster parents took Vivian. (Their relative, Carrie said, had impregnated her through rape.) Vivian died in infancy from measles.

Historian Nancy Isenberg understands the Buck women as textbook examples of "white trash" at a time when Americans had become class obsessed.[148] Justice Oliver Wendell Holmes's opinion bears out this thesis. He "described the Buck family, this family with cascading problems . . . a series of people who've had illegitimate children."[149] The court intervened to stop cycles of nonmarital birth. Historian of science Stephen Jay Gould denounces *Buck v. Bell's* legacy, which involved sterilizing unknowing women like Doris Buck, Emma's natal sister, who tried for years to get pregnant after doctors told her she had undergone an appendectomy. Gould expresses indignation at Supreme Court justices for denying such women the experience of pregnancy. He does not discuss how prejudice against bastards shaped Holmes's decision.[150]

Marriage and Morals?

Where divorce received validation, it was often to enable marriage. England's President of the Probate, Divorce, and Admiralty

Division, Sir Gorell Barnes, chaired a 1912 government commission that suggested making divorce accessible in order to discourage nonmarital sex: "A working man whose wife leaves him to live with another man, is practically compelled to take a housekeeper . . . immoral relations almost inevitably result."[151] England did give soldiers' girlfriends financial support at the outset of World War I. As casualty numbers increased, a committee formed to determine eligibility for death benefits. It distinguished between wives and all other partners. Soldiers' girlfriends got temporary support but not the lump-sum payments widows received to cover funeral expenses. (Sound familiar?) Eight years later, the British army no longer accepted nonmarital lovers as allowance beneficiaries.[152]

World War I also generated a system of American support: "mother's pensions" for women running households as their partners served. Compensation went to wives and widows only.[153] Philosopher Bertrand Russell's treatise, *Marriage and Morals* (1929), denounces such nepotism. Russell argues for the state-sponsored dissemination of contraceptive information and the respectful treatment of sex workers. He claims that sexual jealousy is the result of cultural obsessions with legitimacy: "The discovery of fatherhood led to the subjection of women as the only means of securing their virtue." So, "there has in most civilized communities been no companionship between husbands and wives."[154] Relationships between men and women were tainted early by the mandate to produce "legitimate" children, which generated norms of lifelong monogamy and possessiveness. *Marriage and Morals* makes a case for open relationships. Russell's beliefs cost him a professorship in philosophy at the City College of New York. In 1940 the New York State Supreme Court ruled that he was morally unfit to teach.

In 1951 the Royal Anthropological Institute of Britain defined marriage as "a union between a man and a woman such that children born to the woman are the recognized legitimate offspring of both partners."[155] In this spirit, unwed Englishmen lost access to children. In 1956 the English Court of Appeal punished unmarried biofathers by ruling that biomothers would receive automatic custody. Natal fathers were to have no contact with their progeny.[156]

Elsewhere, truly horrifying fates awaited nonmarital children. Inventor Doris Drucker's autobiography describes a middle-class childhood in Cologne on the brink of World War II, where her parents' sterile marriage offered protection, if not inspiration. Their neighborhood's nonmarital infants were regularly deposited with a woman known as the "Angelmaker," who starved them to death.[157]

Throughout the 1950s, American birth certificates and school records classified nonmarital children as "illegitimate."[158] Between 1940 and 1970 though, most states revamped their statutes, allowing men to leave money and property to nonmarital children.[159] And, "In 1975, the European Convention of the Legal Status of Children Born Out of Wedlock recommended that all countries abolish discrimination between children born in and out of marriage."[160] By stating that those born within and outside of wedlock were equals, this proposal dealt marriage a significant blow. Still, in 1980, Supreme Court Justice William Brennan wrote smarmily that "modern society shrinks from the application of the Old Testament (Exodus 20:5) commandment 'visiting the iniquity of the fathers upon the children . . . ' as we progress to the more humanitarian view that there are no illegitimate children, only illegitimate parents."[161]

An Unwholesome Preoccupation with the Sexuality of Others

In 1993 the Dublin convent Sisters of Charity sold some of its land to a real estate developer. Beneath a section of the plot, 133 corpses were unearthed. These were remains of Magdalene laundresses: nonmarital female children, sexually active teenage girls, unwed pregnant women, and prostitutes imprisoned as slave laborers. The Magadelene movement began as a Catholic/Protestant enterprise aimed at improving "fallen women." It quickly Catholicized, opening its first home, the 1765 Magdalen Asylum for Penitent Females, as a halfway house that gave short-term vocational training. More laundries opened throughout Ireland; they became jails, secretly funded by the government and overseen by nuns. Presiding authorities determined inmates' sentences, which varied widely. Prisoners often had to shave their heads, wear standard-issue uniforms, and maintain silence. They worked backbreaking hours and survived on meager rations; one in ten died.[162]

Magdalene laundries operated in Europe, Australia, and North America for 231 years. The number of women tortured within their walls is uncertain, since records have been obscured. Cultural studies scholar Rebecca Lea McCarthy contends that the laundries were numerous in Ireland because of that country's traditional conflation of femaleness with wedlock. Clearly, the laundries' overseers qualified children in terms of marital birth. In 2014, 796 "illegitimate" infants' remains were discovered in the septic tank of Tuam's Bon Secours Mother and Baby Home.

News of these institutions has recently reached the public. Former inmates now come forward with their stories and meet at survivors' conventions. The Waterford Institute of Technology has made numerous accounts available through online archives. Filmmaker Stephen O'Riordan captured the Magdalene experience in his beautiful short documentary, "The Forgotten Maggies" (2009).

Four orders ran the Irish laundries: The Sisters of Charity, the Sisters of Mercy, the Sisters of Our Lady of Charity, and the Good Shepard Convent. No representative of these orders would speak with O'Riordan when he was filming. Worse, Church apologists characterize the laundries as relics of a distant era. This is absurd; the last laundry closed in 1996. Thousands of Magdalene women remain alive. One is Kathleen Legg, a retired air force medic from Bournemouth, England. Born nonmaritally in Lisvernane, Legg was placed in a laundry on Dublin's Stanhope Street at age fourteen with the promise of a good education. She did not see a classroom for four years, though the presiding nuns sent glowing academic reports home. They named Legg "Number Twenty-Seven" and ordered her to work twelve-hour stints. "There were big heavy rollers," she recalls. "The sheets would be white hot." Prisoners sustained injuries from mangles, primitive spin dryers.[163]

Historian Frances Finnegan avers, "This unwholesome preoccupation with the sexuality of others is an aspect of the system curiously ignored by its apologists . . . Such apologists seem unaware of the fact that even in the mid-nineteenth century . . . the imposition of enforced celibacy and confinement with hard labour were punishments normally reserved for felons."[164]

An unwholesome preoccupation with the sexuality, or asexuality, of others forms the basis of much relationship-status discrimination. The United States still has more laws regulating sex than all European nations combined. In Virginia, for instance, it is illegal to masturbate in another adult's presence with consent. Mississippi forbids the demonstration of condom use in sex-education classes.[165] Alabama illegalizes the sale of vibrators for genital use.[166]

This preoccupation underlies distinctions between marital and nonmarital children. Legal scholar Solangel Moldonado has shown that American immigration law treats the two types of children differently. A marital child of an American biofather and a noncitizen routinely receives US citizenship. But according to Section 1409 of the Immigration and Naturalization Act, nonmarital children of American biodads must be legitimized before age eighteen to access the same right. The man must acknowledge his paternity in an oath or written document and get a court order. In *Nguyen v. INS* (2001) the Court ruled that a Vietnamese biomother and her American partner's child could be denied citizenship, even though he had resided in the United States, with his father, since age five. But the man had not legitimated him by age eighteen. Since no marital child would lose citizenship on such a technicality, Nguyen's team argued (unsuccessfully) that the young man's constitutional right to equal protection had been violated.[167]

Contemporary mental health professionals have carried the marital standard. In 2005, attorneys arguing for same-sex wedlock in New Jersey gathered quotes from the American Psychological Association and the New Jersey Psychological Association. Psychiatrists and psychologists had an opportunity to state that happy, gay, nonmarital households were excellent places for kids and deserved every legal benefit.[168] Instead, they tarred nonmarital children: "Being born to unmarried parents is still widely considered undesirable . . . children of parents who are not married may be stigmatized by others . . . This . . . will not be visited upon the children of same-sex couples when those couples can legally marry."[169]

This survey provides a mere glimpse of disciplinary tactics used to enforce marriage. They include the following:

- policing nonmarital eroticism and punishing sex outside marriage with penalties that include public shaming, fines, institutionalization, imprisonment, indentured servitude, torture, and execution;
- establishing matrimony as the prerequisite for independent living;
- establishing matrimony as the prerequisite for citizenship;
- treating the act of leaving marriage as a crime;
- treating nonmarriage as a symptom of failure;
- celebrating marriage as an emblem of success;
- treating wedded people as adults and never-married people as children;
- zero-sum thinking about relationships, according to which one person must be the sole recipient of another's amorous love, since that emotion is presumed to come in limited quantities;
- zero-sum thinking about relationship status, according to which legal benefits cannot extend to nonmarital relationships because this would weaken the link between wedlock and entitlement, dimming spouses' sense of specialness;
- invalidating nonmarital alliances and thereby increasing wedlock's importance.

I hope that at the very least, my discussion of "illegitimates'" shows that it is impossible to understand marriage without understanding bastardy. My goal is to encourages viewing marriage with greater skepticism than it usually invites. When people step back and evaluate matrimony, a theoretical space forms in which they can ask themselves what, if any of its parts are worth preserving and whether they want their lives circumscribed by marital dictates.

Coontz notes that legitimacy-obsessed cultures tend toward elaborate weddings.[170] Such nuptials reward adherence to conjugal convention, and they do so indirectly. Wedding ceremonies stress phenomena that sound beneficial: companionship, intimacy. A wedding in Oregon will not begin, "We gather to celebrate the fact that Steven will be the assumed biological father of Molly's child, while unwed Oregonian men must sign paternity papers." It will not continue, "These two will be each other's next of kin when it comes to health decisions. They've known each other for three months; lovers of thirty years lack this option . . . and Steven and Molly's kids won't be bastards!"[171]

Instead, marriage ceremonies traffic in "love" and "commitment." These benign-sounding nouns can send guests drifting into a comfortable mental fog. Even those of us who dislike being manipulated in this way find ourselves responding emotionally. And because wedding nomenclature is polysemous, officiants and onlookers often understand it differently. By love, the ceremonial script does not denote personal attachment of different sorts. It means *conjugal* love. By devotion it refers to *marital* devotion. The rhetoric is so familiar, however, that precise definitions seem unnecessary.[172] In some ways, the seventeenth-century announcement of wedlock as "a remedy against sin and to avoid fornication" was better because it was honest. Contemporary nuptials camouflage their outcomes by celebrating matrimony's insiders without mentioning its outsiders. Traditionally, its outsiders have been an entire class of innocent children.

I have argued elsewhere that contemporary weddings display their principals' discomfort with conformity through demonstrations of ethnicity. Ethnic flourishes represent muted assertions of individualism. Multicultural decorations, cuisine, and poetry are used to distinguish the principals from others making an identical relationship choice. Often the additions come from a smorgasbord of options presented by wedding planners rather than either spouse's background. A non-Jewish groom will smash a glass with his foot. A non-Indian bride will wear a sari. A non-black couple will jump over a broom. Regional menus and rings handcrafted by indigenous artists contribute gently to a wedding's ambience; detailing foreign cultures' practices might not. An American bride and groom who dance to hauntingly gorgeous rhythms of the Bedouin El Oud, a traditional stringed instrument, probably don't know what intense shame Rwala Bedouins attach to nonmarital birth: "If a woman gave birth to a child before her wedding, she was cast out of her group or killed by her own kin."[173] Anthropologist Aref Abu-Rabia attributes Rwala Bedouin intolerance of bastardy to the culture's "inculcation of chastity codes in girls at an early age" in preparation for wedlock.[174] Appreciating, or in academia's current list of no-no's, "appropriating" another culture's positive artifacts, seems fine to me. But a *wedding* that uses any society's most beautiful productions without mentioning its brutal cruelty toward nonmarital people buries the lead. This omission cries out for attention.

I will argue that during periods rife with relationship experimentation, the emphasis on legitimacy becomes stronger. Marriage evangelists fight to secure wedlock's survival by idealizing it. They strain to prove that licensed sexual relationships are splendid, other erotic ties are second rate, and all partnerships pale beside the spousal connection. But as long as marriage remains our society's dominant organizational mode, people who live nonmaritally will be disadvantaged. And American children will remain vulnerable to vicious relationship-status discrimination.

(Endnotes)

1   I borrow this phrase from Victor Turner. *The Ritual Process: Structure and Anti-Structure* (New Brunswick, New Jersey: Aldine Transaction, 1969), 155.
2   Gen. 21:11–14, Gen. 21: 19–21.
3   Zech. 9:6.
4   Wisd. 3:16–17.
5   Stephanie Coontz, *Marriage, A History: How Love Conquered Marriage* (New York: Penguin Books, 2005), 65–6.
6   Ibid., 76. Marilyn A. Katz, "Daughters of Demeter: Women in Ancient Greece," *Becoming Visible: Women in European History,* ed. Renate Bridenthal, Susan Mosher Stuard, and Merry E. Wiesner (Boston: Houghton Mifflin, 1998), 54.
7   1 Cor. 7:9.
8   1 Cor: 7:33.
9   Jo Ann McNamara, "Matres Patriae/Matres Ecclesias: Women of Rome," *Becoming Visible,* 83.
10 Coontz, *Marriage,* 80.
11 *Love for Sale: A World History of Prostitution,* trans. Richard Daly (New York: Grove Press, 1997), 95.
12 McNamara, "Matres Patrias," 83.
13 Mary Beard, *SPQR: A History of Ancient Rome* (New York: Liverlight Publishing Corporation, 2015), 308–9.
14 Ibid., 359.
15 John Witte, Jr., *The Sins of the Fathers: The Law and Theology of Illegitimacy Reconsidered* (Cambridge: Cambridge University Press, 2009), 53–4.
16 Ibid., 56.
17 Ibid., 56.
18 Rosemary Rader, *Breaking Boundaries: Male/Female Friendship in Early Christian Communities* (New York: Paulist Press, 1983), 83. Matthew: 19:11–12.
19 Christopher Brooke, *The Medieval Idea of Marriage* (Oxford: Clarendon Press, 1989), 65–7.
20 Derwas J. Chitty, *The Desert a City* (Crestwood, New York: St. Vladimir's Seminary Press, 1966), 8–11. Peter Brown, *The Making of Late Antiquity* (Cambridge: Harvard University Press, 1978), 80.
21 Palladius of Aspuna, *The Lausiac History,* trans. John Wortley (Collegeville, Minnesota: 2015), 123–4.
22 *The Making,* 86, 64.

23   "Matres Patrias," 91.
24   Laura Swan, *The Forgotten Desert Mothers: Sayings, Lives, and Stories of Early Christian Women* (New York: Paulist Press, 2001), 39.
25   *Breaking Boundaries*, 62–5.
26   Ibid., 66–8.
27   *Against Jovinianus*, trans. W. H. Fremantle (Delcassian Publishing, 2017), 55.
28   Ibid., 85.
29   Augustine, *Confessions*, trans. R. S. Pine Coffin (London: Penguin, 1961), 131.
30   Peter Brown, *Augustine of Hippo: A Biography* (Berkeley: University of California Press, 1967), 50–5.
31   Henry Chadwick, *Augustine* (Oxford: Oxford University Press, 1986), 44.
32   Ibid., 176.
33   Ibid., 136. Augustine wrote his softer treatise, "On the Good of Marriage" (401), a manual for nuns, largely to distinguish himself from St. Jerome, whose ferocious attack on matrimony was discomfiting fellow clergy.
34   Ibid., 89.
35   Brown, *Augustine of Hippo*, 470–7. Chadwick, *Augustine*, 102.
36   *Medieval Europe: A Short History* (New York: John Wiley & Sons, 1964), 46.
37   *Marriage*, 103.
38   Witte, Jr., *The Sins*, 71–2, 53–9.
39   Ibid., 54–9.
40   Gen. 21:8–10.
41   Frances and Joseph Gies, *Marriage and the Family in the Middle Ages* (New York: Harper & Row, 1989.
42   Anonymous, *Beowulf*, trans. Seamus Heaney (New York: W. W. Norton & Company), 3.
43   Ibid., 3–5.
44   Quoted in Ruth Mazo Karras, *Unmarriages: Women, Men, and Sexual Unions in the Middle Ages* (Philadelphia: University of Pennsylvania Press, 2012), 35.
45   J. M. Wallace-Hadrill, *The Barbarian West: The Early Middle Ages, A.D. 400–1000* (New York: Harper & Row, 1962), 110–11.
46   Valerie L. Garver, *Women and Aristocratic Culture in the Carolingian World* (Ithaca: Cornell University Press, 2009), 70–7. George Duby, *The Knight, the Priest, and the Lady: The Making of Marriage in Medieval France*, trans. Barbara Bray (New York: Pantheon Books, 1981), 30–3

47 xxxix Garver, *Women*, 131,133.

48 Jacques Boussard, *The Civilization of Charlemagne* (New York: McGraw Hill Book Company, 1968), 24–42, 157–66.

49 Garver, *Women*, 161–3.

50 Frances and Joseph Gies, *Marriage and the Family*, 78.

51 Duby, *The Knight*, 44–5.

52 "From the Laws of Cnut," *The Broadview Anthology of British Literature*, Vol. 1, ed. Joseph Black, et al. (Peterborough, Ontario: Broadview, 2015), 386–8.

53 Diarmaid MacCulloch, *Christianity: The First Three Thousand Years* (New York: Viking, 2009), 373.

54 Hollister, *Medieval Europe*, 132.

55 Mazo Karras, *Unmarriages*, 47.

56 *Historia calamitatum, Heloise and Abelard: The Letters and Other Writings*, trans. William Levitan (Indianapolis: Hackett Publishing, 2001),12.

57 Mazo Karras, *Unmarriages*, 48–52.

58 *Letters of Abelard and Heloise, Heloise and Abelard*, 56.

59 Coontz, *Marriage*, 112.

60 Mazo Karras, *Unmarriages*, 165–208.

61 Ibid., 9–10. John Boswell's *Same-Sex Unions in Premodern Europe* (New York: Random House, 1994) argues for the existence of a medieval marriage ceremony between men. Historian Alan Bray finds this unlikely, since the documented ritual did not involve lovers or exclude already married participants. *The Friend* (Chicago: University of Chicago Press, 2003), 316.

62 Quoted in *The Broadview Anthology*, 407.

63 Alan Bray, *The Friend* (Chicago: University of Chicago Press, 2003), 81–3.

64 Witte, Jr., *The Sins*, 84–6.

65 Ibid., 99. Oblation—the medieval practice of placing children in monasteries—included those born within marriage. See John Boswell, *The Kindness of Strangers: The Abandonment of Children in Western Europe from Late Antiquity to the Renaissance* (Chicago: The University of Chicago Press, 1988) especially Part III, Chapter 8.

66 Witte, Jr., *The Sins*, 132.

67 *The Trouble with Normal: Sex, Politics, and the Ethics of Queer Life* (Cambridge: Harvard University Press, 1999), 218.

68 *The Village Voice*, November 15, 1983, 14.

69 Kathleen Manning, "What is the History of Marriage?", *U.S. Catholic*, October 9, 2012, https://uscatholic.org/articles/201210/what-is-

the-history-of-marriage.

70 Coontz, *Marriage*, 110.

71 Geoffrey Chaucer, *The Canterbury Tales*, *The Riverside Chaucer*, ed. Larry D. Benson (Boston: Houghton Mifflin Company, 1987), 79.

72 Ibid., 79.

73 Mazo Karras, *Unmarriages*, 141.

74 Coontz, *Marriage*, 108.

75 Ruth Mazo Karras, *Common Women: Prostitution and Sexuality in Medieval England* (New York: Oxford University Press, 1996), 97–8.

76 MacCulloch, *Christianity*, 608.

77 Ibid., 555–6.

78 See John Farrell, *Paranoia and Modernity: Cervantes to Rousseau* (Ithaca: Cornell University Press, 2006), 60–6.

79 Witte, John, Jr., *From Sacrament to Contract: Marriage, Religion, and Law in Western Tradition* (Louisville: Westminster John Knox Press, 2012), 119.

80 Quoted in Coontz, *Marriage*, 134.

81 Gen. 1:28.

82 Martin Luther, "The Estate of Marriage," *Luther's Works*, Vol. 45, trans. Walter Brand (Minneapolis: Fortress Press, 1962), https://pages. uoregon.edu/dluebke/Reformations441/LutherMarriage.

83 Steven E. Ozment, *The Age of Reform, 1250–1550: An Intellectual and Religious History of Late Medieval and Reformation Europe* (New Haven, Yale University Press, 1980), 435.

84 *Paranoia and Modernity*, 78.

85 Geoffrey Moorhouse's *The Last Divine Office: Henry VIII and the Dissolution of the Monasteries* (Katonah, New York: Blue Bridge, 2008) shows how English monasteries' popularity as pilgrimage sites spurred this initiative. Discouraging Catholicism by suppressing pilgrimages combined with a royal mandate to seize valuables housed within the monasteries.

86 Witte, Jr., *The Sins*, 126–7.

87 Mazo Karras, *Unmarriages*, 197.

88 Parliament's 1536 Second Act of Succession changed this by empowering the monarch to name successors in wills or by written executive order. It also retroactively annulled Henry's marriage to Ann Boleyn, with whom he had sired Elizabeth. Hence, the queen's enemies would derogate her as a bastard. Thomas Regnier, "Did Tudor Succession Law Permit Royal Bastards to Inherit the Crown?", *Brief Chronicles* IV (2012–13), 48.

89 Seventeen-year-old Henry FitzRoy died in 1536 of what is recorded

as consumption. Peter Beauclerk-Dewar and Roger Powell, *Royal Bastards: Illegitimate Children of the British Royal Family* (Brimscombe Port: The History Press, 2006), 28–33.

90 See Mark Rohrs, "Elizabeth Tudor: Reconciling Femininity and Authority," unpublished master's thesis, University of South Central Florida, 2005.

91 Coontz, *Marriage*, 113.

92 Sheilagh Ogilvie, *The European Guilds: An Economic Analysis* (Princeton: Princeton University Press, 2019), 109.

93 Ibid., 110.

94 Ogilvie, *The European Guilds*, 124.

95 Keith Thomas, *In Pursuit of Civility: Manners and Civilization in Early Modern England* (New Haven: Yale University Press, 2018), 328.

96 Amy M. Froide, *Never Married: Singlewomen in Early Modern England* (Oxford: Oxford University Press, 2007), 19-27.

97 *Witches, Witch-Hunting, and Women* (P.M. Press, 2018), 31.

98 Ibid., 19.

99 Ibid., 40.

100 Brian P. Levack, *The Witch-Hunt in Early Modern Europe* (London: Routledge, 1987), 129.

101 Rolf Schulte, *Man as Witch: Male Witches in Central Europe*, trans. Linda Froome-Döring (Palgrave Macmillan, 2009), 1–3.

102 Witte, Jr., *The Sins*, 109–10.

103 Ibid., 115–19.

104 Ibid., 170-7

105 John R. Gillis, *For Better, For Worse: British Marriages, 1600 to the Present* (New York: Oxford University Press, 1988), 211–14.

106 Tim Stretton, "Marriage, Separation, and the Common Law in England, 1540–1660," *The Family in Early Modern England*, Ed. Helen Berry and Elizabeth Foyster (Cambridge: Cambridge University Press, 2007), 21.

107 Ibid., 24–5.

108 Capp, Bernard, "Republican Reformation: Family, Community, and the State in Interregnum Middlesex, 1649-1660," *The Family in Early Modern England*, Ed. Helen Berry and Elizabeth Foyster (Cambridge: Cambridge University Press, 2007), 46.

109 Coontz, *Marriage*, 111–12.

110 Eleanor Leacock, "Montagnais Women and the Program for Jesuit Colonization," *Women and Colonization: Anthropological Perspectives*, ed. Eleanor Leacock and Mona Etienne (New York: Praeger, 1980), 30-1.

111 Helen King, *The Disease of Virgins: Green Sickness, Chlorosis, and the Problem of Puberty* (London: Routledge, 2004), 29.

112 *Characters*, trans. Jean Stewart (Harmondsworth, Middlesex, England: 1970), 68.

113 Ibid., 157.

114 Froide, *Never Married*, 157.

115 Quoted in Bridget Hill, *Women Living Alone: Spinsters in England, 1660-1850* (New Haven: Yale University Press, 2001), 146.

116 Quoted in Hanne Bank, *Straight: A Surprisingly Short History of Heterosexuality* (Boston: Beacon Press, 2012), 67.

117 Alan Bray, *Homosexuality in Renaissance England* (New York: Columbia University Press, 1982), 90.

118 Anonymous, "The Women-Hater's Lamentation," 1707, in *Homosexuality in Eighteenth-Century England: A Sourcebook*, ed. Rictor Norton, December 1, 1999, http://www.rictornorton.co.uk/hater.

119 Lisa Zunshine, *Bastards and Foundlings: Illegitimacy in Eighteenth-Century England* (Columbus: The Ohio State University Press, 2005), 98.

120 Quoted in Zunshine, *Bastards and Foundlings*, 5.

121 Hannah Wooley, *Gentlewoman's Companion or, a Guide to the Female Sex* (Devon, England: Prospect Books, 2001), 134-5.

122 Ibid., 183.

123 Full text of *Sermons to Young Women in Two Volumes by James Fordyce, https://bl.uk/collection/sermons-to-young-women*.

124 Witte, Jr., *The Sins*, 119-20.

125 Dominik Lasok, *"Virginia Bastardy Laws: A Burdensome Heritage," William and Mary Law Review* (9:2) 1967, 409.

126 Ibid., 411.

127 Ibid., 419.

128 Ibid., 417-18.

129 Nathaniel Hawthorne, *The Scarlet Letter*, ed. Brian Harding (Oxford: Oxford University Press, 1990), 43.

130 Witte, Jr., *The Sins*, 140.

131 Edmund S. Morgan, *The Puritan Family: Religious and Domestic Relations in Seventeenth-Century New England* (New York: Harper & Row, 1944), 39.

132 Ibid., 27.

133 *Anne Orthwood's Bastard: Sex and Law in Early Virginia* (Oxford: Oxford University Press, 2003), 34–5.

134 Ibid., 50.

135 *The Devil in the Shape of a Woman: Witchcraft in Colonial New England* (New York: W. W. Norton & Company, 1998), 198.

136 Cindy Peyser Safranoff, *Crossing Swords: Mary Baker Eddy VS. Victoria Woodhull and the Battle for the Soul of Marriage* (Seattle: This One Thing, 2015), 88–9.

137 Froide, *Never Married*, 179.

138 *Principles of Moral and Political Philosophy*, https://oll.libertyfund.org/titles/paley-the-principles-of-moral-and-political-philosophy.

139 Coontz, *Marriage*, 307.

140 *Two Treatises of Government*, ed. Peter Laslett (Cambridge: Cambridge University Press, 1960).

141 The Honorable Michael Kirby, AC CMG, "The Sodomy Offence: England's Least Lovely Criminal Export," *Journal of Commonwealth Criminal Law* 1 (2011), 6.

142 Coontz, *Marriage*, 152.

143 "Familiar Letters of John Adams and His Wife During the Revolution," *Feminism: The Essential Historical Writings* (New York: Vintage Books, 1972), 2.

144 "Feminism and the Methodology of Women's History," *Liberating Women's History*, ed. B. A. Carroll (Urbana: University of Illinois, 1976), 370.

145 Witte, Jr., *The Sins*, 147.

146 Ibid., 155.

147 Ibid., 147.

148 *White Trash: The 400-Year Untold History of Class in America* (New York: Penguin Books, 2016), 201–3.

149 Paul Lombardo, "Emma, Carrie, Vivian: How a Family Became a Textbook Case for Sterilization," interview with Shankar Vendantam, NPR, Washington, DC, April 23, 2018: https://www.npr.org/transcripts/604926914.

150 *The Mismeasure of Man* (New York: W. W. Norton & Company, 1981;1996), 365–6.

151 Quoted in Rebecca Probert, *The Changing Legal Regulation of Cohabitation: From Fornicators to Family, 1600–2010* (Cambridge: Cambridge University Press, 2012), 119.

152 Ibid., 158.

153 Cott, *Public Vows*, 171.

154 Bertrand Russell, *Marriage and Morals* (London, Allen & Unwin Ltd., 1976), 26–7.

155 Quoted in Coontz, *Marriage*, 27.

156 Probert, *The Changing Legal*, 157.

157 Doris Drucker, *Invent Radium or I'll Pull Your Hair Out: A Memoir* (Chicago: University of Chicago Press, 2004), 16.

158 Coontz, *Marriage*, 257.

159 Ibid., 153.

160 Quoted in Coontz, *Marriage*, 257.

161 Quoted in Witte, Jr., *The Sins*, 157.

162 Erin Blakemore, "How Ireland Turned 'Fallen Women' Into Slaves," History.com, July 21, 2019, https://www.history.com/news/magdalene-laundry-ireland-asylum-abuse.

163 Naomi Greenway and Luisa Metcalfe, "'It Will Be with Me Until the Day I Die," *Daily Mail*, May 26, 2015, https://www.dailymail.co.uk/femail/article-3097186/Magdalene-laundry-survivor-reveals-s-haunted-fear-breaking-labour-loneliness-ordeal-60-years-later.

164 *Do Penance or Perish: Magdalen Asylums in Ireland* (Oxford: Oxford University Press), 243.

165 Janice Zarro Brodman, *Sex Rules! Astonishing Sexual Practices and Gender Roles Around the World* (Coral Gables, Florida: Mango, 2017), 79.

166 Lester Haines, "Alabama Judges Take a Hard Line on Dildos," *The Register*, September 14, 2009, https://www.theregister.com/2009/09/14/alabama_ruling.

167 Solangel Moldenado, "Illegitimate Harm: Law, Stigma, and Discrimination Against Non-marital Children," *Florida Law Review* 63 (2011), 345–95.

168 Drawing on research by Dr. Charlotte Patterson, Coontz reports that "Lesbian couples . . . have greater parenting awareness skills on average, than heterosexual parents," and, "Unlike the documented cases of fathers who encourage sons to 'prove' their heterosexual masculinity, there is no evidence of gay and lesbian parents doing anything comparable with their children." *The Way We Really Are: Coming to Terms with America's Changing Families* (New York: Basic Books, 1997), 161–2.

169 Brief for American Psychological Association and New Jersey Psychological Association as Amici Curiae in Support of Plaintiffs—Appellants, *Lewis v. Harris*, http://www.lambdalegal.org/binarydata/LAMBDA-PDF/pdf/320.pdf.

170 Coontz, *Marriage*, 307, 30.

171 For a celebratory list of marital entitlements see Michelle M. Winner, "A Guide to the Legal Benefits of Getting Married," *Brides*, July 16, 2021, https://www.brides.com/legal-benefits-of-marriage.

172 For a crystalline analysis of obfuscating language's role in propaganda, see the introduction to Jason Stanley, *How Propaganda Works* (Princeton: Princeton University Press, 2015).

173 Lewellyn Hendrix, *Illegitimacy and Social Structures: Cross-Cultural Perspectives on Nonmarital Birth* (Westport, Connecticut: Bergen & Garvey, 1996), 1.

174 "Family Honor Killings: Between Custom, State, and Law," *The Open Psychology Journal*, 2011, 4, 34–44.

3

The American Marriage Fixation

"To come with a well-informed mind is to come with an inability of administering to the vanity of others."

—JANE AUSTEN, *NORTHANGER ABBEY*

Matrimony as a Harmonizing Blend of Opposites

In 1788 New Hampshire became the ninth state to ratify the United States Constitution, thereby ushering in a new era of American government. One year later, the French Bastille was stormed. English speakers largely favored defiance of what they considered a corrupt regime.[1] In 1792, however, the revolutionary Commune was established; it declared France a republic. King Louis XVI was tried for tyranny, convicted, and executed. Under the aegis of a subgroup called the Committee for Public Safety, mob violence raged for two years. Some 2,000 French citizens were murdered in the notorious Terror.[2] By the time France outlawed Catholicism, Anglophone opinion had turned against the revolution. However, a band of intellectuals known as the Jacobins continued to (partially) support revolutionary programs. It included William Godwin (1756–1836), whose 1793 treatise, *Enquiry Concerning Political Justice and its Influence on Moral Happiness*, denounces marriage, and his lover Mary Wollstonecraft (1759–1797). Faced with her unintended pregnancy, Godwin conceded to wedlock so the child would be "legitimate"; after marrying they continued to live and socialize separately in London.[3]

Wollstonecraft authored *A Vindication of the Rights of Woman* (1792), the first published secular argument for sexual equality. It argues that women are not inherently dependent or coquettish but acquire these qualities through socialization. Wollstonecraft advocates formal education and work (including military service) for women, insisting that sexual parity will upgrade matrimony: "The affection of husbands and wives cannot be pure when they have so few sentiments in common . . . when their pursuits are so different."[4] The *Vindication* recommends schooling as preparation for maternity.

Wollstonecraft ventures repeatedly into dangerous territory only to take cover behind two cultural icons: the capable wife and the good mother. Nevertheless, her work and life were considered scandalous. Those who never read the *Vindication* knew that prior to her unusual relationship with Godwin, Wollstonecraft had been impregnated by an American Revolutionary War soldier named Gilbert Imlay and born a nonmarital child.[5]

This period's clashing ideas led to what some historians view as a compromise.[6] Men and women were cast as opposing types. Clergy, courtesy book writers, and other advisors described the sexes as so different that they required assessment on disparate registers. The question was no longer superiority or inferiority but variance.

Medieval and Renaissance culture had deemed women the lustier sex. This was no compliment; traditional Europe was not, in contemporary parlance, sex positive. Church writers described erotic insatiability as a distaff flaw—like fickleness. The eighteenth century, however, gave rise to the idea that males were highly libidinous and females weakly sexed. A woman's sexual appetite, once congruent with her unreliable nature, "now became abnormal and unwomanly."[7] Scottish medical author, Dr. John Gregory (1724–1773), explains in *A Father's Legacy to His Daughters* (1774), "A virtuous girl often hears very indelicate things with a countenance no wise embarrassed, because in truth she does not understand them."[8] Some, raised on what historian John Tosh calls "an unquestioning belief in the purity and innocence of womanhood,"[9] probably misunderstood the sexual basics. Others surely grasped the imperative to misunderstand, at least publicly.[10]

Now a woman who enjoyed sex betrayed her own quiddity. Folk wisdom upheld marriage and motherhood as femininity's actualization. Armed with the handy art of forgetting, pundits claimed that this had always been the case, and everyone knew it. Unique sensitivity qualified women for wedlock and disqualified them for much else. Early modernity's decarnalized female lacked lust, "competitive desires and worldly ambitions that consequently belonged—as if by some natural principle—to the male."[11] This justified woman's exclusion from the university, the market, and the battlefield. It situated her in the conjugal home, where she could manage emotional matters, instill values in children, and set standards of taste.

Literary critic Nancy Armstrong remarks that "the most powerful household is the one we carry around in our own heads."[12] Many early moderns seem to have internalized a belief that the sexes blended harmoniously in wedlock, where men flourished as breadwinners and women thrived as nurturers. A preference for separate, gender-based spheres hardened into ideology: evidence-resistant belief that demands acquiescence. Men, with their rational capacities, belonged in academia and politics. Constitutional toughness made them natural businessmen, ready to "cope with the hard, dirty public work of the industrial city . . . maneuvering in the rough and ready new world of capitalism."[13] But never-married men were defective. A 1795 poem, "The Bachelor," published in the newspaper *Philadelphia*, deprecates a phlegmatic youth who is "stupidly free from Nature's tenderist ties."[14]

The marriage ethos embraced by Britain and America's middle class found expression in literature. Fictional representations of affective marriage proliferated throughout the eighteenth and nineteenth centuries. Hannah More's *Coelebs in Search of a Wife* (1809), for example, features Charles, an Englishman searching for his other half. He passes on fashionable London ladies before reaching Hampshire, home of eighteen-year-old Lucinda Stanley. Charles becomes entranced by and engaged to this modest country girl. A hit in More's native England and America, *Coelebs in Search of a Wife* went through eleven editions in nine months.[15]

More (1745–1833) prescribes female diffidence. Mentions of her Latin studies make Lucinda blush, but she takes pride in sedulous housekeeping. *Coelebs* ("unmarried" in Latin) suggests that by downplaying their intellects and exuding quiet goodness, women would attract husbands. Conversely, a man who valued modest female virtue would find his just rewards.

Companionate marriage bestowed joint psychological gifts. Men learned that they were intellectual system builders, political agents, economic competitors, and household heads. They could savor the pleasure of being in charge. Women learned that through behind-the-scenes management and childrearing, they were *really* in charge. Both could feel progressive; the new template was said to supersede prior models. Accordingly, marriage-based families were pressed to place their interests above friendship, community, and state. American advice writer Catharine Beecher (1800–1878) declaimed that "the desire for a home of his own, and the hopes of paternity" motivated men's work in the public sphere.[16] This anti-suffragist delivered her culture's extremist message: every American should make marriage their primary emotional investment.

This attitude represented an extraordinarily radical breach with the past. Traditional sources say it best. Viewers of *Orestes*, by Euripedes (c. 480–c. 406 BCE), would have recognized its eponymous protagonist, who commits matricide in the name of justice, as flawed. But his valuation of relationships would have been familiar: "The friendship of a man whose character melds with yours, even if he doesn't belong to your immediate family, is worth more to a man than thousands of relatives."[17] Ancient Greek nomenclature used identifiers like "friend of Pericles."[18] Aristotle (384–322 BCE), who devoted two chapters of *The Nicomachean Ethics* to friendship, treats as uncontroversial the claim that no one without friends would wish to live.[19] He defines three kinds of friendship characterized by, respectively, utility, pleasure, and virtue.[20] Adapting this lexicon to current times, utilitarian friendship might involve someone who provides job leads. The pleasurable friend could be a tennis buddy. Virtuous friendship, however, stems from mutual appreciation of the *arête* (excellence) each friend possesses. Reciprocal encouragement of *arête* gives friendship value; virtuous friendship gives life meaning.

The Renaissance produced an outpouring of friendship writing from which two classic treatises stand out. "On Friendship" (1580) by never-married French essayist Michel de Montaigne (1533–1592) pays homage to the former's relationship with writer Étienne de la Boétie (1530–1563): "such a friendship has no model but itself."[21] For Montaigne great friendship is enigmatic: "If I were pressed to say why I love him, I feel that my only reply could be: 'Because it was he, because it was I.'"[22] "Of Friendship" (1612) by English statesman Francis Bacon (1561–1626) celebrates friendship as the tie most conducive to "the ease and discharge of the fulness and swellings of the heart."[23] Bacon disparages marriage as an obstacle to ambition.[24] These authors would not have understood the phrase, "just friends."

Traditionally, relatives were not automatically friends, but some kin met the standard friendship demanded. This belief was proverbial in Hellenistic, medieval, and Renaissance culture. Early modernity turned it on its head, making marriage-based family the social benchmark. Advisors prescribed paring family down to its nuclear core.

This trend badly injured never-married people. Now every bachelor was a mind without a pulsating heart or a resonant soul. Each spinster was a heart without a directing mind. The fiction of wedlock as mutually perfecting unity began exerting power over people in childhood, when they started to learn that ever-potent lesson: what constitutes normality.

Early modern bachelors' cultural capital plunged lower as wedlock became, increasingly, prerequisite to masculinity. The nascent industrial economy absorbed women's work, including beer brewing, candlemaking, and midwifery. Increasingly, men worked outside the home, so money flowed from an external source, transforming households into insular domains whose methods of support were unseen.[25] Marriage propagandists feminized the conjugal home. Welsh-born author Elizabeth Griffith (1727–1793) wrote, "It is doubtless, the great business of a woman's life to render his home pleasing to her husband."[26] Griffith's big hit was a series of letters between she and her spouse that spans six volumes, describing their courtship and marriage in mind-numbing detail. By 1849 the introduction to an anthology of female poets could state that different did not imply better or worse: "It is easy enough to understand that the sphere of woman's duty requires powers altogether dissimilar from those which are needed by the male . . . Man rules the mind of the world, woman its heart."[27]

Scholars of early modern marriage emphasize choice, averring that affective matrimony involves people selecting each other rather than being thrust together.[28] I think this notion appeals to moderns because it validates contemporary courtship. It also appears autonomous; "choice" became an organic self-willed act. Actually, betrothal still responded to various pressures and incentives. Husbands could expect accolades and households that provided uplifting moral agendas. Elevated to a pedestal that excluded sensuality, wives could await admiration within and outside the home. But early modern wedlock's most powerful inducement may have been freedom from the embarrassment of being never-married; bachelors, spinsters, and nonmarital children could anticipate contempt. Surely, wedlock's enhanced status influenced much decision-making, as it does today. Realistically, all marriage was, and is, somewhat coerced. Whatever private discussions couples have, wedlock occurs in a public context and bestows copious advantages. There is a spectrum, with forced marriage on one end and encouraged marriage on the other.

Liberating Enslaved People by Regulating Their Personal Lives

When nineteenth-century proslavery writers justified an institution under attack, they often described African promiscuity. The journal *Debow's Review*, which circulated throughout the American South from 1846 to 1884, characterizes enslaved people as excessively carnal. An anonymous Mississippi farmer laments the difficulty of imparting marriage's sacredness to his charges: "I know of no means whereby to regulate them, or to restrain them."[29] Resisters of abolitionism's rising tide also claimed that enslaved people's disesteem for matrimony signaled low morality. This claim would live on as a racist truism.

Defenders of slavery portrayed it as a benign institution in which white masters safeguarded dependents who could never negotiate a competitive world. Such ideologues found a useful template in wedlock. After all, they insisted, marriage was another unequal, legally binding relationship. The protective husband and dependent wife exemplified benign asymmetry, slaveholders argued, insisting that ownership did not demean an enslaved person as marriage did not compromise a wife. Erasure of their surnames and legal identities actually benefitted wives, as did the presumption of sexual obedience. (Husbands could not be charged with raping their wives.)[30] As social theorist George Fitzhugh wrote, "Marriage is too much like slavery not to be involved in its fate."[31] This Virginian envisioned the two institutions interlocking to promote civic stability.

During the Civil War, runaways and enslaved people freed by Union soldiers found temporary refuge in contraband camps. General Grant's army established these encampments in, among other states, Alabama, Florida, Mississippi, North Carolina, South Carolina, and Tennessee. When the 1861 Confiscation Act freed any enslaved person in a Union area, many seized their liberty. Imprecise data make it difficult for historians to gauge how many landed in contraband camps. Some researchers estimate between 400,000 and 500,000 freed-people. Others put the number at half a million.[32]

Presbyterian minister John Eaton served as Contraband Camp Superintendent. His records describe "men, women, and children in every stage of disease and decrepitude . . . with flesh torn by the terrible experiences of their escapes."[33] Getting them married was a priority. Officials were told to give refugees shelter, schooling, and paid work—while imposing matrimony. Reading contraband camp volunteers' accounts, one finds it inconceivable that wedlock factored in. How could nuptial vows matter for malnourished people scarred from beatings and clothed in rags, whose shoeless feet were covered with sores?

Contraband camp directors had a twisted logic. They saw desperate human beings. But rather than cite slavery's depredations as the cause, many officials stressed nonmarriage to explain formerly enslaved people's "uncivilized" quality. This malady had to be remedied before other issues were addressed. Eaton ordered camp officials to enforce wedlock on any pair of lovers seeking shelter.[34]

Matrimaniacal policing of black families continued after the Emancipation Proclamation. By the spring of 1864, a Union decree empowered all army clerics to perform weddings among and supply marriage certificates for freed people. Formerly enslaved men who had been soldiers were required to marry female partners if they had them. The Freedmen's Bureau, established by Congress in 1865, upheld this policy and enjoined formerly enslaved people to assemble marital families. By 1865 it had codified a set of "Marriage Rules," which illegalized romantic cohabitation.[35]

In 1866, Georgia passed a law that declared its cohabiting freedmen and women married. Thousands of people who may never have planned to marry were suddenly wed. No one stopped by to announce the legislation, so many formerly enslaved people probably did not know about it. Yet a man living with two women, or vice versa, could be arrested for bigamy.

Other states reentering the Union that took this automaticizing measure include Mississippi, North Carolina, South Carolina, and Virginia.[36] Throughout the South untold numbers of formerly enslaved people were married without their consent. We know their predicament mainly from annals of institutions that punished them. Court registers recorded outcomes without providing much context. One must assume, however, that many formerly enslaved people had minimal information about the new restrictions on their intimate lives.

The story of Sam Means, a blacksmith living in Georgia, is illuminating. He could not have researched his home state's laws since he neither read nor wrote. "Keeping company" with a woman named Ellen Johnson, Means probably did not know that he was her spouse. This fact came up twenty-six years later, in 1890, when Means was arrested after visiting an Oxford, Georgia resident named Frances Slaton. At trial Means's attorney argued that his client had lived with a different woman years earlier and remained her husband. So, the local definition of fornication—intercourse between unwed adults—did not apply. This strategy failed. Means was found guilty and ordered to pay the state lawyer's fees, which he could not afford. This probably lengthened his sentence when he was incarcerated. Considering Means's fate, we see someone caught in the flypaper of racism and marriage law: hindered by regulations he had no hand in shaping, which were not explained to him until his trial. This freedman was anything but free.[37]

Historians report that despite such practices, many formerly enslaved people—understandably—wanted to marry. For some, wedding vows represented a first: taking legal oaths as enfranchised adults. Additionally, in times of war material benefits are dear. Wives of black soldiers killed in battle could petition for back pay. However, postmarital sex disqualified them from receiving war pensions. An 1882 legal amendment stated that black widows taking lovers "in open and notorious adulterous cohabitation" would lose their compensation.[38]

Congressman Thomas D. Eliot of Massachusetts and Senator Jacob Howard of Michigan rhapsodized that marriage would give formerly enslaved people dignity. The humblest freedman would become king of his own connubial castle.[39] Policymakers made no space for informal erotic alliances. They held formerly enslaved people to a single conjugal standard and complained that it was often ignored. For Mississippi (and then Texas) Freedman Bureau agent Alvan Gillem, getting these people married was an *idée fixe.* Gillem's reports express shock at freedmen and women's sense that they could "take up" with each other and separate if a relationship ran its course. The practice of having more than one sexual partner seemed to him distressingly widespread. Gillem regularly reported offenders to local law enforcement.[40]

A Florida law gave "colored" cohabitants nine months to marry. North Carolina allowed freedmen and women six months to show county clerks marriage certificates. Every month missed formed a discrete, prosecutable crime.[41]

In some southern states divorce was illegal. Wherever they resided, formerly enslaved people must have found it largely inaccessible. Divorcing meant finding a lawyer, paying him, and covering court fees. Often it required taking time from work and traveling. Those who managed such feats faced another obstacle: no-fault divorce did not exist. An initiating party had to prove the other's erotic meandering, sexual dysfunction, cruelty, alcohol abuse, or desertion. The campaign on behalf of black marriage, therefore, must have shoehorned countless freed people into arrangements from which there was no exit. For many postbellum black adults, what would later be celebrated as the "right" to marry must have felt more like a disciplinary measure.

The imposition of wedlock was not limited to formerly enslaved people. In 1879, E. A. Hayt, Commissioner of Indian Affairs, demanded that male lovers of Native American women living on reservations marry their partners. Derogatively termed "squaw men" who failed to comply faced eviction."[42]

The initial draft of the Constitution's thirteenth amendment stated, "All persons are equal before the law." Probably smelling a threat to paternalistic relations, Senator Lazarus Powell objected. Had the amendment's original wording survived, its implications could have been broader than this Kentucky Democrat imagined. Nonmarital Americans might have made a case for receiving privileges reserved for marrieds. Children who found their living situations intolerable could have established the right to seek other arrangements. The amendment's language was narrowed: "Neither slavery nor involuntary servitude . . . shall exist within the United States."[43]

Bolstering Marriage While Informing Nonmarital People That They Are Worthless

The 1867 Kansas Marriage Act illegalized sexual cohabitation. Transgressors were fined between five hundred and one thousand dollars or imprisoned for up to three months. This was no moribund law. In 1886 journalist Edwin Cox Walker and publisher Lillian Harman had what would today be called a commitment ceremony. No judge or cleric presided; no license was issued. The two affirmed their feelings for each other, stressing the relationship's privacy. Harman vowed to not make promises she could not keep—presumably oaths of sexual exclusivity. She kept her surname.

Local authorities arrested both parties for the crime of pretending to be husband and wife—just what they had not done. Walker and Harman were tried and convicted. He got seventy-five days in prison; she got forty-five.[44]

Spinsters like Alice Paul (1885–1977), who served three separate prison terms for the cause of suffrage, and Hallie Quinn Brown (1849–1949) remain unfamiliar to most Americans. But it is generally understood that at one time women could not vote, activists protested, and a series of constitutional amendments rectified the problem. The relationship between voting rights and marriage is less known. In 1882 Congress criminalized the practice of living nonmaritally with more than one person. According to the Edmunds Act, a man guilty of "bigamous unlawful cohabitation" lost the abilities to hold public office and vote. Supreme Court judges ruled that a governing body could "declare that no one but a married person shall be entitled to vote."[45] (The decision was repealed in 1983.)

Nineteenth-century politicians found that denigrating nonmarriage helped their careers. Indiana's Republican senator Albert J. Beveridge had a high profile in the early twentieth century. In 1905 he published a homiletic primer for young men. Here is a tidbit of Beveridge's wisdom: "The . . . man who is not enough of a man to make a home need not be counted. He is a 'negligible quantity,' as scientists put it. So, if your arm is not strong enough to protect a wife, and your shoulders are not broad enough to carry aloft your children in a sort of grand gladness, you are not really worthwhile."[46]

In 1917, Congress passed a law requiring literacy of every immigrant over age sixteen. It exempted male immigrants' wives. Two interlocking beliefs undergirded this law. First, wives were better than other women. Second, bachelors were a hazard. A husband whose wife lived abroad became, effectively, a bachelor. Without an on-site spouse to restrain his larcenous tendencies, he might become dangerous, so allowing wives' entry into the country was paramount.

This policy responded to waves of European and Asian immigration. It legally crystallized beliefs about wedlock's alchemizing power. President Theodore Roosevelt announced, "The first essential for a man's being a good citizen is his possession of the home virtues."[47] Women lacking these virtues included girlfriends, best friends, females cohabiting with men nonmaritally, and prostitutes. All were unwelcome. No relationship other than marriage earned a woman entry into the United States. Sadly, this is still true.

Matrimony was deemed so important that students could get college credit for learning to do it. Sociologist Ernest R. Groves taught marriage preparation courses at Boston University (in 1922) and the University of North Carolina (in 1927). With his wife, Gladys, he coauthored the 1931 handbook, *Sex in Marriage.* An expanded version called *Sex Fulfilment in Marriage* appeared in 1942, five years after the American Medical Association endorsed contraception, green-lighting marital intercourse for nonprocreative purposes.[48] The belief that men had a monopoly on lust still held, but advice-givers touted women's enjoyment of—or at least responsibility to—married sex. The Groves' told readers that meaningful eroticism was vital to marriage, and marriage was essential to life. Writing, lecturing, and counseling together, they acted the part.

The Social Security Act took effect in 1935, largely in response to 1929's economic crisis. President Franklin Roosevelt crowed: this was no handout but a compensation system. Deductions from workers' wages would fund a federal retirement plan. Employees would receive amounts commensurate with what they put in.

Would they? Amended in subsequent decades, the act created a category of "survivor benefits" for wives whose husbands died before age sixty-five. These were not extended to nonmarital partners. A wife could tap into payments based on her husband's contributions. Never-wed women had no comparable option. Once a man turned sixty-five, his benefits increased by 50 percent if a wife lived with him.[49] So, a sixty-five-year-old husband working in an office alongside a bachelor of the same age, who performed identical tasks and put the same amount toward Social Security, reaped 50 percent more from the system. Policymakers understood that unwed male employees' taxes were subsidizing married couples. This was perceived as a positive, because it encouraged bachelors to marry.[50]

Brave World War II soldiers heard that they were protecting matrimony. The government-sponsored 1942 radio show, "To the Young," features an earnest youth telling a young woman that the war effort is "About love and gettin' hitched and havin' a home and some kids, and breathin' fresh air out in the suburbs."[51] One war-bonds advertisement features the painting of a woman perusing a fashion magazine. The framed photograph of her soldier beau sits on a table behind her. "Will you do without an evening gown today—FOR A WEDDING DRESS TOMORROW?" the copy reads.[52] Investing in war bonds, not clothing, meant investing in marriage, such ads insisted. "Bridal gowns, like wedding rings, were seen as part of the war effort—what the country was fighting for," explains historian Vicki Howard.[53]

Midcentury exaltations of marriage are especially offensive because so many nonmarital people participated in the war effort. Rita Levi-Montalcini (1858–1940) grew up in Turin. She earned an MD degree at the University of Turin but lost her job when Benito Mussolini's 1938 Manifesto of Race robbed Italian Jews of their livelihoods. She persevered, building a makeshift laboratory in her bedroom and studying chicken embryos' nerve fibers. Levi-Montalcini then practiced as a physician in Florence, treating refugees who poured in from Northern Europe. After the war, she resumed her cellular biology research at Washington University in St. Louis, ultimately isolating a protein that stimulates nerve growth. She won the Nobel Prize for Medicine in 1986.

Marriage propagandists tout wedlock as a health enhancer

that extends life expectancy. Levi-Montalcini confounds their claims. She remains the oldest enduring Nobel recipient, having died in 2013 at age 103.[54]

In 1944 German forces invaded Hungary. During their occupation, a Swedish "diplomat" named Rauol Wallenberg (1912–1945, disappeared) arrived and began issuing counterfeit passports to Jews, whom he identified as Swedish subjects awaiting repatriation. Working from the Swedish Legation, Wallenberg rented some thirty buildings and designated them extraterritorial, which gave their occupants diplomatic immunity. Omitting to mention his connection to the Allies, the never-married Wallenberg hung signs advertising these buildings as research facilities. No one knows how many lives he saved before his disappearance, probably at the hands of Soviet captors. The buildings alone housed 10,000 Jewish people.[55]

Such heroism did not dent wartime matrimania. Film scholar Jeanine Basinger writes that movie audiences "not only *wanted* to believe in marriage in those years; they *needed* to believe in it."[56] Hollywood obliged. Director William Wyler set his film, *Mrs. Miniver* (1942), in a London suburb, where architect Clem Miniver (Walter Pidgeon) and his wife Kay (Greer Garson) deal with their oldest, Vin, joining the army. They diligently care for Toby and Judy, the two youngsters still at home. Both forty-two when the film was shot, Pidgeon and Garson look youthfully, maturely handsome. This fit Wyler's conception of responsible people made more responsible by wedlock. In one scene Clem and Kay respond to a German air attack by ushering the kids into an Anderson bomb shelter. A finely synchronized team, they coolly help each child through the ordeal. Wyler's message is clear; while soldiers fought on the front lines, marrieds preserved stability at home.

Postwar clinicians gave marriage the hard sell. Paul Popenoe authored a 1950s *Ladies Home Journal* column thrillingly titled,

"Can This Marriage Be Saved?" A college dropout who boldly designated himself, "Dr. Popenoe," he founded the Hollywood-based American Institute of Family Relations, where clients received advice about how to become more desirable, dependable spouses. Sometimes called "the Mayo Clinic of Marriage," this facility employed thirty-seven counselors and advised over 1,000 couples per year at its peak. Popenoe set its tone, philosophizing that "a motherhood-fixation is responsible for the celibacy of many old bachelors who might otherwise have been superior husbands."[57] Stereotypes of unwed men as oddballs stunted by mommy-love allowed him to bachelor-bash ad libitum.

David M. Levy, a Columbia University clinical psychiatry instructor, claimed that marital eroticism protected children's mental health. Levy's book, *Maternal Overprotection* (1943), differentiates between submissive and domineering mothers, suggesting that married sex cures both maladies: "A wife devoted to her husband cannot be exclusively a mother . . . the release of libido through satisfactory sexual relationship shunts off energy that must otherwise flow . . . in the direction of maternity." Levy based his statements on a survey of twenty women, with no comparative focus group.[58]

By making prejudice sound scientific, figures like Popenoe and Levy became doyens. They benefitted from the widespread respect accorded Sigmund Freud, whose theories loomed large. Even those who had never read *Interpretation of Dreams* (1899) felt as if they had. Americans heard that dreams opened passage-ways to reservoirs of feral desire. They knew that a prestigious treatment involved lying on a couch and talking to a credentialed shaman who could extract subterranean motives from the asso-ciative ramblings.

Freud's theories have since been discredited. A model of the mind based on metaphors—id, ego, superego—is quackery.[59]

Freud claimed that male maturation involved falling in love with one's biological mother and having this reverie shattered by a menacing father figure, who would become an emulative model. He did not discover this "Oedipus complex" in a research environment but recalled it. In an 1897 letter to a friend, Freud wrote, "I have found, in my own case too, [the phenomenon of] being in love with my mother and jealous of my father, and I now consider it as a universal event of early childhood."[60] Note that Freud did not attribute this process to other Austrian men or other Austrian Jewish men. He generalized it to all men, claiming that his theory ran the entire ethnographic and historical gamut. Postwar America was mesmerized and equally enchanted by Freud's fable in which the pivotal moment in every female's life involves realizing that she lacks a penis. This recognition frays attachment to her mother, whom she considers the castrator. Not to worry; maternal identification can resurface when a woman marries and gives birth.[61] Surprise, surprise.

American clinicians normalized Freud's astonishingly weird version of childhood, accepting it as a series of phases that made people marriageable. Here is America's preeminent postwar childrearing expert, Doctor Spock: "We believe that a boy's attraction to his mother in the three-to-six-year-old period is vital in establishing an idealistic romantic pattern for his future life as an adult."[62]

Freudian psychoanalysis constructed females as wives and childbearers. She who accepted her biologic/psychic femininity embraced these roles. "Neurotic" women rejected castrato status. Their unconscious desire to be men manifested in intellectual or professional ambition. Because formative events occurred in early childhood's terra incognita, they could not be verified. One simply had to trust an analyst's intuition.

Legitimated by Freud, midcentury marriage propagandists had a field day. Psychiatrist Marynia Farnham and journalist

Ferdinand Lundberg's 1947 hit, *The Modern Woman: The Lost Sex*, characterizes an independent female as "a contradiction in terms." They labelled feminism "a deep illness" caused by wrong-headed women's desire to emulate men. Married female professionals were driven by—what else?—the wish to castrate their husbands.[63] Farnham and Lundberg told women to cease all this career-building and penis-snipping. It distracted from their true vocation: matrimony.

These luminaries considered never-married women emotionally unfit to teach children and suggested putting an official ban in place. They overlooked countless nonmarital female educators. Lucy Craft Laney (1854–1933), for instance, was born to formerly enslaved people and founded the Haines Normal and Industrial School in Augusta, Georgia. America's first black school, its curriculum included English, math, physics, chemistry, German, and French. Laney's fundraising sustained the school; she served as its principal for fifty years, inaugurating America's first African-American kindergarten class.[64]

Matrimonial advisors downplayed such pioneers and focused on helping women hook husbands. "It's up to you to *earn* the proposal," declared journalist E. Michel in 1951. Michel explains that any gal with a beau must promote herself in particular and wedlock in general.[65] In 1953 psychiatrist Sidonie Gruenberg warned that "a girl who hasn't a man in sight by the time she is 20 is not altogether wrong in fearing that she may never get married."[66] In colleges, marriage classes achieved unprecedented popularity with female students. Textbooks like *Toward a Successful Marriage* met coeds' demand for matrimonial instruction. Curricula of schools like Stephens College, University of Iowa, and Boston College included nuts-and-bolts marriage preparation.[67]

Network television was similarly prescriptive. Set in the fictitious town of Springfield, *Father Knows Best* (1954–1960) starred Robert Young as Jim Warren, an insurance company manager married to Margaret (Jane Wyatt). Jim sagaciously counsels the three Warren kids, cloyingly nicknamed "Princess" (Elinor Donohue), "Bud" (William Thomas Gray), and "Kitten" (Kathy Anderson). Margaret appears in the morning fully made up, wearing a wide-skirted dress, heels, and a pearl necklace, as if heading to a gala. This is quite an ensemble for the task of handing Jim his briefcase. But advice columns told wives to rise early and prettify themselves for their husbands.[68] When she is not caring for her brood, Margaret sits on a sofa reading magazines. This was the good life, postwar American style.

Two thirds of females who began college in the 1950s dropped out, usually to marry.[69] Belief in the husband-breadwinner/wife-homemaker household had never been so widely shared by people from different regions, classes, and cultures. Sociologists liken this consensus to a bulldozer that obliterated every alternate view.[70] It razed a path from America's cities to its suburbs. The suburban population increased from thirty-six million to seventy-two million denizens.[71] Concurrent birth rates rose; by 1957 America saw 129 births per every thousand women, a sharp increase from the previous decade.

By the century's end, 95 percent of Americans were marrying.[72] Sitcoms normalized the separate spheres ideal. However, a backlash may have occurred. Some historians believe that media representations of domestic bliss generated discontent with actual life, contributing to divorce rates. These began rising in 1957. One out of every three couples who wed in the 1950s, American marriage's "golden age," eventually divorced.[73]

Still, glad-to-be-married propaganda proclaimed a glorious era of conjugal enmeshment. It told unmarrieds that their lives were hollow. The tax code solidified this message. In the initial dictate for federal income tax, relationship status played no role. Each person was taxed independently. In 1948 Congress decided to give wedded couples a combined tax-return option. Spouses could file as split-income households, dividing their lump-sum earnings in half, which generally resulted in lower federal taxes.[74]

In his bestseller, *The Naked Ape* (1967), English zoologist Desmond Morris claims that naked apes (i.e., human beings) couple monogamously because fidelity keeps peace between males. His chapter on sexuality gives marriage as the answer to virtually every question. Why do women have orgasms? To produce warm feelings between spouses. Why do pregnant women have sex when many female primates don't? Again, to keep husbands happy. Morris designates the female orgasm a "borrowed male pattern."[75] How do women climax? Missionary position intercourse with lots of in-out thrusting. Morris blathers that "everything possible has been done to . . . ensure the successful evolution of a pattern as basic as pair formation."[76]

After reading *The Naked Ape*, one feels very sad for Mrs. Morris. This makes it easy to view the book as a dated, feeble attempt at satire. Actually, Morris retains a following. In 2011, *Time* magazine included *The Naked Ape* on its list of the greatest and most important pieces of English-language nonfiction written since 1923.[77]

Much evolutionary biology combines Morris's idea with bleak gender essentialism. It envisions different objectives hard-wired into men and women. Compelled to secure fidelity, men shelter and feed biological children. Seeking status, women want commitment, sustenance, and male protection. So, men are sexually jealous, women threatened when lovers share emotional intimacy with other women. This perspective shows matrimony blending unsavory agendas. Males spread their genes through sole sexual access to women. Women get practical support and prestige. Evolutionary biologist Robert Wright intones, "In every human culture . . .

marriage . . . is the norm, and the family the atom of social organization."[78] He recklessly maps social observation onto evolving
bodies of prehistoric ancestors. With colleagues Helen Fisher and
Sarah Blaffer Hrdy, he has furthered notions of marital inevita-
bility. Touting a biological explanation, these determinists resemble
preachers who claim that God favors wedlock. They present
matrimony as something over which human beings have minimal
control. This strips critics of the ability to reshape or discard it.

Medieval and Renaissance Europe evinced numerous, over-
lapping kinds of love. Regard for parents, lords, and monarchs;
affection between siblings, natal and nonnatal; intellectual frisson
between tutors and students; longing for the divine; Petrarchan
desire for an unattainable desideratum; and passion between
sexual partners. Eighteenth-century advice-givers singled out
love between spouses as nonpareil. They extolled companionate
marriage as an enlightened relationship predicated on gender
difference. Two hundred years later their vision culminated in a
short period of marriage-centric prosperity that Americans associated with tradition, having lost touch with Augustine's para-
digmatic belief that love should be channeled toward God and
one's neighbors. When the new model was eventually challenged,
its defenders positioned themselves as traditionalists. As Coontz
explains, "they could not understand why this kind of marriage,
which they thought had prevailed for thousands of years, was
being abandoned by the younger generation."[79]

Cohabitation—or Something Else?—Generates Outrage

"An Arrangement: Living Together for Convenience, Security,
Sex," proclaimed a 1968 *New York Times* headline. Its subject,
Barnard sophomore Linda LeClair, had lived with her boyfriend,

Peter Behr, for two years. When their circumstances came to light, Iphigene Ochs Sulzberger threatened to stop donating to the college unless LeClair was expelled. Ochs Sulzberger was not just any alumnus; she stood to inherit the *New York Times* fortune.

LeClair appeared before a school judicial committee. Reporters "called her a 'whore' and an 'alleycat'; they called Barnard 'Barnyard.'" In his widely syndicated column, William F. Buckley, Jr. maligned LeClair as "an unemployed concubine" who was "gluttonous for sex and publicity."[80]

In photographs LeClair looks like she's smiling for her high-school yearbook. Wearing neutral-colored cardigan sweaters, with no makeup and dirty blonde hair falling past her shoulders, this Hudson, New Hampshire native may be the least concubinish concubine in history. Her technical infraction was lying on a registration form. Journalist Moira Weigel explains, "According to Barnard regulations, students could live off campus only with family or an employer."[81] LeClair had moved into Behr's apartment on 110th Street, eight blocks from Columbia University, where he attended school. On her housing form LeClair claimed to be the nanny of a Manhattan-based married couple with whom she lived. She provided the contact information of friends who agreed to cover for her.

As hate mail poured into the college, Behr and LeClair distributed an anonymous questionnaire on which 300 Barnard students admitted to falsifying housing information. Sixty identified themselves in letters to the administration. LeClair got a slap on the wrist: Barnard president Martha Peterson barred her from its dining halls. LeClair withdrew from Barnard, and Behr left Columbia in solidarity with her.

In cohabiting nonmaritally, these two did something that had become common. Their unapologetic stance galled marriage fundamentalists, who accused them of flaunting a nonmarital setup—an odd allegation, since LeClair had taken pains to conceal the relationship.[82] Reporter Maggie Astor argues that student's rights fueled the "LeClair Affair"; Barnard undergraduates did not want the college operating *in loco parentis*.[83]

Some students surely felt infantilized by Barnard's rules. LeClair took more heat than Behr did, which shows the 1950s sexual double standard in operation. A woman living nonmaritally with a man was doing so, largely, for sexual access to him. To Buckley and other commentators, this made her tawdry, while Behr was a regular American guy. But analysts of this episode don't consider a counterscenario. What if LeClair had moved into a Morningside Heights apartment alone? She would have been in equal violation of Barnard's by-laws. Students were to remain in their (presumably) marital households-of-origin until marriage. The liminal period between "legitimate" childhood and wedlock was deemed so perilous that colleges had to supervise. This shows relationship-status discrimination as the LeClair Affair's key subject. As often happens in nonmarital news, the lead got buried.

Marriage Garners (Some) Criticism

In women's studies circles the LeClair incident generates discussion as an event that foreshadowed Second-wave Feminism. Like all expansive social movements, this one resists precise characterization, but clearly, many second-wavers were marriage-critical. Kate Millet objected to the assumption that wedlock provided an optimal, validating childrearing environment.[84] Germaine Greer mocked husbandly exceptionalism—the claim of having found one man in a million.[85] Psychologist Phyllis Chesler exposed mental health professionals' malfeasance. Acknowledging that men and women fell victim to psychiatric maltreatment, Chesler found clinicians interpreting female self-reports more skeptically. Too often, psychotherapy involved nudging renegade wives back to their marriages.[86] Each of these thinkers perceived wedlock as flawed. Each understood conjugal sentimentality as a screen that concealed power. Each tried, in her way, to pull that screen back.

Betty Friedan took a more forgiving stance, presenting suburban housewives' boredom through a women's rights lens. Friedan prescribed "mature" matrimony. This meant spouses sharing childcare and jointly pursuing careers. Wedlock would fulfill both sexes, who "marry, of course, but on a much more mature basis."[87]

In 1966 the National Organization for Women held its kickoff conference in Washington, DC, elected Friedan president, and confirmed a "Statement of Purpose." It endorsed a reformed version of wedlock: "A true partnership between the sexes demands a different concept of marriage, an equitable sharing of responsibilities, of home and children . . ."[88] "The Statement," as it became known, articulated centrist feminism's view that marriage was salvageable. Husbands would share childcare, enabling women to pursue formal education and build meaningful careers. Never-married women were—the word stuck around for decades—"valid."

This analysis elided wedlock's infliction of harm on nonmarital people and sidestepped key questions. Why did America isolate matrimony as *the* "true partnership?" What rulebook made it part of childrearing—and how would intramarriage parity eliminate widespread "moral horror at the idea of unwed pregnancy?"[89] If power disparities between husbands and wives were corrected, egalitarian sexual possessiveness—not everyone's ideal—would remain. NOW posited a via media between rigorous investigations of wedlock and marital triumphalism. This centrist position, put forth by "liberal feminists," basically prevailed.[90]

Fanciful authors grasped for an epoch of matriarchal rule. Here is Gloria Steinem writing in 1972: "For five thousand years or more, the gynocratic age had flowered in peace and productivity. Slowly, in varying stages . . . the social order was painfully reversed. Women became the underclass . . . "[91] Simultaneously, prudent historians noted the absence of historical evidence for anything resembling matriarchal history.[92] Gerda Lerner spearheaded the discipline of women's history at Sarah Lawrence College. She explained patriarchal government as the result of Middle Eastern agricultural expansion that began in 8,000 BCE. Lerner argued that legal marriage emerged as a means of differentiating between respectable (wedded) and nonrespectable (sexually unfettered) women.[93]

Liberal feminists focused on wedlock's oppressive aspects while ignoring the massive terrains of privilege it afforded men and women. They criticized matrimony for its sex-based inequities and presented a solution: balance the tables. A fuller reckoning would have analyzed asymmetries between husbands and wives while considering how marriage benefitted both, disenfranchising nonmarital people. Subsequent generations of writers have repeated this error. I count myself among them.

Royal Weddings Cast a Spell

In October 1981, Ronald Reagan granted Rauol Wallenberg posthumous, honorary American citizenship. Another event overshadowed the tribute to this nonmarital hero. That July, 750 million viewers observed the televised wedding of Charles, Prince of Wales, and Lady Diana Spencer, at St. Paul's Cathedral in London. The British throne's heir apparent looked morose. Peering from beneath her veil encumbered by a grotesquerie of taffeta, pearls, and sequins, the princess appeared stupefied. She marched slowly forward in her gown, with its twenty-five-foot trail, followed by a phalanx of attendants.

"The people's princess" was actually aristocratic; her ancestors included King Charles II (1630–1685). She and Prince Charles travelled in the same circles; their rapport was hardly electric. Diana was thirteen years the prince's junior: nineteen on her wedding day. She botched his name when uttering her vows but compensated by providing an heir: Prince William, born in 1982. Two years later she produced the requisite "spare," Prince Henry (aka Harry).

By their 1996 divorce, Charles and Diana's dramatis personae were well known. They included the Prince's companion, Camilla Parker Bowles; her ex-husband (and Charles's friend), army officer Andrew Parker Bowles; and Diana's lover, James Clifford Hewitt. Wedding aficionados knew the dimensions of Diana's gown and two backup dresses. Briton's taxes paid for these garments and the event's twenty-seven cakes.

Decades later, the spectacle of a seemingly empty relationship generates fascination—at least among reporters. It reminds us that princess imagery still dominates the formal wedding, with its regally attired brides and solicitous bridesmaids. *Vanity Fair* magazine's April 2018 issue featured "Charles and Diana's Fairy-Tale Wedding," an article enhanced with photographs of the procession, the vows, and Queen Elizabeth alongside the couple on a Buckingham Palace balcony, where Charles stares distractedly away. Colossal media attention given subsequent Windsor nuptials of Prince William to graphic designer Catherine Middleton (on November 16, 2010 at Westminster Abbey) and Prince Harry to actress Meghan Markle (on May 19, 2018 at Windsor Castle) shows an unabated obsession with royal weddings. In September

2019 *Marie Claire* magazine offered an explanation: "When you turn on the news and Brexit has been so divisive, a royal birth or wedding can bring the country together in a way few other stories can."[94]

Religious Matrimania Takes Off

As marriage critics gained visibility, opposing forces gathered. In 1977 psychologist James C. Dobson founded the NGO Focus on the Family. This marital supremacist organization disseminated filmed lectures, instructional videos, and ten separate magazines. It also broadcast Dobson's daily radio show on more than 2,000 stations and marketed his primers, including *What Wives Wish Their Husbands Knew About Women* (1975), which argues for reinvesting the word "housewife" with dignity. Focus on the Family has been described as Dobson's "media empire."[95] The Christian right's most influential 1980s spokesperson, he commanded up to sixty million viewers for one lecture series. His books sold over sixteen million copies.

Focus on the Family's headquarters still sit on eighty acres in Colorado Springs. Its website explains, "We believe that the institution of marriage is a sacred covenant designed by God to model the love of Christ for His people and to serve both the public and private good as the basic building block of human civilization."[96] For Dobson, protecting civilization has meant zealously guarding nuclear family autonomy. In 1994 he helped defeat a bill that would have forced homeschooling instructors to earn certification in subjects they teach. Single-sex gatherings also appear to threaten civilization; Dobson called the Bejing-based 1995 World Conference on Women "the most radical atheistic, antifamily crusade in the history of the world."[97]

In 2003 Dobson resigned as Focus on the Family's CEO to concentrate on his radio program. "Dr. James Dobson's Family Talk" kicked off in 2010. The group continued to accept staggering donations. In 2004, for instance, Focus on the Family received $118,263,318 million in grants and contributions.[98]

Dobson's message remains static: "If homes are going to survive, it will be because husbands and fathers again place their families at the highest level in their system of priorities."[99] What of nonmarital households and families? Simple: they don't exist. Or they exist as dens of depravity.

Dobson's chum Ted Haggard, founder of Colorado Springs's New Life Church, agrees. With his wife, Gayle, a proud college dropout who spends her time being married, Haggard coauthored the primer, *From This Day Forward: Making Your Vows Last a Lifetime* (2006). This illustrated tome attempts to demonstrate the Christian wedding's glory. In the year of its publication, news broke of Ted Haggard's three-year relationship with Mike Jones, a Denver-based sex worker. Haggard had also behaved "inappropriately" with twenty-two-year-old church volunteer, Grant Haas. "Inappropriately" means masturbating in a Cripple Creek, Colorado hotel room Haggard shared with his protégé. If one keeps these events in mind, *From This Day Forward* becomes a delightful read.[100]

The Christian men's group, Promise Keepers, also evangelizes fervently on behalf of wedlock. Founded in 1990 by sports-coach William McCartney, this group aims to make men better husbands. Like Focus on the Family, Promise Keepers is headquartered in Colorado Springs. Its members make seven pledges. Here is the fourth: "A promise keeper is committed to building strong marriages and families, through love, protection, and biblical values."[101]

This approach is common among marriage-evangelizing

groups. Getting their members hitched is not enough; outsiders have to marry, and they have to stay that way. Toward this end, missionaries are dispatched. I don't know how they operate. Maybe they stand guard over marital homes, protecting them from intruders. Perhaps they knock on doors and thunder, "Keep biblical values!"

At home the promise keeper makes things good by functioning as a "servant leader." This oxymoron has two possible explanations. Either Mr. Promise Keeper heads the household as a retainer of God, or he is selflessly Christ-like, acceding to his wife's preferences. Both modes rely on what sociologist John P. Bartkowski calls "tender warrior imagery."[102]

Promise Keepers does not fit into Catholicism or any branch of Protestantism. Its nondenominationalism renders cryptic phrases like "biblical values." Generic Christianity hangs like a diaphanous veil over this group's real obsession: marriage and men as husbands. Promise Keepers' theological looseness allows it to situate matrimony at the center of male identity.

Before dismissing it as an umbrella under which nostalgists gather, one should consider that in 1993 Promise Keepers brought 50,000 proselytes to Boulder's Fulsom Field. The year 2000 saw sixteen Promise Keepers conferences in, among other cities, Denver, Baton Rouge, and Pittsburgh. These events featured "side-by-side training for fathers and sons."[103] In 2008 clergy-training workshops ran in several cities, including Atlanta, Dallas, and Cleveland.

Promise Keepers' crescendo moment arrived in October 1997, when it hosted one of the largest religious gatherings in American history, bringing approximately one million men to Washington, D.C. The organization continues to disseminate books, CDs, and other forms of glad-to-be-married propaganda. According to one astute journalist, "Promise Keepers has tapped into the current angst about the disintegrating traditional family by preaching that 'godly men' take responsibility for their families."[104] With its radically limited definition of family, this organization has attracted thousands of proselytes.

When marriage evangelism gains momentum, abstinence-only programs flourish. These initiatives differ from voluntary religious celibacy regimens, which stress spiritual enhancement. Marriage evangelists peddle abstinence in preparation for wedlock, urging teenagers to withhold sex until their wedding nights. Toward this end, ignorance is perpetuated. Throughout the 1990s, 400,000 schools used an abstinence-only curriculum called *Sex Respect*, which contained an unusual workbook. It featured an illustration of the female anatomy with a vagina, ovaries, uterus, and cervix—but no clitoris. According to author Leora Tanenbaum, "Girls in *Sex Respect* classes are kept shamefully ignorant of their own bodies."[105]

Predictably, these programs have been debacles. A 2005 study of 12,000 teenagers revealed that those who vowed abstinence until marriage were likelier to engage in oral sex than nonabstinence committed adolescents. The "abstinent" teens were more likely to have anal sex. Less liable to practice safe sex, they contracted just as many STDs as did their unapologetically sexually active peers. Eighty-eight percent of the subjects who promised abstinence conceded that they had not kept their pledges.[106]

To note abstinence-only programs' lameness is not to suggest that teenagers become swingers. But obliviousness will not extinguish youthful libidos. Psychologist Christopher Ryan and psychiatrist Cacilda Jethá praise Mangaia, a southerly Cook Island where teens are encouraged to experiment erotically "with particular emphasis on the young men learning to . . . take pride in the pleasure they can provide a woman."[107] This helps young people learn about sex, with men discovering the gratifications of treating women attentively.

What makes the Mangaian practice seem so un-American? One aspect above all: it does not incentivize marriage. The Mangaian goal is to ease young people into an understanding of eroticism. American abstinence-only programs are stick-and-carrot scams, intended to lure adolescents into lifelong commitments, the legal implications of which they cannot possibly understand.

"A Little Bit Nutty and a Little Bit Slutty:" Anita Hill and Non-marriage Under Fire

John N. Doggett, an Austin-based management consultant, described lawyer Anita Hill as "somewhat unstable." This law-school classmate of Supreme Court Justice Clarence Thomas claimed, at the latter's 1991 judicial confirmation hearings, that Hill nursed a grudge because men, including himself, kept rebuffing her. "She was having a problem with being rejected by men she was attracted to," Doggett opined during sessions in which Hill said Thomas had asked her out and discussed sex at their workplace (Washington DC's Equal Opportunity Employment Commission) eight years earlier.[108]

Doggett smeared Hill as a gal who couldn't get a date. A gal who can't get a date won't land a husband. When a never-wed person discredits a spouse, the former is often shamed in such terms. Traducers portray the never-married whistleblower as someone with a case of sour grapes. Doggett went further. He reached back a few centuries into the arsenal of antispinster stereotypes, for the image of someone living in her own paradise, where every man desires her. When rejection upsets her fantasies, she becomes aggressive. I think this is why Doggett said "somewhat unstable" rather than "unstable." He suggested that Hill's steadiness depended on a set of illusions. Undisturbed, they held her together. Touched by reality, they loosened, and she turned, becoming dangerous. "You know the type," Doggett hinted. In his "nudge, nudge; wink, wink" account, this was not a woman recalling her then boss's inappropriate behavior but a spouseless loser seizing the Thomas hearings as an opportunity for comeuppance.

Hill calmly testified, explaining that there had been no attraction to Doggett or Thomas. Her credibility seemed to exacerbate opponents, who assaulted Hill with chop-logic. Senator Arlen Specter asked if Thomas had upset her with the words, "large breasts," implying that Hill was too repressed to brook body parts spoken aloud. "No," she replied. "The most embarrassing aspect was his description of . . . the acts that those particular people would engage in . . . it was the continuation of the story about what happened in those films with the people with this . . . physical characteristic."[109] According to Hill, Thomas had enjoyed recounting pornographic video plots for his staff.

Utah's Republican senator, Orrin Hatch, characterized Hill as a political operative working with unnamed special interest groups. As a polygraph test affirmed her account, reporters enshrined Thomas and his attorney wife, Virginia. A September 1991 *Washington Post* article praised Judge and Mrs. Thomas as the "perfect couple": "intellectual soulmates."[110] The November 1991 cover of *People* magazine featured a photo of them arm in arm, their unctuous grins accentuated by the headline, "Anita Hill 'was probably in love with my husband.'"

The contrast with Hill, who was generally photographed alone, made a point; this individual had no soulmate. In the years since Thomas's confirmation hearings, Hill has been lauded for raising awareness of workplace sexual harassment. Her ordeal can be viewed from an additional angle. Hill was insulted, specifically, as an unwed person. Two years after Thomas's confirmation, author David Brock published a salacious exposé that peddled another stereotype: the unwed, wanton sensualist. Brock maligned Hill as "a little bit nutty and a little bit slutty."[111] Nineteen years after Thomas's confirmation hearings, Hatch demanded that Hill apologize to Justice and Mrs. Thomas for disrupting their conjugal harmony: "I think this had probably grated on Ginny all these years."[112]

If she cares, Hill can take comfort in the fact that few people lose sleep over what grates on "Ginny" Thomas. Hill might find satisfaction in Brock's retractions. In a round of 2001 interviews he admitted to making uninformed statements about Hill and vilifying her supporters, most of whom he had not met. Brock also acknowledged that his denial of Thomas's penchant for X-rated videos was false.

What gave Hill the intrepidity to stand down power brokers intent on dragging her through the mud? It was not a connected insider's stridency. Descended from enslaved people, she grew up in Okmulgee County, Oklahoma, a small farming community with an economy centered on the local peanut plant.[113] "We did not travel, we did not take vacations or go to the movies," Hill has written of her childhood. "We were farm people."[114] She spent every Sunday at the Lone Tree Missionary Baptist Church, to which she walked three miles.

This self-made woman held up for eight hours of browbeating. Of the Senate Judiciary Committee's fourteen members questioning Hill, twelve were married. One (Massachusetts's Democrat senator Ted Kennedy) was between wives. Vermont's Democrat senator, Patrick Leahy, remains a favorite of reporters, who applaud the devotion he shows his nurse wife, Marcelle. Leahy calls her "the best political sounding board I have." Journalists praise Leahy's habit of beginning sentences, "Marcelle and I . . . "[115]

Hill, by contrast, appeared to have no sounding board. She used the first-person pronoun, "I," unapologetically, refusing to be discredited as a never-married adult. Reading between the lines of negative articles about her, one sees this as the real accusation. It surely riled her interlocuters as she dispassionately described a supervisor who imagined pubic hairs on Coke cans: the jurist who remains linked in Americans' minds with adult film star, "Long Dong Silver." I think this same pluck characterizes Hill's personal life. Brought up Baptist, she has had the courage to never marry.

In the years since Thomas's hearing, various players have backpedaled. Hill has not. After teaching commercial law at the University of Oklahoma, she accepted a position at Brandeis in 1999. Her publications include "The Scholarly Legacy of A. Leon Higginbotham: Voice, Storytelling, and Narrative," in the 2001 *Rutgers Law Review* and "The Embodiment of Equal Justice Under the Law," in the 2007 *Nova Law Review*.[116]

She continued to brook resentment, including an angry 2010 voicemail from Clarence Thomas's intellectual soulmate. But current photographs show a professional who soars above the insults hurled at her. With a sheen of grey in her now short hair, Hill looks even more beautiful than she did twenty-seven years ago, sitting across the table from a group of senators and fielding their embarrassing questions. She exemplifies the degree to which nonmarital life need not be solitary. "Since age six, except for the three years in Washington, DC, I have been part of an academic community," she explains.[117] She maintains an LAT relationship with businessman Chuck Malone.[118]

Marriage-Centrism Lurks in Unexpected Corners

Unwed men eager to share their homes with children know first-hand the prejudice that bachelors are immature. Robert Klose's 1999 *Adopting Alyosha: A Single Man Finds a Son in Russia*, chronicles the suspicion its author met when trying to adopt.

A biology professor, Klose had a résumé that seemed custom-designed for adoption agencies. He possessed a stellar education, a secure job, and a flexible academic schedule. Klose had the friends a university position often provides and a house in Maine. Yet he hit barrier after barrier. These obstacles "existed mostly in the form of adoption agencies that had little or no experience working with single men."[119] Unofficially, he was treated as an interloper. During his first visit to an agency in Lewiston, Maine, Klose sat in a lobby full of marrieds; spouses whispered to each other. "The couples," he writes, "were looking at me as if I'd crashed their party."[120]

Thailand had many needy children and low adoption fees. It would not consider Klose—or any unwed applicant. Adjustments have since been made. Thailand's policymakers now match what they consider the least worthy adults with the least lovable children. Straight married couples have no restrictions, but according to the Thai Embassy, "Single women can petition to adopt special-needs children only." Unwed men—apparently lowest in this caste system—cannot adopt.[121]

How Much Are Nonmarital Lives Worth?

After the September 11, 2001 attacks, Congress established a fund to compensate families of people who had been killed. Fund employees had to determine a figure for each person and based their main calculations on salary—what each victim would have earned if the attacks had not occurred. In addition, each spouse of a deceased victim received $50,000. No survivor who loved but was not married to a victim got that amount. With this policy, the American government stated unequivocally that a married person's life meant more than a nonmarital one.

Attorney Kenneth Feinberg served as Special Master of the September 11[122] Victim's Compensation Fund. Feinberg had an onerous task: assigning a cashvalue to people's lives.[122] In privileging married lives over unmarried ones, he failed. But where were the marchers asserting the value of nonmarital life? Where were the press conferences? Nowhere, because the decision did not make headlines.

It is easy to imagine premoderns as a mass of naïve bigots. Contemporary Americans might bracket this condescension and consider how marriage-centrism will look in five hundred years. Future Americans may well gasp reading about the September 11th Victim Compensation Fund's knee-jerk marriage-centrism. They may not believe that a store manager with renal failure had to marry when she lost her job and health insurance. A native of Lake Charles, Louisiana, Brandy Brady was thirty-eight when her dialysis treatments stopped working. She liked plumber Ricky Huggins but did not want to marry him after two months of dating. But his insurance would cover the kidney replacement she needed, so they moved forward. In 2008, Brady's culture deemed her more valuable if she married. Not coincidentally, as a wife, her progeny would be "legitimate."[123]

A Very Carefully Crafted, Controlling Narrative

Several years ago, a writer from the *Atlanta Journal Constitution* contacted me for an interview. A never-married thirty-something, she lived in Atlanta. We spent two successive Sunday afternoons on the phone, chatting about nonmarriage's pleasures. She seemed excited about the article that came from these four or five hours of conversation, but it never ran. I got no clear explanation as to why; apparently it had to do with timing or the content not being what her editors expected. This was not the last time I would hear such nebulous excuses. I doubt that I'm the only marriage critic to be—not censored but placed on hold.

I mention this experience because it fits with a trend described by journalist Betsy Israel, who researches media representations of unwed women from the nineteenth through the twenty-first centuries. She finds a remarkable similarity in these accounts. Reporters portray unwed women who say they are happy as dissemblers trying to conceal empty lives. An unmarried female reader will "eventually find a story about her uncertain future" that includes a photograph in which she pathetically clutches her cat.[124]

Editors seeking an isolate who lives vicariously through pets find something else in women like me. But this condescension extends to all varieties of nonmarital women, including those with SEEPs. In a venomous article, Phoebe Eaton details the last days of fashion designer L'Wren Scott, who committed suicide in 2014. Eaton portrays Scott as the archetypal desperado who can't wrangle a ring from her beau—in this case, Rolling Stones frontman Mick Jagger. "L'Wren Scott appeared to have it all," Eaton begins, setting her subject up for a fall. But she was turning fifty and "may have been premenopausal, say friends, who add that this is something women can't bear to admit." Eaton snipes, "Of course she had wanted to marry him," adding, "It was her funeral that finally got Jagger to the chapel."[125]

Actually, Scott and Jagger met in Paris, where she worked as a stylist. They began dating and at first kept things quiet at *her* insistence. Jagger purchased the house in Chelsea, London where they lived and bought Scott a Midtown Manhattan coop. He was the silent partner in her fashion line, which launched in 2006. They spoke daily—maybe even about perimenopause. Yet this is how Eaton depicts her death: "It was a cold cloudy day in March when Scott stood before a window of a chic condo . . . she had in New York City—whose very purchase, she had figured out by now, meant that Jagger would never marry her. Knotting an ascot . . . she knelt down and hanged herself from the balcony door-knob."[126]

Jagger called Scott his "lover and best friend."[127] Receiving news of her suicide, he cancelled Rolling Stones tours of Australia and New Zealand. At Scott's Los Angeles funeral he eulogized, "You know, it's not very easy . . . to be a stepmother to seven chil-dren."[128] Five of these kids flew to California, so they could help Jagger plan her memorial. He has since established a scholarship in Scott's name at Central Saint Martins, a London art school.[129] Clearly, these two considered each other family. Narrating her death with a scene in which nonmarriage triggers suicide is beyond presumptuous. It is obscene.

It is also unbelievable. People eager to marry do not typi-cally commit suicide when no spouse appears. Nor do candidates vying for a job kill themselves when it goes to another applicant. According to the National Institute of Mental Health, clinical depression or other psychiatric disorders, chronic physical pain, a genetic propensity for suicide, and recent release from prison are among the main reasons people end their lives. However, "No one takes their life for a single reason."[130] Scott's best friend cannot explain her actions. By spinning a yarn in which nonmarriage pushes a successful woman over the edge, Eaton suggests that female nonmarital life is unendurable.

Those who chronicle women jettisoning ambivalence toward marriage are almost guaranteed celebratory publication. College administrator Patricia Payette describes her anxiety about matri-mony in a maudlin essay that appears in an anthology representing the contemporary women's movement. After some feminist hand-wringing Payette embraces wedlock: "When our wedding finally arrives I savor each moment: getting ready with my closest girl-friends . . . carefully and lovingly delivering each word in my vows to Ed . . ." Less schmaltzy but more depressing is an article by blogger Jessica Valenti, wife of digital media executive Andrew Golis:

> As I grew up . . . there were plenty of issues that continued to make me question marriage: the father "giving" the bride away, women taking their husband's last name, the white dress . . . I remember reading one study that said that even couples who had been living together for years in equitable bliss ended up with a more "traditional" division of house-hold labour if they got married
>
> But never underestimate the power of being in love.[131]

Jill Corral and Lisa Miya-Jervis's anthology of essays, *Young Wives Tales: New Adventures in Love and Partnership* (2001), is a treasure trove of such doublespeak. It includes Bhargavi C. Mandava's account of rejecting an arranged marriage, heading to New York University, and deciding to never marry . . . until she meets Mark. Engaged, they find themselves "whirling down a limitless corridor of spiritual possibility." These lovebirds stop pirouetting at the Vedic section, moved by Hindu vows that present "the bride and groom as two halves of one whole . . . "[132]

Noelle Howey, on the other hand, has daddy issues. With psychoanalytic confirmation bias, she reports that these surfaced in her dating life. Howey describes a series of bad liaisons with language that could come from any number of postwar marriage primers, branding herself the "Doomed Modern Woman." As it turns out . . . she's not doomed! She meets shy Christopher in an acting class. Christopher worries (perhaps unnecessarily) that he's not intellectual enough for her. Daddy dilemmas dissolve; clichés ensue: " . . . I feel blessed. He is nothing that I had ever been looking for, and yet he is everything I could have wanted."[133]

Juhu Thukral writes, "I compromised my principles and begged/forced Jeff into having a wedding neither of us wanted." After a series of negotiations with her convention-bound Indian relatives, the dreaded nuptials occur. Thukral is led into a bridal shower or *sangeet,* at which point she realizes that her battle for individuation has failed. Then comes a conclusion that someone else appears to have written: "My role as an Indian daughter transcended any other facet of my identity until my family properly gave me away on that elaborate night."[134]

One must marvel at a collection that advertises its newness while celebrating the ancient practice of handing a woman—or her reproductive system—over to a man. In any case, these are hardly "new adventures." The sudden turnaround to marriage was a stock narrative by 1815 when Jane Austen tweaked it in *Emma.* Eliza Haywood (1693–1756) used it in *The History of Miss Betsy Thoughtless* (1751). Charlotte Lennox (1730–1840) deployed it in *The Female Quixote* (1752). Plays, essays, and especially, novels about nonconforming females who surprise themselves by marrying are too numerous to list.

Medievalist Candace Barrington has followed this "I'm getting married, but it's not what it looks like" phenomenon. Barrington shrewdly analyzes one account from *The New York Times* "Vows" section:

Each one insists upon the couple's individuality, yet each one follows a very carefully crafted, controlling narrative. At first glance, a known leader in sex-positive feminism resists the master narrative. With her former lover, she brought up their daughter in a three-parent family. Nevertheless, there it is: thirty-plus years of principles set aside for financial exigency neatly explained in the final sentences as "love wins."[135]

This narrative shapes Elizabeth Gilbert's *Committed: A Skeptic Makes Peace with Marriage* (2010). Gilbert recounts her attraction to Felipe, a nonprofit–organization employee with Australian citizenship, who reciprocates. They vow to never marry. His visa restrictions kick in, providing the opportunity for a journalist and a political activist to publicize unjust immigration policies. Instead, they marry. Gilbert rhapsodizes incoherently: "That's what I've needed . . . a clamorous song of self-persuasion about marriage belted out on my own street, underneath my own window, until I could finally relax into my own acceptance."[136]

"Hugh Grant Says He was Plain Wrong About Views on Marriage and Children," blares a recent newspaper headline. Behind uppercase black print is a photo of the actor with his television producer wife, Anna Eberstein. For six years Grant and Eberstein repeatedly told reporters that marriage did not interest them. It's unclear what changed their minds. Grant sputters, "It was very nice getting married . . . very nice being married. Very nice."[137]

America's best-known marriage convert is Gloria Steinem, who vocally criticized wedlock before marrying in 2000 at age sixty-five. Steinem explained that when she and South African environmentalist David Bale noted various legal reforms that had softened matrimony's sexism, they felt comfortable getting engaged. Native American Charlie Soap conducted the Oklahoma wedding in Cherokee by a burning sage fire.

As journalist Rebecca Traister shows, there was more to this story. Congress had eliminated the kind of visa that allowed Bale to live in the United States: "The pair consulted with lawyers and was told that the surest way for Bale to secure a green card was through marriage."[138] By viewing matrimony through a women's rights rather than a nonmarital rights lens, Steinem could tell the public (and perhaps herself) a story about progress. Realistically, countless people cannot or will not get visas through wedlock. Cherokee blessings and sage fires cannot obscure the fact that Steinem put forty years of antimarriage principles aside for a benefit that should have no relationship to marriage.

Here, I hope to reignite Payette's anxiety. I wish to shift Valenti's focus from "the power of being in love" to the power of loving one's nonmarital family. I want to interrupt Gilbert's tone-deaf rendition of "My Way" by informing her that marital supremacism thrives in America's military. "I have always wondered why a marriage saves you money but never really cared . . . until I joined the Army," one soldier wrote to *The Atlantic* in 2016. "Then I got angry."[139] A twenty-six-year-old college graduate who called in airstrikes, the anonymous soldier lived in dormitory-like barracks with eighteen-year-olds. Married soldiers had better options: tax-free housing stipends and food allowances. They could rent or buy homes off base.

So, an educated twenty-six-year-old sergeant often earned less than an eighteen-year-old private with no college degree. The military labelled unwed soldiers "single," discounting girlfriends, boyfriends, or best friends. Achieving the rank of staff sergeant, this serviceman found a boon in his situation; he was happier than wedded colleagues: "Being single is financially unfair but emotionally better for me as a solider . . . I do have a girlfriend . . . and we've already talked about why marriage doesn't need to happen for us to be happy. We don't need a piece of paper and a tax break to reinforce our relationship as valid and enduring."[140]

Universities Peddle Marriage-Centric Clichés

In George Orwell's Oceania, war is peace, freedom slavery, and ignorance strength. Judging by their policies, in contemporary colleges marriage is everything. When myriad universities dropped civil and domestic partnerships as benefit-qualifying categories, they left untold numbers of academics in a "default to marriage or lose everything" situation. Meanwhile, academics like Maike Ingrid Philipsen recommended accommodating married faculty by reshaping jobs to better fit their spouses' credentials. Special treatment is prejudicial; prejudice is wrong. Also, we're all equal, but some of us are more equal than others.

Philosopher Elizabeth Brake offers a remedy: "Supports for caring relationships, with no assumptions about sexual interaction, procreation, number of parties, reciprocity of all legal rights, shared totality of lives, or union." Brake's suggestion of "eroding the legal distinction between marriage and life-structuring friendships" may sound unrealistic.[141] Actually, France has basically implemented it since 1999 with *pacte civil de solidarité*, commonly known as PACS. Pairs who sign a PACS agreement qualify for many rights conventionally reserved for marrieds, including shared health insurance and Social Security benefits. PACS is not tailored for romances but remains open to partners of all kinds.

What do today's undergraduates learn, formally, about nonmarriage? According to Bella DePaulo, almost nothing, and what they learn is biased. In a recent psychology textbook DePaulo found explanations for women not marrying that ranged from choosing career over matrimony to postponing wedlock until most candidates had died. The authors don't consider women embracing nonmarital life as a serious possibility.[142]

David G. Myers's textbook, *Social Psychology* (2008), regurgitates falsehoods about marriage generating improved health and contentment, omitting to mention practices that make American wedlock a status enhancer. Thinking cogently about matrimony requires weighing the morality and efficacy of its social mechanisms. Students cannot do this without knowing what those mechanisms are.

The 2015 *Norton Anthology of Short Fiction* contains 152 stories representing a range of periods and ethnicities. Used in fiction and creative writing classes, this is probably the most popular collection of its kind. It includes Peter Taylor's 1971 "A Spinster's Tale." From old age, the protagonist, Elizabeth, recalls her childhood in Nashville. She peered out the window at the local drunk, Mr. Speed, who stumbled by her house every afternoon, swearing at trees. The story describes Elizabeth's eventual association of all men with Speed, which causes her to fear males as violent brutes. Again, a woman's nonmarital status signifies psychological disturbance.[143] With reading like this, is it any wonder that undergraduates equate matrimony with health and happiness?

This is a false equivalency. Despite formidable obstacles, nonmarital men and women have an extraordinary history. Out of deep-seated disadvantages we have contributed powerfully to Western culture. We have made it a real culture, with depth, variety, and brilliance no purely married civilization could achieve.

(Endnotes)

1   William Doyle, *The French Revolution: A Very Short History* (Oxford: Oxford University Press, 2001), 3–4.
2   Ibid., 55–8.
3   Pamela Clemit and Gina Luria Walker, Introduction, *Memoirs of the Author of a Vindication of the Rights of Woman*, ed. Pamela Clemit and Gina Luria Walker (Toronto: Broadview, 2001), 29–30.
4   Mary Wollstonecraft, *A Vindication of the Rights of Woman*, ed. Miriam Brody (London: Penguin, 1982), 317–18.
5   Miriam Brody, Introduction, *A Vindication*, 19.
6   Coontz, *Marriage*, 153.
7   Clare A. Lyons, *Sex Among the Rabble: An Intimate History of Gender and Power in the Age of Revolution, Philadelphia, 1730–1830* (Chapel Hill: University of North Carolina Press, 2006), 293.
8   London: Wood & Innes, 1808, https://www.gutenberg.org/files/50108/50108-h/50108.
9   John Tosh, *A Man's Place: Masculinity and the Home in Victorian England* (New Haven: Yale University Press, 2007), 68.
10 Coontz, *Marriage*, 159.
11 *Desire and Domestic Fiction: A Political History of the Novel* (New York: Oxford, 1987), 59.
12 Ibid., 251.
13 Robin W. Winks and Joan Neuberger, *Europe and the Making of Early Modernity: 1815–1914* (New York: Oxford University Press, 2005), 113.
14 Quoted in Lyons, *Sex*, 295.
15 Cheryl Turner, *Living by the Pen: Women Writers in the Eighteenth Century* (London: Routledge, 1992), 113.
16 Quoted in Kathryn Kish Sklar, *Catharine Beecher: a Study in American Domesticity* (New York: W. W. Norton & Company, 1976), 265.
17 Trans. Robin Waterfield (Oxford: Oxford University Press, 2001), 806–9. References are to lines.
18 Quoted in B. S. Strauss, *Athens After the Peloponnesian War: Class, Faction, and Policy 406–386 BC* (London: Croom Helm, 1986).
19 *Nicomachean Ethics*, 141.
20 Ibid., 143–6.
21 *Essays*, trans. J. M. Cohen (London: Penguin, 1958), 97.
22 Ibid., 95.
23 *A Selection of His Works*, ed. Sidney Warhaft (Indianapolis: The Odyssey Press, 1965), 113.

24   Ibid., 62.

25   Armstrong, *Desire*, 73.

26   Griffith's conduct book, *Essays, Addressed to Young Married Women*, appeared in 1782. Quoted in Turner, *Living*, 44.

27   Frederic Rowton, ed., *The Female Poets of Great Britain, Chronologically Arranged, With Copious Selections and Critical Remarks* (Philadelphia: Carey and Hart, 1849), xiv.

28   The historian who most famously argues for companionate marriage's emergence in early modernity is Lawrence Stone. See *The Family Sex and Marriage in England: 1500–1800* (New York: Harper & Row, 1977).

29   Quoted in J. W. Blassingame, *The Slave Community: Plantation Life in the Antebellum South* (New York, Oxford University Press, 1972), 153.

30   Stone, *Uncertain Unions and Broken Lives: Intimate and Revealing Accounts of Marriage and Divorce in England: 1660–1857* (Oxford: Oxford University Press: 1992), 18–19. Polikoff, *Beyond (Straight and Gay)*, 12–13.

31   *Sociology for the South, or, The Failure of a Free Society* (Richmond: A. Morris Publisher, 1854), 205–6.

32   Rick Beard, "Disunion: Grant's Contraband Conundrum," *The Opinion Pages* (blog), *New York Times*, November 14, 2012, https://opinionator.blogs.nytimes.com/2012/11/14/grants-contraband-conundrum.

33   Quoted in Katherine Franke, *Wedlocked: The Perils of Marriage Equality* (New York: New York University Press, 2015), 122.

34   Ibid., 124.

35   Ibid., 86–7.

36   Ibid., 129.

37   Ibid., 117–20.

38   Ibid., 118.

39   Ibid., 94.

40   Ibid., 127–9.

41   Ibid., 130.

42   Sheila McManus, *The Line Which Separates: Race, Gender, and the Making of the Alberta-Montana Borderlands* (Lincoln: University of Nebraska Press, 2005), 101.

43   Quoted in Nancy F. Cott, *Public Vows: A History of Marriage and the Nation* (Cambridge: Harvard University Press, 2000), 80.

44   Wendy McElroy, *Individualist Feminism of the Nineteenth Century: Collected Writings and Biographical Profiles* (Jefferson, North Carolina: McFarland, 2012), 126. Cott, *Public Vows*, 127.

45 Cott, *Public Vows*, 118. These measures were part of a government campaign against plural marriage as it was practiced by Mormons. However, the Court's language extended to other sexual non-conformists. Since the statute was repealed, no subsequent case was necessary to challenge it.

46 *The Young Man and the World* (New York: D. Appleton and Company, 1905), 156.

47 Quoted in Cott, *Public Vows*, 142.

48 Christina Simmons, *Making Marriage Modern: Women's Sexuality from the Progressive Era to World War II* (Oxford: Oxford University Press, 2009), 185, 181.

49 Cott, *Public Vows*, 176–7.

50 Coontz, *Marriage*, 220.

51 Quoted in Elaine Tyler May, "Rosie the Riveter Gets Married," *The War in American Culture: Society and Consciousness During World War II*, ed. Lewis Erenberg and Susan E. Hirsch (Chicago: University of Chicago Press, 1996), 137.

52 Reprinted in Vicki Howard, *Brides, Inc.: American Weddings and the Business of Tradition* (Philadelphia: University of Pennsylvania Press, 2006), 169.

53 Ibid., 168.

54 Ronald Gerstl, *The Super Achievers: The Remarkable Jewish Contribution to Science and Human Well-Being Highlighted by Nobel Prize Winners* (Excelsis Press, 2020), 79–80, 202–3. *The Nobel Prizes, 1986*, ed. Wilhelm Odelberg (Stockholm: The Nobel Foundation, 1987), https://www.nobelprize.org/prizes/medicine/1986/levi-montalcini.

55 Jewish Telegraphic Association, "Reagan Confers Honorary Citizenship on Wallenberg," October 7, 1981, https://www.jta.org/1981/10/07/archive/reagan-confers-honorary-citizenship-on-wallenberg.

56 *I Do and I Don't: A History of Marriage in the Movies* (New York: Vintage Books, 2012), 94.

57 Jill Lepore, "FIXED: The Rise of Marriage Therapy and Other Dreams of Human Betterment," *The New Yorker*, March 29, 2010, http://www.newyorker.com/magazine/2010/03/29.

58 Quoted in Barbara Ehrenreich and Deirdre English, *For Her Own Good: 150 Years of the Experts' Advice to Women* (Garden City, NY: Anchor Books: 1979), 72.

59 See John Farrell, *Freud's Paranoid Quest: Psychoanalysis and Modern Suspicion* (New York: New York University Press, 1996) and Frank Cioffi, *Freud and the Question of Pseudoscience* (Chicago: Open Court, 1998).

60 Quoted in Frederick Crews, *Freud: The Making of an Illusion* (New York: Metropolitan Books, 2017), 516.

61 Sigmund Freud, "Femininity," *New Introductory Lectures on Psycho-analysis*, trans. and ed. James Strachey (New York: W. W. Norton & Company), 139–67.

62 Ehrenreich and English, *For Her Own Good*, 249.

63 Kristin Celello, *Making Marriage Work: A History of Marriage and Divorce in the Twentieth-Century United States* (Chapel Hill: University of North Carolina Press, 2009), 281–2.

64 Richard Wormser, *The Rise and Fall of Jim Crow*, "Lucy Craft Laney," https://www.thirteen.org/wnet/jimcrow/stories_people_laney.

65 "How to Make Him Propose," *Coronet*, December 1951, 30.

66 Quoted in Coontz, *Marriage*, 227.

67 Beth L. Bailey, *From Front Porch to Back Seat: Courtship in Twentieth-Century America* (Baltimore: The Johns Hopkins University Press, 1989), 127–132.

68 Celello, *Making Marriage Work*, 281–2.

69 Ibid., 236.

70 Ibid., 229.

71 Ruth Rosen, *The World Split Open: How the Modern Women's Movement Changed America* (New York: Penguin, 2000), 9.

72 Coontz, *Marriage*, 226.

73 Ibid., 252.

74 Cott, *Public Vows*, 193.

75 *The Naked Ape* (Toronto: Bantam, 1967), 70.

76 Ibid., 71.

77 Susanna Schrobsdorff, "*The Naked Ape*," "All-Time 100 Nonfiction Books," *Time*, August 17, 2011, http://entertainment.time.com/2011/08/30/all-time-100-best-nonfiction-books/slide/the-naked-ape-by-desmond-morris.

78 *The Moral Animal: The New Science of Evolutionary Psychology* (New York: Pantheon, 1994), 53–4.

79 Coontz, *Marriage*, 228.

80 Moria Weigel, *Labor of Love: The Invention of Dating* (New York: Farrar, Straus and Giroux, 2016), 129.

81 Ibid., 129.

82 Ibid., 129.

83 Maggie Astor, "In Another Era, a Barnard Student Makes National Headlines After Moving in with Boyfriend," *Columbia Spectator*, April 2008, https://spectatorarchive.library.columbia.edu.

84 *Sexual Politics* (Urbana: University of Illinois Press, 1969), 34–5.

85   *The Female Eunuch* (Toronto: Bantam Books, 1971), 227.

86   *Women and Madness* (San Diego: Harvest/HBJ, 1972), 66–72.

87   *The Feminine Mystique* (New York: Dell, 1974), 353.

88   Quoted in Rosen, *The World Split Open*, 79.

89   Kingsley Davis, "Illegitimacy and Social Structure," *American Journal of Sociology* 4 (1939), 227. I deliberately quote Davis, who defended this attitude, out of context.

90   Menoukhah Case and Allison V. Craig define liberal feminism as a movement aimed at "women's social empowerment, social well-being, and personal freedom through legislative and cultural change." *Introduction to Feminist Thought and Action* (New York: Routledge, 2020), 12.

91   Quoted in Cynthia Ellen, *The Myth of Matriarchal Prehistory: Why an Invented Past Won't Give Women a Future* (Boston: Beacon Press: 2000), 2.

92   Ibid., 93–116.

93   *The Creation of Patriarchy* (New York: Oxford University Press, 1986).

94   K. J. Yossman, "Royal Gossip," *Marie Claire*, September 2016, 206.

95   Frances Fitzgerald, *The Evangelicals: The Struggle to Shape America* (New York: Simon & Schuster, 2017), 443.

96   "The Permanence of Marriage," Focus on the Family, https://www.focusonthefamily.com/about/foundational-values.

97   Quoted in Fitzgerald, *The Evangelicals*, 450.

98   Amie Newman, "Focus on the Family: Funding Extremism Millions of Dollars at a Time," Rewire News Group, February 2, 2019, https://rewirenewsgroup.com/article/2010/02/02/focus-family-funding-extremism-millions-dollars-a-time.

99   James C. Dobson, *Straight Talk to Men: Principles of Leading Your Family* (Tyndale House Publishers, Inc., 2014), 58.

100 Jim Spellman and Eric Manapodi, "New Haggard Accuser: 'He Really Thought He Was Invincible,'" CNN, January 27, 2009, https://www.cnn.com/2009/CRIME/01/28/colorado.church.haggard. Kevin Roose, "The Last Temptation of Ted," *GQ*, January 26, 2011, https://www.gq.com/story/pastor-ted-haggard.

101 Wayne Jackson, "What's Wrong with the Promise Keeper's Movement?", *Christian Courier*, https://www.christiancourier.com/articles/110-whats-wrong-with-the-promise-keepers-movement.

102 *The Promise Keepers: Servants, Soldiers, and Godly Men* (New Brunswick, New Jersey: Rutgers University Press, 2004), 101.

103 "PK History," Promise Keepers, https://promisekeepers.org/pk-history.

104 Laurie Goodstein, "A Marriage Gone Bad Struggles for Redemption,"

New York Times, October 29, 1997, https://www.nytimes.com/1997/10/29/us/a-marriage-gone-bad-struggles-for-redemption.

105 *Slut: Growing up Female with a Bad Reputation* (New York: Seven Stories Press, 1999), 243–4.

106 D. J. Fortenberry, "The Limits of Abstinence-Only in Preventing Sexually Transmitted Infections," *Journal of Adolescent Health* 36 (2005), 269–357.

107 Ryan and Jethá, *Sex at Dawn*, 285.

108 Sam Howe Verhovek, "A New Forum for a Onetime Newsmaker," *New York Times*, March 25, 1997, https://www.nytimes.com/1997/03/25/us/a-new-forum-for-a-onetime-newsmaker.

109 Anita Hill, *Speaking Truth to Power* (New York: Anchor Books, 1997), 179.

110 Laura Blumenfield, "The Nominee's Soulmate," *The Washington Post*, September 10, 1991, https://www.washingtonpost.com/archive/lifestyle/1991/09/10/the-nominees-soul-mate.

111 Howard Kurtz, "Author Who Trashed Anita Hill Now Confesses to Lies," *Los Angeles Times*, July 3, 2001, http://articles.latimes.com/2001/jul/03.

112 Michael O'Brien, "Hatch: Clarence Thomas Does Deserve an Apology from Anita Hill," *The Hill*, October 21, 2010, http://thehill.com/blogs/blog-briefing-room/news/125135-hatch-clarence-thomas-does-deserve-an-apology-from-hill.

113 Hill, *Speaking Truth*, 47.

114 Ibid., 29.

115 Emillie Teresa Stigliani, "Marcelle and Patrick Leahy: A Vermont Love Story," *Burlington Free Press*, February 14, 2016, https://www.burlingtonfreepress.com/story/news/politics/2016/02/14/marcelle-patrick-leahy-vermont-love-story.

116 "Anita Hill," Brandeis University, http://www.brandeis.edu/facultyguide/person.

117 Hill, *Speaking Truth*, 318.

118 Abcarian, "Anita Hill's Still Standing."

119 *Adopting Alyosha: A Single Man Finds a Son in Russia* (Jackson: University Press of Mississippi, 1999), 6.

120 Ibid., 13.

121 "Thailand Adoption Requirements," https://www.thaiembassy.com/family/thailand-adoption.

122 DePaulo, *Singled Out*, 228.

123 Kevin Sack, "Health Benefits Inspire Rush to Marry, or Divorce," *New York Times*, August 12, 2008, https://www.nytimes.com/2008/08/13/us/13marriage.

124 *Bachelor Girl: The Secret History of Single Women in the 20th Century* (London: Aurum Press, 2003), 246.

125 "Unravelling the Mystery Behind L'Wren Scott's Path to Self-Destruction," *GQ*, November 11, 2014, https://www.gq-magazine.co.uk/article/lwren-scott-suicide-death-mick-jagger-fashion.

126 Ibid.

127 Elizabeth Day, "L'Wren Scott: The Mysterious Suicide of Mick Jagger's Girlfriend," *The Observer*, June 22, 2014, https://www.theguardian.com/fashion/2014/jun/22/lwren-scott-mysterious-suicide-of-mick-jaggers-girlfriend.

128 Eaton, "Unravelling the Mystery."

129 Veronique Hyland, "Mick Jagger Establishes a Scholarship in Memory of L'Wren Scott," *The Cut*, January 16, 2015, https://www.thecut.com/2015/01/mick-jagger-establishes-lwren-scott-scholarship.

130 "What Leads to Suicide?", https://afsp.org. "Risk Factors," https://www.nimh.nih.gov/health/topics/suicide-prevention/index.

131 "My Big Feminist Wedding," *The Guardian*, April 23, 2009, https://www.theguardian.com/lifeandstyle/2009/apr/24/feminist-wedding.

132 "A Suitable Union," *Young Wives Tales: New Adventures in Love and Partnership*, ed. Jill Corral and Lisa Miya-Jervis (Seattle: Seal Press, 2001), 82, 88–9.

133 "Sex Scenes," *Young Wives Tales*, 195.

134 "Reluctant Bride and Groom," *Young Wives Tales*, 218, 225, 226.

135 Letter to author, August 10, 2020.

136 *Committed: A Skeptic Makes Peace with Marriage* (New York: Viking, 2010), 267.

137 Sabina Barr, *The Independent*, December 16, 2019, https://www.independent.co.uk/life-style/love-sex/hugh-grant-marriage-children-chris-evans-virgin-radio-interview.

138 *All the Single Ladies*, 264.

139 Chris Bodenner, "Why Should Married Soldiers Get Extra Support?", *The Atlantic*, March 21, 2016, https://www.theatlantic.com/notes/2016/03/why-should-married-people-get-extra-support-contd.

140 Ibid.

141 "Equality and Non-hierarchy in Marriage: What Do Feminists Really Want?", *After Marriage*, ed. Elizabeth Brake, 120.

142 "What Are College Students Taught About People Who Are Single?", *Singlism*, ed. Bella DePaulo, 92–3.

143 *The Norton Anthology of Short Fiction*, ed. Richard Bausch and R. V. Cassill (New York: W. W. Norton & Company, 2015), 1498–1513.

4

The American Marriage Crusade

"Genuine research seeks explanations, not just examples; its goal is understanding, not reassurance."

—ROBERT ASAHINA, "SOCIAL SCIENCE FICTION"

"Good Families"

A 1996 welfare reform bill prioritized getting Americans living at or below the poverty line married; states implemented various stratagems. West Virginia's welfare department offered unwed biomothers one hundred dollars per month for marrying. Oklahoma invested seventy million dollars of federal funding in programs that included "marriage education" curricula and pro-wedlock rallies. Journalist Mike McManus cofounded the federally subsidized marital supremacist organization Marriage Savers. Based in Kilmarnock, Virginia, it aims "to push down divorce and cohabitation rates and raise marriage rates."[1] Marriage Savers pairs "mentor couples" with restive newlyweds, so the former can quash the latter's doubts. Sociologist William Julius Wilson published *When Work Disappears: the World of the New Urban Poor* (1996), which suggests a WPA-style job program for inner-city males, to make them marriageable. Instead of generating outrage with his suggestion that "women should marry themselves out of poverty," Wilson was named one of *Time* magazine's twenty-five most influential Americans.[2]

Marshall Miller and Dorian Solot—the cohabitors denied San-Francisco housing—note that magical thinking characterizes such initiatives. The government tells Americans that wedlock will solve their problems, including financial difficulties. "You can't feed your children wedding rings and pay your electric bill with your marriage license," Solot and Miller write in their study, *Let Them Eat Wedding Rings: The Role of Marriage Promotion in Welfare Reform* (2002).[3] Indeed, one year of postsecondary education reduces by half the poverty rate of households run by women of color. Yet the 1996 bill discouraged schooling, required recipients to work, and pushed wedlock.[4]

In 1998, President Bill Clinton's relationship with White House intern Monica Lewinsky came to light. The press bombarded Americans with reports of semen-stained dresses, taped telephone conversations, and equivocal definitions of sex. There was a special prosecutor's report, an impeachment proceeding, and a five-year suspension of the president's law license.

Through it all there was Hillary Clinton, failing to convince in her performance as Wronged Wife. Television had accustomed people to teary, hyperemotional, "betrayed" women. Clinton seemed bored. The look in her dry eyes that said, "When can I get back to work?" suggested that politicians wed to meet public expectations—not because they believe in fidelity.

Retaliation was swift and enduring. In a 2008 speech on behalf of her husband, Hillary's competitor for the Democrats' presidential nomination, Michelle Obama declared, "One of the things about this race, is role modeling what good families should look like. And my view is that if you can't run your own house, you certainly can't run the White House."[5] This statement equated nonmonogamy with degeneracy while disparaging Hillary as the proverbial career woman who can't keep her man happy. The exemplar of, "When they go low, we go high," delivered the lowest blow possible.

More recently another Hillary competitor, Vermont Senator Bernie Sanders, descended into paralepsis when he promised not to "go back into the early 1990s and cast judgment" on Bill Clinton. Sanders told journalist James Hohmann that "The Lewinsky affair cast a very long shadow."[6] These insults go beyond realpolitik. Married politicians for whom wedlock has, in conventional terms, worked out, often display brazen moral one-upmanship as they judge others' relationships. "But when we get down to it," Carrie Jenkins observes, "the nuclear family simply does not have the right to disparage and erase every other model of what a good life can look like."[7]

In 2000, the American Law Institute (ALI), a group of legal experts that creates prototypes for state legislatures, articulated new tenets for domestic partnerships. Like civil unions, domestic partnerships provide certain benefits without putting sexual relationships under full governmental control. Ending a domestic partnership requires no legal divorce. ALI suggested making these arrangements more marital. If two lovers cohabited long enough, they should become subject to matrimonial law—just what myriad domestic partners sought to avoid.[8]

Why didn't ALI suggest that spouses fill out a form affirming their satisfaction every five years? If they neglected their paperwork the marriages would be automatically dissolved. ALI members did not make this recommendation because its members considered wedlock a centering norm. Their logic should remind nonmarital Americans how often we are perceived as deviant and substandard.

Determined to Seize What They Already Have, Marriage Activists Galvanize

By this time a discrete group of marriage evangelicals had emerged. It called itself the Marriage Movement. Its 2000 "Statement of Principles" describes "a grass-roots movement to strengthen marriage," adding, "a healthy marriage culture benefits every citizen in the United States."[9] An outpouring of Marriage Movement publications included David Blankenhorn and Dana Mack's *The Book of Marriage: The Wisest Answers to the Toughest Questions* (2001). Ignoring copious evidence that proves otherwise, they present wedlock as a venue for "the true meaning of community, of tolerance, of mutual understanding, of responsibility, and of spiritual cultivation."[10]

To demonstrate that marriage synchronizes humanity's noblest qualities, movement spokespeople needed a master narrative. They crafted one about civilization's conquest of barbarism, averring that savagery (i.e., nonmarriage) was, at some indeterminate point, vanquished by culture (i.e., matrimony). Movement leaders like Barbara Dafoe Whitehead made this story a broad explanatory tenet. They avoided historical specifics and cross-cultural comparison: marriage inaugurated civilization. When? Long ago. Where? Everywhere. How? By being marriage. Restating the mantra, movement members certainly appeared to convince themselves.

Anthropologist Claude Lévi-Strauss (1908–2009) theorized that myth offers solutions to contradictions within a society's conceptual frame of reference.[11] Here we see his idea at work.

How could wedlock be a love affair and a legal document, something instinctual and the distillation of culture's finest elements, a desideratum and an institution that needs roadblocks to prevent escape? Easy: marriage was synonymous with the birth of civilization. Actually, it was the birth of civilization.

The claim that any behavior marks a historical dividing line requires an explanation for why people started doing it. Scholars of the Neolithic Near East, who work in medias res, have no such rationale for matrimony. No sodality stepped forward to announce the end of prehistory and the beginning of history. The oldest recorded laws reflect ongoing practices. The first code, from Sumeria's Kingdom of Ur-Nammu, dates to approximately 2100 BCE. Its seventh law dictates execution for wives who sleep with men other than their husbands.[12] According to Mesopotamia's Code of Hammurabi (c. 1754 BCE), any husband of a woman who had extramarital sex could cut her nose off, kill her, and castrate the lover.[13] Middle Assyrian law from the fifteenth through the eleventh centuries BCE punished women who deliberately miscarried with impalement.[14] Middle Assyrian laws of the twelfth and eleventh centuries BCE required wives to wear veils and forbade concubines from veiling. An unwed woman who upgraded her status by veiling could receive fifty lashes, have hot tar poured on her head, and have her ears cut off.[15]

The Ptolemies, who ruled Egypt during its Hellenistic period (323 BCE–30 BCE), encouraged biological siblings to wed. The seventeen-year-old pharaoh Cleopatra (69 BCE–30 BCE) married her ten-year-old brother, Ptolemy XIII. Her liaison with Roman general Julius Caesar produced a child, Caesarion. When Ptolemy XIII died, she married the next sibling in line, Ptolemy XIV, who perished in 44 BCE, probably at Cleopatra's order of execution. She then placed Caesarion on the throne.[16]

By the time Rome conquered Egypt in 30 BCE, blood siblings

from all social strata regularly married each other.[17] Roman authorities succeeded unevenly in suppressing this practice. Of course, Roman children depended on paternal authorization. A Roman man conventionally signaled his acceptance of each newborn by holding it. If he refused, the infant was exposed.[18] At least through the time of Vergil (70–19 BCE), "Roman society . . . appears to have accepted without question the right of a father to execute even a grown son."[19]

Do Marriage Movement leaders believe that such practices epitomize refinement?

Why was early marriage so *uncivilized*? The Marxist answer has become a popular fallback: matrimony was a property-transferring venue when nation-states coalesced over 5,000 years ago. Farming techniques had created surpluses: the foundation of private property. Passing it to one's own biological children became a preoccupation, especially for males, who coopted women's reproductive systems through marriage. Husbands and governments policed female chastity to ensure heirs' "legitimacy," imposing monogamy on wives. Until Christianity's ascension, husbands had open sexual access to prostitutes and slaves. So, bastardy was not wedlock's outcome but its *raison d'être*. Later kingdoms and nation-states would focus on women but monitor all sexual relations, imposing draconian laws on men as well.[20]

Stephanie Coontz proffers a kinder theory: "In early human societies, marriage was primarily a way to extend cooperative relations and circulate people and resources beyond the local group. When people married . . . it turned strangers into relatives and enemies into allies."[21]

These explanations are speculative. Friedrich Engels, promulgator of the first theory, does not explain why men would care who inherited their assets posthumously. Nation-states' intervention remains more mysterious. Yet this is his theoretical linchpin. Coontz does not describe what made the legal couple, a closed and prohibitive unit, necessary for broadening communal relations. There are countless ways to forge familial alliances. Such groupings might have grown from friendships, nonmonogamous lovers, or agricultural partnerships, to name a few.

Such questions did not faze Marriage Movement founders, who simply claimed civilization's backing—a stance that gave them infinite a priorism. Their formula was simple: start by assuming that nonmarriage causes, and marriage fixes, most problems: escalating crime, lowered rates of high school graduation . . . gingivitis. The solution had four steps: pathologize nonmarital people, sometimes highlighting particular celebrities as degenerates; chastise married couples for not being married enough; and call for weddings en masse as well as events in which nuclear-family commitments are renewed. Finally, implore government to "strengthen the family."

President George W. Bush was game. In 2001, he made Wade Horn Assistant Secretary for Children and Families at the Department of Health and Human Services. Horn had authored a paper recommending preferential treatment of married couples in public housing. Bush vowed to allocate 1.5 billion dollars for marriage promotion. Legislation that passed earmarked 750 million.

Marriage Movement operatives tend toward stridency and self-confidence. They tell nonmarital people that our strengths—inclusiveness, creative family configuration, nonconformity—are weaknesses. (Particularly suspect is our penchant for privacy; marriage fundamentalist Charles Murray objected to housing plans with small apartments that accommodated solo living.)[22] They preach that wedlock preserves love and contentment, as if these qualities could be stashed in a container. Their analyses, which incorrectly locate cause at every turn, are nonqualitative and nonanalytic—executed to show that wedlock alone deserves government benefits.

The movement's *locus classicus, The Case for Marriage: Why Married People Are Happier, Healthier, and Better Off Financially* (2000) works from this model and merits discussion. If nonmarital people want to reject stereotypes with which our attackers misrepresent us, we must know what they are.

The authors, Linda Waite and Maggie Gallagher, assume wedlock's "naturalness." Ideologues of all stripes use the word "natural" to brand insider/outsider members of a culture. Natural is quasibiological; unnatural deviates from biology. Natural is the majority; unnatural is everyone else. Marriage Movement writers use the word cagily, aware that feelings about wedlock's rightness remain potent in America's popular imagination. (Indeed, political scientist Adolph Reed, Jr. observes that "all too many people who identify with the left nonetheless maintain blind spots about the intrinsic superiority of the two-parent, 'intact,' nuclear form of household organization."[23]) Waite and Gallagher argue that wedlock's naturalness renders suspect all households other than the marital. What Michelle Obama calls "good families" get top billing. To show how good they are, the authors evoke a landscape in which weakening marriage bonds create turpitude.

From its inception the Marriage Movement demonized unwed mothers. Defoe Whitehead argues that they impair children. The never-married man, however, is Waite and Gallagher's bête noir. In a segment entitled, "The Wild Lives of Single Men," they encapsulate wedlock's pluses for men with a jingle: "fewer stupid bachelor tricks."[24] They envision men as gluttonous, boozy delinquents who need matrimonial constraints. Contradicting the Center for Disease Control, they claim that husbands are healthier than bachelors because wives "discourage drinking, smoking, and spending."[25] Wives also prepare wholesome meals. So, men can either wed and ingest salubrious fare cooked by women (who still inhabit the kitchen) or live "warped lives."[26] "Men who aren't married voluntarily behave in ways that endanger their own life and health," Waite and Gallagher state.[27]

As someone with unwed male friends, I boil over with replies. Personal anecdotes are best left aside in favor of examples from the public domain. In 2008, four New York University alumni in their thirties commandeered two floors of a Queens office building. They set up a communal kitchen and living room. Four bedrooms would afford privacy to visit with friends and dates.

This household offers what one denizen calls "the benefits of a family with very little of the craziness."[28] Its garden, from which vegetables go straight to the kitchen, would surely puzzle Waite and Gallagher. With a loving home life offset by reasonable rent, these housemates have pursued careers in filmmaking, game design, and fitness instruction. Indeed, residents of the building dubbed "Fortress Astoria" thwart *The Case for Marriage*'s claim that unmarried cohabitants' commitments to each other are flimsy. By 2012, when the *New York Times* interviewed Rick Brown, Luke Crane, Danahar Dempsey, and Shyaporn Theerakulsit, they had been together, in various dwellings, for eighteen years—longer than many marriages. They shared a checking account for home expenses.

Journalist Rod Dreher disapproves. He predicts that Fortress Astoria's "man children" auger civilization's demise.[29] Dreher worries that all nonstandard homes accelerate this worrisome event. His fuddy-duddyism shows Marriage Movement priggishness at its worst. Dreher contends that nonmarital households, whose residents help each other and hurt no one, imperil culture. History tells a different story. The sixth-century-BCE philosopher, Pythagoras, assembled a household of like-minded individuals dedicated to the precept that friends enjoy unique intimacy that makes resource-sharing easy. Discerning no essential differences between the sexes, Pythagoras included women in his friend-centered homes. Several mixed-sex Pythagorean fellowships appeared in southern Italy; they probably inspired Plato to create an academy—the first western university.[30] No institution is more basic to civilization.

Waite and Gallagher praise wives who interrupt. If hubby is watching television, Mrs. can intrude, summoning him to the bedroom. ("I didn't get married to be in bed alone," says one stern wife.)[31] Scheduling medical checkups and arguing with insurance companies offer additional pleasures. Badgering someone while functioning as his secretary isn't enough for those who want husband hunting's ultimate reward: living as a leisured wife. Waite and Gallagher approve: "Higher income gives [married] women access to better housing and safer neighborhoods and the security and social prestige that comes with . . . owning one's own home. Marriage also gives women access to private health insurance, an increasingly precious commodity in the United States."[32]

American wives do have better insurance options than their nonmarital counterparts. But no country should make medical care a "precious commodity" contingent on one relationship. Nor should newlyweds get first dibs on safe neighborhoods. Waite and Gallagher seem unaware that health care and optimal housing's greater availability to marrieds and lesser availability to nonmarital people should not be used as a sales pitch because it is morally objectionable.

The claim that women need husbands for housing must confuse twenty-six-year-old software developer Amanda Starling, whose career was going well. She purchased a home in Tampa, Florida, for $142,000. Waite and Gallagher's view would likely amuse Patricia Ramos, a sixty-three-year-old medical clerk who spent eight years re-establishing the credit rating her ex-husband destroyed when he defaulted on a loan that carried both their names. In 2017, she purchased a St. Petersburg, Florida condo for $89,000 "I'm proud of myself," she asserts. "It took a little bit to get here, but I did."[33]

These two represent a trend. In 2018, the National Association of Realtors, Home Buyers, and Sellers reported that one in every five American home buyers is an unmarried woman. Escalating divorce rates among people fifty and older partly explain this development; many American women buy as singletons, seeking equity and a fresh start.[34] Waite and Gallagher's cherished "prestige" still exists. But home ownership patterns are draining this topos of power as America's lifespace pioneers reject matrimonial scripts.

The Case for Marriage cites resource-sharing as a marital benefit.[35] Living part-time with a boyfriend and a housemate—who is much more than that to us—I know firsthand that combining resources is not restricted to spouses. I can pay an electricity bill while Jim does a home repair. In ten minutes, Heidi can fold a load of laundry that would take me a half hour. Jim and I can split a grocery bill while Heidi provides extras like wine.

Of course, economizing provides an excuse to be together. I hope to spend many years with these people. I may not have that chance, so I try to maximize the time we have. The possibility of permanence is all love ever promises. Stating such obvious truths seems strange. It is necessary to counter Marriage Movement superciliousness. And countering this group is important. The Marriage Movement can seem comical, which furthers an argument—ubiquitous in northeastern circles—that the United States has more urgent concerns than relationship-status discrimination. If this group shows anything it is the extent to which no equalizing initiative is complete unless its agenda includes nonmarital rights. The Marriage Movement continually advances modest goals that are intended to expand. Congress enacted a 2006 law granting $150 million per annum for research ventures that encourage wedlock and married fatherhood. These monies funded marriage-preparation training, pro-wedlock advertisements, and matrimony-promoting high school programs.[36]

Nonmarital Americans receive no monies to enhance our relationships, encourage our choices, or prepare bachelors and spinsters for nonmarital life. No federal grants fund publicity campaigns on our behalf. This will not change unless nonmarital people lobby for funding, forcing politicians to face their marriage-free constituents. Until then, the federal government will allot resources to marriage-centric causes as it taxes bachelors, spinsters, and people living-apart together (LATs) to pay bills like that $150 million check.

Resistance is also essential because any Marriage Movement goal's realization energizes the entire crusade. David Blankenhorn cofounded the Marriage Opportunity Council in 2015. "New Group Brings Together Right and Left, Gays and Straights." a press release reads: "Once seemingly at odds, the pro-family and pro-equality agendas have converged."[37] After years of opposing same-sex marriage, Blankenhorn embraced it, founding a group that strove to make wedlock more widely accessible. It rejected myriad gay families and households like mine. But in a polarized nation, even the specious promise of unity is seductive. And Blankenhorn explained his conversion with a word that same-sex marriage advocates would overemploy: "dignity."[38] Wedlock, Blankenhorn averred, makes people dignified; it classes them up.

Blankenhorn and other movement propagandists' key weakness remains ignorance of specific history and more generally, what history is. Waite and Gallagher (a journalist without academic training) fail to discuss social institutions in light of the milieus where they develop. They present wedlock as unvaryingly, perpetually beneficial. Never mind that early medieval female celibates commanded respect withheld from their wedded counterparts. And pooling is traditionally a nonmarital phenomenon. Among Europe's medieval villages, "Several households in a community would get together to build a water mill, put up a fence . . . or set up a blacksmith forge."[39] Townspeople grazed animals in common pastures. A prosperous landowner would stock his neighbors' larders with apples. Town committees were tasked with providing poor relief.

Thirteenth-century Europe witnessed an efflorescence of female mysticism, which included the emergence of beguines: laywomen who eschewed marriage without taking church vows. Especially in the Low Countries, they cohabited in houses called beguinages, which offered greater freedom than convents. While this makes it hard to determine their numbers, it allowed beguines mobility as merchants. Sister Laura Swan characterizes beguines as shrewd businesswomen whose profits went directly to the poor.[40]

Lepers, thought to be divinely punished for sin, were banned from cities and reduced to begging from outlying areas. Assisting them was a key beguine project. Purchasing land for use as *"leprosaria,"* beguines built leper communities with huts, hospices, and churches.[41] Beguinage declined in the fourteenth century, but one Huy collective lasted until the French Revolution.

Between the 1300s and the 1600s, from 10–20 percent of northwestern European women never married. In fifteenth-century York, England, 17 percent of non clerical women who had wills drafted were never married.[42] These are substantial percentages. Civilization rolled on.

Impervious to such information, the Marriage Movement invokes cartoonish spousal roles. Men can't feed themselves or get to bed on time. Women cook, wag their fingers, and dispute medical bills. Their reward is prestige, which culminates in the feathering of a conjugal love nest. Marriage Movement members beg the question by defending wedlock as a set of norms and prohibitions; those norms and prohibitions are what need to be explained. They stand at the edge of a flowing current of nonmarriage, shrieking at it to stop, so the cloak of myth and pseudoscience in which they wrap wedlock will not be soiled. You'll get sick, Waite and Gallagher tell nonmarital people: you'll devolve into a decrepit loner; you'll go broke. Outlandishly, they claim that living unwed is more dangerous than having heart disease or cancer.[43] To prove how happy married couples are, they use a study whose researchers manipulated data, failed to track subjects over time, and excluded all life factors other than romantic attachment.[44]

Contemporary authors who confirm damning stereotypes applied to members of a disadvantaged group usually take heat. A handful of scholars have challenged the Marriage Movement. Most Americans have left it alone. Their silence encouraged Marriage Movement psychologist Judith S. Wallerstein, who appeared on television throughout the late twentieth and early twenty-first century, looking matronly and sagacious. Her book, *Second Chances: Men, Women, and Children a Decade After Divorce*, reached the *New York Times* Bestseller List in 1989. It adumbrates Wallerstein's central argument; while divorce can feel liberating for adults, it damages children. Her second effort, *The Unexpected Legacy of Divorce: A 25 Year Landmark Study* (2001), features a series of emotional train wrecks: "commitment-phobes," needy teens, and spouses terrified of abandonment.

Like *Second Chances* and *The Unexpected Legacy of Divorce*, Wallerstein's next two releases were hits. Taken as a whole, these books are a curious orgy of dogmatism and mythmaking. Wallerstein basically asks unhappy spouses to remain together because even cold, fractious marital households benefit kids. Each volume reiterates this idea, creating a false dilemma in which there are two categories of child-caretaker: married or divorced. In a reality that was making itself felt when Wallerstein launched her one-note career, multiple household configurations for childrearing exist. Conceding that relationship quality matters more than relationship iconography opens endless possibilities for thriving families.

Wallerstein's slipshod methodology has been widely criticized. *Second Chances* generalizes from a tiny sample group: 131 middle-class children from California, most of whom were white. She assembled no corresponding control group of kids from married households, let alone nonstandard families.[45]

Wallerstein interviewed her allegedly doomed subjects. Personal interview studies are problematic because interplay inflects responses. Imagine a child with divorcing bioparents describing stress at home. Indeed, transitions are stressful. Influenced by pundits like Wallerstein, the subject's caretakers comport themselves as failures rather than people undergoing a life change. The child describes this (temporary) home environment; the therapist takes notes, screening out multiple factors that influence personal outcomes. This interview, which says nothing about who the child will become and whether divorce will have negative, positive, or nugatory effects, becomes evidence for a bluntly simplistic explanation of personality. Wallerstein insisted that parental separation injured children well into adulthood, leaving them desperately fragile: "Children of divorce are more eager to be loved and more frightened of being rejected and pushed outside." [46]

Wallerstein disregarded research that contradicted her conclusions. Sociologist Kathleen Gerson surveyed Americans who came of age in the 1980s and 1990s. Among those from divorced homes, "Close to half concluded that while not ideal, parental separation was better than living in a conflict-ridden or silently unhappy home." Of Gerson's respondents from nondivorced households, "four out of ten felt that their parents might have been better off apart.[47] Researcher Joan Berlin Kelly gathered studies on Americans from married versus divorced households conducted throughout the 1990s and found that "the long-term outcome of divorce for the majority of children is resiliency rather than dysfunction."[48] According to legal scholar Michael Wald, the impact of divorce on children is unexceptional. This finding, "which is consistent with the great majority of the research, belies the often hysterical claims of some commentators that divorce and single parenthood are destroying the lives of large numbers of children and the cause of major social problems."[49]

One prominent researcher concludes that America's divorce maven was a total fraud: "Her books sold . . . but as science they are useless; all families she studied sought counseling and all were getting divorced. There was no control group of intact or self-sufficient families with which to compare the children of her patients and no way to filter out professional biases."[50]

In 2009 the National Marriage Project (NMP) found lodging at Charlottesville's University of Virginia (UVA). Founded by Thomas Jefferson in 1819, UVA had as its second rector James Madison. It has since established itself as one of America's leading research institutions. Presumably, any organization it houses publishes research. David Popenoe, scion of postwar marriage guru, Paul Popenoe, founded the NMP, which purports to conduct academic studies. But NMP's director, Brad Wilcox, produces articles like, "Don't be a Bachelor: Why Married Men Work Harder, Smarter, and Make More Money" and "Knot Now: The Benefits of Marrying in Your Mid-to-Late Twenties (Including More Sex)."[51] NMP is not a think tank but an advertising agency.

In 2011, an Iowa based Marriage Movement subgroup called the Family Leader demanded that politicians sign a contract called "The Marriage Vow." It contained a section for presidential candidates helpfully titled "The Candidate Vow." Its authors sought to block any unwed person from running for office. They stipulated that each presidential hopeful promise sexual fidelity to their spouse. The document mandated "support for prompt reform of uneconomic, antimarriage aspects of welfare policy, tax policy, and marital and divorce law, and 'second chance' or 'cooling off' periods for those seeking a 'quickie divorce.'"[52]

Like Jonathan Swift's satire, "A Modest Proposal" (1729), "The Marriage Vow" reads as madness thinly veiled by civic leadership's staid language. Its writers seem poised to suggest that Americans kill, grill, and eat nonmarital citizens. Yet Michelle Bachman, Newt Gingrich, Rick Perry, and Rick Santorum—ambitious elected officials—all signed.[53] Gingrich's two divorces did not hinder him from trying to impose restrictions on others.

In religious communities matrimania is not limited to the extreme fringes. Thirty-seven-year-old bachelor Mark Almlie had studied history at Sonoma State University and earned an MA in divinity from Fullerton Theological Seminary, also accumulating pastoral experience. Job hunting in 2010, Almlie encountered advertisements that read, "Preferably married," and "Is married (preferably with children)." Interviewers doubted an unwed pastor's ability to meet licensed couples' needs. They assumed that a wedded pastor *could* administer to nonmarital congregants—after all, marrieds have the answers. Never mind that two never-married men—Jesus Christ and Paul the Apostle—generated Christian ethics. No job materialized. Unable to support himself, Almlie moved home to Petaluma County, California.[54] His ordeal alerts us to the danger of an organized campaign against nonmarriage.

In *Don't Divorce: Powerful Arguments for Saving and Revitalizing Your Marriage* (2017), Divorcée Diane Medved reiterates

Waite and Gallagher's claim that unmarrieds end up poorer than marrieds.[55] Often they do. As Almlie learned, America rewards wedlock economically. Medved might as well say that people hit on the head with baseball bats get more concussions than those who aren't.

If it liberates adults and spares children a Technicolor view of misery, keeping two homes is worth the additional expense. Reforming the marriage system's economic imbalances can address drops in income some ex-spouses experience. Pooling resources with friends and chosen family can redistribute them to meet children's needs.

These solutions have no place in Diane Medved's marriage-centric universe. "Above all, stick to your partner like glue!" she adjures.[56] Medved proceeds to judge unwed adults, especially those who leave marriage, in two categories: pathetic and cunning. She cheers the first group with statements like, "You're not as young as you were when you made your first commitment" and, "Age comes with illness. A chronic health problem makes you less desirable."[57] Actually, at its best age brings self-awareness; wisdom; professional expertise; career advancement; increased earning potential; greater economic security; for those who exercise, fitness; for people immersed in scholarship, erudition; and for the most blessed, sureness about who one's family is. These blessings accrue over time. Few twentysomethings have them.

Medved expresses "sympathy for . . . people seeking someone with whom to complete their lives."[58] Her diction betrays a radical failure of understanding. Maturity is, largely, the sense of having a complete life. According to the matrimaniac's script, someone meeting a potential spouse tingles with excitement about having found their other half. A marriage-free adult meeting a romantic partner can feel excited while asking different questions: "What kind of relationship might we have?" or, "Will this person gel with my chosen family?"

Medved's take on "singles" life reads like a drugstore fantasy novel; her scenarios may indeed be fictional. She describes "enthusiastic sex freaks" like Jefferson, a divorcé who hosts bimonthly orgies.[59] Her rancor is strongly directed at women who sleep with married men—like fortyish Claire, who attends a professional conference and drops her pen so an older male participant bumps into her when he bends down to retrieve it: "It was an invitation, and Chet knew it."[60] Soon they're FaceTiming and fornicating; Chet leaves his wife and becomes a pariah, rejected by people from his past and longing to backtrack "with my head down and my tail between my legs."[61] Having known myriad divorced people and interviewed many more for my research, I can say that this story feels totally inauthentic. Marriage refugees who suffer horrendous outcomes do not wax sentimental about their former spouses. Typically, they regret formalizing a relationship, not leaving it.

Medved presents herself as an astute logician who makes "airtight" cases.[62] Actually, her book is a concatenation of fallacies, especially appeals to fear and bandwagon appeals. "Don't you know some incredible, intelligent, achieving women who can't seem to find a mate?" she queries provocatively. Let me translate: high-powered women, stick to those husbands with Super Glue. Finding someone else who will appreciate—or tolerate—your achievements, is unlikely. The interrogative, "Don't you know," leaves Medved's sample group of smart unwed women numerically vague. And her entire argument assumes that nonmarital life is terrifying. "Women who click with notably younger men—'cougars,' we call them—are simultaneously admired and reviled,"[63] she pontificates. So, what? Medved mistakes popularity for pertinent authority. Like the high school writer who begins an essay, "Most Americans believe that," she invokes a faceless collective and accords it wisdom. This featureless herd is exactly what people should not care about. All Medved shows here is that she overvalues image.

Finally, Medved abandons civilized discourse and characterizes "singleness" as a contagion: "Even working with [unwed] people who are of the same sex as yourself can be dangerous to marriage."[64] In a section titled "Friendship's Ulterior Motives," Medved introduces Stephanie, who is considering divorce. Her "friend," Becky, approves. Briana (Becky's swinging housemate) enlists Stephanie as her dating buddy. Rachel shacks up with a boyfriend.[65] All give advice that alienates Stephanie from her spouse. This phalanx confirms matrimaniacs' worst suspicions about what unwed women are (catty troublemakers) and want (to poison true love).

As Marriage Movement dogmatists revile nonmarital people, divorce itself is changing. Terms like "conscious separation" have become part of America's lexicon. Some adults formally celebrate the end of their marriages. Sylvia Beckerman, founder and CEO of the women's social networking platform Life Après, was married for four-and-a-half years. She divorced in 2014 and gave her furniture and housewares to charity. Beckerman then threw herself a divorce party that included the important people in her life. Beforehand, she enrolled with a bridal registry and sent the link to invitees.

Beckerman refused to consider herself a failure or feel embarrassed about asking for what she needed. She cast her divorce as a fresh beginning rather than a dismal ending. This lifespace pioneer lives in Fairfield, Connecticut with Marshall, whom she calls her partner. ("Boyfriend sounds a little silly after age sixty," she recently joked with me.) She hosts the podcast, "Sylvia and Me," which features women who creatively meet life's challenges.[66]

Diane Medved cannot squelch such people's confidence. Perhaps this is why she seems permanently enraged.

Bogus Science and Belinda Luscombe, the Most Married Woman in America

In November 2010 the following quotation appeared in *Time* magazine: "A successful marriage increasingly becomes the relationship equivalent of a luxury yacht—hard to get, laborious to maintain, but a better vessel to be on when there are storms at sea."[67] This metaphor suggests that married couples have durable relationships, while unmarrieds sail life's oceans in rickety rowboats. Those loving friendships, life-changing mentorships, and wonderful sexual relationships are illusory. When the weather gets rough, nonmarital people end up treading water alone.

Belinda Luscombe, who authored the article containing this quote, uses such analogies to scare nonmarital readers. They don't frighten me. In December 2015, abdominal surgery left me temporarily unable to walk or dress independently. Heidi flew from Washington, DC, minimizing my concern for the three children remaining at home: "They'll be fine." She hoisted me up steps and helped me into my clothes. She wasn't the only one. Spend two weeks with a few partners like this, and you'll see the fatuousness of Luscombe's statement. Superior material and an excellent navigation system make a vessel seaworthy. A splashy title painted on the front means nothing.

By 2016 Luscombe was enjoining readers to embrace wedlock. "How to Stay Married (and Why)," appeared in *Time's* June edition. Supplemented by a sophisticated-looking graph, its message is actually simple: married life is good, unmarried life not so good. The lesson: if you're unhappily married—unless your spouse is a batterer—hang in; things will improve.

When amassing "proofs," marriage-evangelizing reporters use a few ploys—what my undergraduates call "dick moves." These include tendentious evidence selection and statistical sleight of hand. In "How to Stay Married (and Why)" Luscombe posits the existence of new information that proves how matrimony is health and life enhancing. This is a boldfaced claim; evaluating it requires guidance by statisticians. A project scientist at the University of California, Santa Barbara, Bella DePaulo has the requisite expertise. She holds a PhD in psychology from Harvard and teaches research methodology classes. DePaulo explains, "Random assignment is at the heart of scientific research that tries to establish a causal relationship and not just some murky correlational link."[68]

Luscombe cites various marriage-affirming studies, including one by gerontologist Karl Pillemer, but doesn't explain if their execution included random assignment or met criteria for medical-inquiry standards, which require four social determinants: where someone lives, works, and plays and their access to services. "Happily married people are less likely to have strokes, heart disease, or depression," Luscombe writes. Happily married people from which zip codes, who have access to which doctors? Then, "Mostly, the health effects apply only for happy marriages."[69] Here Luscombe angles; she mentions no "happily marriage-free" cohort group. These two types are not comparable. For a study to yield meaningful results it would have to use sample groups that include married and unmarried people who are basically content. Bracketing the problem of social determinants, one can see that omitting unhappily married respondents renders the experiments pointless.

A hypothetical scenario illuminates this error. Imagine a physician who learns that an emergent drug may prevent coronary artery disease. The medication has been associated with low incidence of coronary artery disease in one patient database. The doctor obtains an NIH grant to fund a clinical trial that will test this drug's efficacy. The study's outcome: observing an absence or presence of coronary artery disease based on clinical evidence. This requires assembling two randomly assigned groups; one will get the medication, the other a placebo.

His study runs and shows that the population who took this drug does not indicate a preventive effect on coronary artery disease. So, the physician, whom I will call Poindexter Schmendrick, decides to "explore" his data. He excludes obese subjects from the group given the drug. The remaining patients without obesity (analogous here to happy marrieds) exhibit less coronary artery disease. This happens because the study removed patients with a leading risk factor (analogous here to depressed marrieds). It's no surprise that obese adults developed more coronary artery disease. They would have done less well whether they took the drug or not. Nevertheless, Schmendrick writes an article on the medication's beneficial effect.

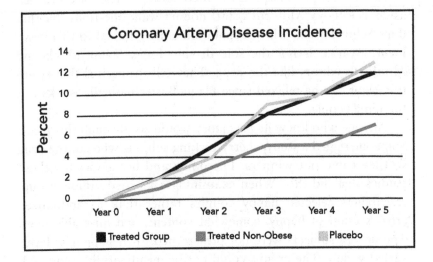

The doctor publishes his article in a minor medical journal. Meantime, the pharmaceutical company advertises its drug, now called PlaqueBuster. Sales improve. Then *Moment* magazine calls: "Dr. Schmendrick, I'm working on a special issue: 'How to Stay Heart Attack Free for Life.' Your findings are exciting. Could you summarize them for lay readers?"

"How about, 'Heart disease is the number one killer in the United States, and people who take PlaqueBuster enjoy lower rates of coronary artery disease?'"

"Sounds good."

Moment gives the piece top billing. Its headline reads, "How to Decrease Your Chance of Heart Disease with PlaqueBuster (And Why You Should Take It)." Featured in newsstands, bookstores, and airports, this special issue flies off the shelves. Everyone knows someone with heart disease; no one wants to get it. *Moment* has told many readers exactly what they want to hear.

A few skeptics question the methodology. They are brushed aside as killjoys. *Moment*'s staff doesn't want questions. Neither does Schmendrick, whose reputation is now linked to this treatment. Avarice is not the sole driving force. Schmendrick and *Moment*'s editors like the drug. They tell themselves that scientific rigor can be relaxed since PlaqueBuster basically works . . . for some people.

Anyone who knew its backstory would see through this piece. Someone rigged a study, cherry-picking subjects who got the drug so they came out winners. Luscombe and her associates chose studies that did this. When examining a married sample group, researchers selected happy couples rather than a randomized cross section of happy, somewhat content, and miserable ones. The unwed subjects were not prescreened; their happiness levels varied widely. The groups could not be meaningfully compared. "If undergraduates, in their very first research methods course, proposed a comparison like that one on another topic, they would get laughed out of class," DePaulo writes.[70]

Because she counsels readers, Luscombe's credentials bear examination. She holds no medical degree or doctorate. The University of Sydney awarded her a Diploma of Education.[71] Trained experts do research marriage, however. Michigan State University psychology professor Richard E. Lucas ran a study containing over 30,000 German participants that spans more than twenty years. It shows that spouses experience a spike in happiness around the time of their weddings but afterward settle into the same contentment levels they had beforehand.[72] Judith P. M. Soons codirected a study that ran from 1987 to 2005, monitoring 5,500 Dutch adults. An organizational psychologist with a doctorate from the Netherlands Interdisciplinary Demographic Institute, Soons found a similar trend; people who marry have inflated happiness levels at first, but these decrease over time. (Soons and her team found that the process took longer.)[73]

In May 2017 the *New York Times* featured University of Amsterdam professor Matthijs Kalmijn. He holds a doctorate in sociology from the University of California at Berkeley. His report, "The Ambiguous Link Between Marriage and Mental Health," draws results from a sixteen-year study of 11,000 Swiss adults chosen as a representative sample of that country's population. He discovered that "people who married reported slightly worse health than they had when they were single. Over time, their health did not improve—it tended to deteriorate, even after taking into account changes in health as people age."[74] In size, longevity, and methodology Kalmijn's study is remarkable—possibly the most important research thus far conducted on health and marriage.

Some of these studies probably demonstrate that a "honeymoon period" provides temporary euphoria. Taken as a group, however, they show that marriage cannot make a dissatisfied person satisfied, an aimless person focused, or a bad relationship good. A wedding is not a conjuring trick.

Behavioral psychologist (and Nobel Prize recipient) Daniel Kahneman interprets his colleagues' findings differently; newlyweds have fresh recollections of their weddings and reach into this positive memory bank when answering questions about their contentment levels. Years later, when asked the same questions, subjects access more recent, nonwedding related memories. So, these studies may show how memory influences people's sense of well-being. For Kahneman, however, the decision to marry is uncanny: "On their wedding day, the bride and groom know that the rate of divorce is high and that the incidence of marital disappointment is even higher, but they do not believe that these statistics apply to them."[75] He finds wedlock as a life-enhancer impossible to evaluate without factoring in individual personalities. Kahneman ultimately rates its significance low in terms of happiness levels.[76]

Such scholarship should interest Belinda Luscombe. So should economists Justin Wolfers and Betsey Stevenson's finding on states that began providing unilateral divorce. These states witnessed a 20 percent drop in female suicides. Men, too, are safer when marital separation is accessible. The Center for Disease Control reports that the number of husbands killed by their spouses dropped by roughly two-thirds between 1981 and 1998 because egress from marriage became more available.[77]

Sean Lauer and Carrie Yodanis have analyzed wedlock's impact on time. These University of British Columbia sociologists found that arguments consume a large part of wedded couples' waking hours, lowering their life-satisfaction levels. Disputes about money are frequent. The researchers' solution: spouses maintaining separate finances and living apart. Lauer and Yodanis believe that most won't make these adjustments because "spouses, despite the fact that alternative arrangements may be more efficient, follow the rules."[78]

Instead of responding to these scholars, Luscombe published a book called *Marriageology: The Art and Science of Staying Together* (2019), which blends exhibitionism with didacticism. Luscombe's husband Jeremy ("He's handsome and strong and great in bed") is an architect—a fact she takes every opportunity to mention.[79] This aesthete (read "genius") frequently interrupts her to help him locate household items. Luscombe finds this annoying and diagnoses their problem as "familiarity:" the condition of knowing someone too well. "Familiarity" is not a medical term, and what follows contains no science. Luscombe suggests that spouses handle each other's irksome habits as they did early on, when the behaviors seemed less irritating. She presents this platitude as if it is the holy grail.

That lovers' passion decreases over time is a murky half truth. Sometimes the first stage involves intensity that gives way to more temperate attraction. But female sexuality is complex; learning what works can take time; relationships where this happens often intensify in successive stages. Emotionally volatile paramours who dislike but won't leave each other come together for periods, separate, and repeat the process in a pattern fueled by passion. Luscombe tries to force various relationship types into the tight space of a single mold.

The belief that spouses should repress mutual annoyance is a worn truism. Jewish folk wisdom recommends that every husband and wife become "a little bit deaf." I imagine that each culture has its version of this adage.

Luscombe recommends that couples befriend other couples in order to bask in coupledness. The 1990s magazine, *Married Woman*, delivered this message in an article called, "Old Friends,

New Friends" and subtitled, "Don't Feel Guilty if You Want to Put Your Single Friends on Hold and Reserve a Table for Four." It wasn't just a matter of dinner reservations; *Married Woman* encouraged readers to purge their lives of unwed people: "It's only natural to feel a strong urge to edit your address book."[80] By encouraging couples ghettos, Luscombe demonstrates her affinity with *Married Woman*, which one scholar calls an expression of "the totalitarian marital outlook of the fifties."[81] By the time Luscombe quotes marriage-maven Esther Perel (on breakfast dates), *Marriageology* has revealed itself as a full-on piece of glad-to-be-married propaganda.

So, it's no surprise when the preaching begins: "Betraying your spouse is a horrible, crappy, selfish and stupid thing to do . . . If you have children, you will break their hearts."[82] By "betraying" Luscombe means sleeping with other people. She ignores romance's long history of shirking monogamy and its defenders like Bertrand Russell. More recently, psychologists Andreas Baranowski and Heiko Hecht redid a 1978 experiment in which most females declined sex when propositioned in night clubs. This seemed to show that women were monogamous or possessed weaker sex drives than men. In the second experiment Baranowski and Hecht created an environment in which subjects were protected from violence by a fictitious dating service that implemented security measures. Without the threat of being beaten up, robbed, or murdered, 97 percent of the women surveyed said they would sleep with prospective candidates. This was only slightly lower than 100 percent of men who answered affirmatively.[83] The earlier study had not shown a sex-based libidinal difference but revealed that women fear attacks by strangers.

Such research indicates that whatever their relationship status, people are not especially monogamous. In Luscombe's view, however, extramarital sex is a grave lapse rather than an option ethical adults might choose. Commentators of this stripe often say that sleeping with someone other than one's spouse is symptomatic of trouble in a marriage. Occam's Razor suggests another explanation: adults like having sex with more than one person.

Any teenager who has hung around a suburban high school, diner, or hair salon, will find Luscombe's statement that marital nonmonogamy breaks children's hearts excessive. Dad's "business trips," mom's "friendship" with the landscaper, and the school secretary's appointments with her "massage therapist" are well-known phenomena. Children and adolescents are observers, not social imbeciles. Speaking from my (nonscientific) experience as a former teenager and current professor, many young people do not view bioparents who have extracurricular sex as fallen gods. Some find the subject icky; others are happy (in the, "Go, Mom!" spirit). Many don't care.

Marriageology is relationship-status discrimination packaged as a cute love story. Indeed, articles about Luscombe feature her marriage to (architect) Jeremy Edmiston, documenting such suspenseful events as the wait for a toilet to be installed in their Manhattan loft.[84]

Why bother with someone who overrates public interest in her domestic life and offers misguided analyses? Because she is salient. Luscombe's articles appear in a widely circulated magazine and demonstrate that major periodicals use reporters who kowtow to prevailing conjugal paradigms. In a special edition of *Time* titled, *The Science of Happiness* (2016), Luscombe's article, "The Marriage Plot," again omits significant research. Where ordinary Marriage Movement insensitivity leaves off, she begins. From one quote readers learn, "**Marriage today offers higher-order benefits. It's as if it used to be a Honda, a perfectly utilitarian ride, but now it's a Benz**" (emphasis Luscombe's). Again, she analogizes wedlock to a luxury vehicle. But here she gloats shamelessly about piled-on nuptial benefits, overlooking how policies that seem benevolent to marrieds appear very different to those whom wedlock dispossesses. Another quote reads, **"Unmarried baby boomers are four times as likely to be poor and twice as likely to have disabilities as married boomers"** (emphasis Luscombe's).[85]

If *Time* continues assessing marriage it should deploy authors who assess marriage, exploring its sanctions, analyzing its penalties for dissent, asking why wedlock carries so much legal weight in the United States while it bears less in many other countries. If *Times*'s editors showcase someone who gushes about her strong handsome husband and believes that nonmarriage causes physical disabilities, they remain partners in an ongoing con.

Sadly, Luscombe is not alone. Couples counselor Sue Johnson asserts, "Seeking and holding onto a life partner has become a pressing organizing principle of our lives, given that other community ties are so marginalized."[86] What Johnson should have said is, the modern West has marginalized relationships that were once central, furthering cultural alienation. Let's reinvest those ties with significance.

But Johnson argues that people are designed for wedlock, and human brain chemistry proves it with the presence of oxytocin, a hormone also found in prairie voles' brains. (They have the rodent version of conjugal bliss.) Citing an animal that shares no major features with human beings is problematic, but prairie voles are not even monogamous. The comparison is absurd. If Johnson shows anything, it's that Marriage Movement ideology has penetrated self-help realms.

In the slick magazine version of relationships, people who wed become happier, healthier, and wealthier. Someone purporting to evaluate the institution promotes it, shunting history aside. Typically, editors give members of this marriage brigade wide berth.

Nonmarital people read that wedlock is the Mercedes Benz of relationships. These images generate doppelganger pictures: the spouseless isolate emptying her cat's litterbox; the aging loner in his cheesy bachelor pad; the lovers whose relationship falters during hard times. Surely, when matrimaniacs like Luscombe treat wedlock as the bond that really counts, it fuels longstanding prejudices.

Clearer journalistic voices are easily missed. Ashton Applewhite, for instance, interviewed fifty divorced women ranging in age, race, class, and circumstance. Her subjects describe a common experience: initial stress followed by increasing independence, pleasure in solitude, and exhilaration.[87] None of Applewhite's respondents hosted orgies. All found themselves "Living as well or better," with time freed for career development.[88] Her interviewees include women who became film archivists and pension fund managers.

Applewhite lives in Brooklyn with her boyfriend, publisher Bob Stein. She kindly made the preface from her book's second edition available to me. I quote from it: "Marriage should not be a gateway to social and economic privilege. I hope we continue to move towards a society that supports the full range of relationships and family forms."[89]

When reporters fetishize wedlock and behave as though it has always been considered the gold standard of human relations, they betray history while sidestepping a fundamental question: is matrimony a deeper, more meaningful bond than any other? In disentangling marriage's philosophical knot, this is the most significant thread. Pull on it, and the rest unravels.

While the knot remains tight, marital supremacism will shape civil law, as wrongful death claims prove. These civil lawsuits aim to help surviving family when someone dies as the result of another's negligence or intentional harm. Marriage entitles survivors to file such suits. San Francisco–based attorney George Khoury admits that this policy may seem unfair to nonmarital survivors but explains that "lawmakers have recognized that marriage . . . is a significant step in a couple's relationship."[90]

Maybe, in their self-interest and/or compliance with collective norms, lawmakers got it wrong. Deepening relationships contain many important moments: the first "I love you"; the decision to live together; the honor of becoming a child's godparent; the first kiss (if the relationship is sexual); the first time sharing a bed if it is platonic; the agreement to become someone's medical proxy; the promise that if one is in trouble, the other will come. Marriage-centrism limits Khoury's thinking and prevents him from considering the host of people who could suffer after someone's demise. He posits that wrongful death claims are correctly restricted to spouses (or blood children). Nonmarrieds shouldn't be offended; our relationships just mean less.

Laws that make wedlock a prerequisite for financial recompense impress one standard on an entire population. They call to mind the United States Constitution, whose Fourteenth Amendment guarantees that no state will refuse citizens "equal protection of the laws." Unfortunately, with Marriage Movement support, a host of public policies does just this.

(Endnotes)

1   Jessica Valenti, *The Purity Myth: How America's Obsession with Virginity is Hurting Young Women* (Berkeley: Seal Press, 2010), 139.

2   Adolph Reed, Jr., "Kiss the Family Goodbye," *Class Notes: Posing as Politics and Other Thoughts on the American Scene* (New York: The New Press, 2000), 115.

3   An updated edition came out in 2007. Visit https://www.unmarried.org/press-releases/let-them-eat-wedding-rings-report.

4   Polikoff, *Beyond (Straight and Gay)*, 70.

5   Kenza Moller, "What Did Michelle Obama Say About Hillary Clinton During the 2008 Election?", *Romper*, October, 2016, https://www.romper.com/p/what-did-michelle-obama-say-about-hillary-clinton-during-the-2008-election.

6   Nicole Goodkind, "Bernie Sanders Says Bill Clinton's Affair with Monica Lewinsky Has 'Haunted That Family Forever,'" *Washington Post*, August 7, 2018, https://www.newsweek.com/monica-lewinsky-bernie-sanders-bill-clinton-affair.

7   *What Love Is*, 145.

8   Franke, *Wedlocked*, 156.

9   See The Institute for American Values website: http://americanvalues.org/catalog/pdfs/marriagemovement.

10 Introduction, *The Book of Marriage: The Wisest Answers to the Toughest Questions,* ed. David Blankenhorn and Dana Mack (Grand Rapids, Michigan: Wm. B. Eerdsmans, 2001), 11.

11 "The Structural Study of Myth," *Structural Anthropology*, trans. Claire Jacobsen and Brooke Grundfest Schoepf (New York: Basic Books, 1963), 226–7.

12 Eric Berkowitz, *Sex and Punishment: Four Thousand Years of Judging Desire* (Berkeley: Counterpouint, 2012), 13.

13 Jean Bottéro, *Everyday Life in Ancient Mesopotamia*, trans. Antonia Nevill (Baltimore, The Johns Hopkins University Press, 1992), 116.

14 Lerner, *The Creation*, 120.

15 Coontz, *Marriage*, 47.

16 Ibid., 62–4. James Trager, *The Women's Chronology: A Year-by-Year Record, From Prehistory to the Present* (New York: Henry Holt, 1994), 20–2.

17 Berkowitz, *Sex*, 21.

18 Coontz, *Marriage*, 78.

19 John Boswell, *The Kindness of Strangers: The Abandonment of*

Children in Western Europe from Late Antiquity to the Renaissance (Chicago: University of Chicago Press, 1988), 59.

20   I condense the argument originally made by Friedrich Engels in 1884. See *The Origin of the Family, Private Property and the State*, intro. Michèle Barrett (London: Penguin, 1986).

21   *Marriage*, 44.

22   Reed, Jr., "Kiss the Family," 114.

23   Ibid., 115.

24   *The Case for Marriage: Why Married People Are Happier, Healthier, and Better Off Financially* (New York: Doubleday, 2000), 53.

25   Ibid., 55.

26   Ibid., 164.

27   Ibid., 53.

28   Hilary Howard, "A Confederacy of Bachelors," *New York Times*, August 3, 2012, https://www.nytimes.com/2012/08/05/nyregion/four-men-sharing-rent-and-friendship-for-18-years.

29   "Four Men and No Babies: is 'Fortress Astoria' the End of the Family?," *The American Conservative*, August 17, 2012, https://www.theamericanconservative.com/four-men-and-no-babies.

30   Rader, *Breaking Boundaries*, 24–5.

31   Waite and Gallagher, *The Case*, 55.

32   Ibid., 60.

33   Kelly Anne Smith, "Single Female Ownership is Baby Booming," *Bankrate*, October 19, 2018, https://www.bankrate.com/real-estate/single-female-homeownership-booming.

34   Renee Stapler, "Led by Baby Boomers, Divorce Rates Climb for Americans 50+ Population," The Pew Research Center, March 9, 2017, https://www.pewresearch.org/fact-tank/2017/03/09/led-by-baby-boomers-divorce-rates-climb-for-americas-50-population.

35   Waite and Gallagher, *The Case*, 30.

36   Andrew Cherlin, *The Marriage-Go-Round: The State of Marriage and the Family in America Today* (New York: Albert A. Knopf, 2009), 27.

37   Institute for American Values, February 23, 2015, https://www.prnewswire.com/news-releases/new-group-brings-together-right-and-left-gays-and-straights-to-fight-marriage-gap.

38   "How My View on Gay Marriage Changed," *New York Times*, June 22, 2012, https://www.nytimes.com/2012/06/23/opinion/how-my-view-on-gay-marriage-changed.

39   Coontz, *Marriage*,128.

40   Laura Swan, *The Wisdom of the Beguines: The Forgotten Story of a Medieval Women's Movement* (Katonah, New York: BlueBridge, 2014), 2.

41 Ibid., 74.
42 Coontz, *Marriage*, 127.
43 Waite and Gallagher, *The Case*, 48.
44 Waite and Gallagher rely on a defective "One-Time Happiness Study" with respondents from seventeen mainly western countries. Its researchers removed every married person who divorced. See *Singled Out*, 41–6.
45 Susan Faludi, *Backlash: The Undeclared War Against American Women* (New York: Crown, 1991), 26–7.
46 Judith S. Wallerstein and Sandra Blakeslee, *Second Chances: Men, Women, and Children a Decade After Divorce* (Boston: Houghton Mifflin, 1989), 246.
47 "Changing Lives, Resistant Institutions: A New Generation Negotiates Gender, Work, and Family Change," *Sociological Forum*, Vol. 24, no. 4 (December 2009), 738.
48 Quoted in Cathy Young, "Dr. Bad News," Salon.com, October 3, 2000, https://www.salon.com/2000/10/03/wallerstein.
49 "Adult's Sexual Orientation and State Determination Regarding Placement of Children," *Family Law Quarterly* 40, no. 3 (2006), 381–434.
50 Judith Rich Harris, *The Nurture Assumption: Why Children Turn Out the Way They Do* (New York: Touchstone, 1998), 305–6.
51 Visit The National Marriage Project website: http://nationalmarriage-project.org/about/director.
52 The Family Leader, "The Marriage Vow," http://thefamilyleader.com/wp-content/uploads/2011/07/themarriagevow.final_.7.7.111.pdf.
53 Maggie Haberman, "Perry Signs Vander Plaats's Marriage Pledge,'" *Politico*, November 11, 2011, https://www.politico.com/story/2011/11/perry-signs-vander-plaats-marriage-pledge.
54 Dan Johnson, "Mark Almlie Finds That Single Male Pastors Face Many Obstacles," *The Press Democrat*, March 27, 2011, http://www.pressdemocrat.com/news/2294600-181/mark-almlie-finds-that-single. Mark Almlie, "From Prejudice to Acceptance: Prejudice is Like a Cockroach," *Singlism*, ed. Bella DePaulo, 69.
55 Diane Medved, PhD, *Don't Divorce: Powerful Arguments for Revitalizing Your Marriage* (Washington, DC: Regnery Publishing, 2017), 114.
56 Ibid., 156.
57 Ibid., 275.
58 Ibid., 277.
59 Ibid., 279.
60 Ibid., 265.

61 Ibid., 266.

62 Ibid., 13.

63 Ibid., 281–2.

64 Ibid., 166.

65 Ibid., 156–7.

66 Conversation with author, October 14, 2020.

67 Belinda Luscombe, "Marriage? What's it Good For?", *Time*, November, 29, 2010, 56.

68 Bella DePaulo, "What's Wrong with Telling People to Stay Married? What TIME Gets Wrong About the Science of Getting Married and Staying Married," *Psychology Today*, *Living Single*, (blog), June 13, 2016, https://www.psychologytoday.com/blog/living-single/201606/whats-wrong-telling-married-people-stay-married.

69 "How to Stay Married," *Time*, June 2016, 39.

70 DePaulo, "What's Wrong with Telling People?"

71 The University of Sydney, BELINDA LUSCOMBE, http://sydney.edu.au/education_social_work/alumni_friends/profiles/belinda_luscombe.

72 Personality & Well Being Lab, Department of Psychology, Michigan State University, https://msu.edu/~lucasri.

73 Judith P. M. Soons, Aart C. Liefbroer, and Matthijs Kalmijn, "The Long-Term Consequences of Relationship Formation for Subjective Well Being," *Journal of Marriage and Family Therapy* 71, no. 5 (December 2009): 1254–70.

74 Bella DePaulo, "Get Married, Get Healthy? Maybe Not," *New York Times*, May 25, 2017, https://www.nytimes.com/2017/05/25/opinion/marriage-health-study.

75 *Thinking Fast and Slow* (New York: Farrar, Straus and Giroux, 2011), 139.

76 Ibid., 400–400.

77 "Til Death do Us Part: Effects of Divorce Laws on Suicide, Domestic Violence, and Spousal Murder and "Bargaining of the Shadow Laws and Family Distress," NBER Working Paper 10175 (2003), http://faculty-gsb Stamford.edu/Wolfers/papers/Divorce. Laura Guan, Daniel Nagin, and Richard Rosenfeld, "Explaining the Decline in Intimate Partner Violence," *Homicide Studies* 3 (1999).

78 *Getting Married: The Public Nature of Our Private Relationships* (New York: Routledge, 2017), 86.

79 Belinda Luscombe, *Marriageology: The Art and Science of Staying Together* (Oneworld, 20019), 4, 5.

80 Quoted in Betsy Israel's *Bachelor Girl: The Secret History of Single Women in the 20th Century* (London: Aurum Press, 2003), 252.

81 Ibid., 252.

82 Luscombe, *Marriageology*, 205.

83 "Receptivity to Sexual Invitations: Gender Differences May Not Be What They Seem," *Archives of Sexual Behavior* 44 (2015), 2257–65.

84 Lucie Young, "I Married a Minimalist," *New York Times Magazine*, November 6, 2015, https://lucieyoung.com/2015/11/06/i-married-a-minimalist.

85 "The Marriage Plot." *Time: The Science of Happiness*, 2016, 64.

86 *Love Sense: The Revolutionary New Science of Romantic Relationships* (New York: Little Brown, 2013), 5.

87 *Cutting Loose: Why Women Who End Their Marriages Do So* Well (New York: HarperCollins, 1997), 161.

88 Ibid., 125.

89 Ashton Applewhite, *Cutting Loose Second Edition*, Preface, 6.

90 "Do You Need to Be Married to File a Wrongful Death Claim if Your Partner Dies?", Find.Law, May 19, 2017, http://blogs.findlaw.com/injured/2017/05/do-you-need-to-be-married-to-file-a-wrongful-death-claim-if-your-partner-dies.

5

Here Comes the Subpoena:
Separation, Litigation, and the Alimony Racket

"After all, the highest form of injustice
is to appear just without being so."

—PLATO, *THE REPUBLIC*

Equal Protection of the Laws?
Not so Much

In Virginia, failure to pay alimony, even when ill or unemployed, is punishable by imprisonment. An out of work man may deplete his savings writing monthly checks to an employed ex-wife. His record counts for nothing if he misses several payments. The recipient of a large inheritance can sue an ex-wife awash in medical bills. If her arrangement is nonmodifiable, the presiding judge has little discretion.

Virginia lawyers speak among themselves about "the grocery rule;" a client who owes back alimony must pay rather than buy groceries with her last few dollars. Her ex-spouse's refrigerator may be full; his education, earning capacity, and financial profile mean nothing. Family law reform activist Sam Brittingham encapsulates the situation: "Virginia awards permanent alimony to young healthy college graduates in established careers who were married for less than 10 years, whether they have children or not. Those who can't afford to pay, go to jail."[1]

Tell people about Virginia marriage law, and they press back. Surely you're mistaken. No developed country has debtor's prisons.

The United States does. And numerous Americans endure something akin to indentured servitude, earning wages that others appropriate. When they fail to meet financial obligations imposed on them by strangers imbued with authority, such individuals can face imprisonment. Jails that incarcerate them do not solely intern debtors, as specific eighteenth-century prisons did. I doubt that the inmate doing time because of a lost job takes comfort in this fact.

Draconian policies are not limited to Virginia. The northeast has its share of payers whose lives are strained to the brink of unmanageability or destroyed. When he ordered biology professor Tom Leustek to pay life alimony, a New Jersey judge said, "It's not fair . . . it's the law."[2] It was not 1950 but 2007. Leustek's ex had not quit college to darn his socks. She was a psychologist starting her own private practice.

Leustek founded an alimony-reform group. It attracted members with a common quandary: supporting employable and employed people. The result was often a bleak future with no savings to retire on, no long-term care insurance, and, in the event of a default, the agony of funding one's own prosecution by covering an ex-spouse's legal bills. Many members of New Jersey Alimony Reform had married during infatuation's first blush: exactly the wrong time to sign a legal contract. Not having researched marriage law, they misunderstood its rudiments. Matrimony contractually binds two adults and a third party: the state. When two people wed, laws of the state in which they marry regulate their relationship.

Louis, a sixty-four-year-old man, got divorced in New Jersey. It was 1995. He was ordered to assume all expenses incurred as a couple, split with the ex-wife his Teamster's annuity, and pay her attorney's bill. He had to purchase life insurance in her name and pay 585 dollars per month in permanent alimony. So this sum could be deducted from his paycheck, the court demanded his driver's license information. Failure to provide it within three months would have resulted in a jail sentence.

I spoke with Louis by phone in December 2019. He lives in Camden, Delaware, where he grew up. His monthly Social Security check is $1,600. Alimony is automatically withdrawn. This leaves him $1,015 per month to live on. "I have food," he told me. "I can pay my heat and electric bill. But that's it."

Playing Bingo at his church, Louis recently met an attorney. Unlike Manhattan lawyers who demanded $5,000 up front, this one seemed interested in filing an appeal—until she learned where Louis divorced. "That's one of the worst states," she explained. "If it had happened outside New Jersey you would have gotten hit, but I suspect the alimony wouldn't be permanent. I don't know if there's any point appealing."

Louis's life shows what can happen if bad luck coincides with the termination of a legal marriage. He graduated from public high school and attended Delaware State University, switching majors from chemistry to business. After commencement he worked as a manager for several retail home improvement stores located throughout New Jersey. Eating in a diner one morning, he met a waitress named Daniella. He found her shy and sweet—qualities he liked as a young man.

Daniella had not attended college. The traditional Italian home in which she grew up discouraged advanced education for women, stressing the idea that husbands provide. She had never questioned this belief. She and Louis dated for six months before getting engaged. They married in 1980.

Within a few months Daniella began having emotional problems. A psychiatrist prescribed various medications. She ended up on Haldol and started getting counseling at a women's center. As traumatic childhood memories she had kept secret came to the fore, her physical relationship with Louis ended. She had taken part-time waitressing shifts, but depression now prevented this. Louis assumed all of their expenses. "It was more like having a teenage daughter than a wife," he explained. "But the depression was not an act. She was incredibly traumatized."

Thirteen years in, Louis decided to end a relationship that had not turned out well. Daniella agreed but demanded a $125,000 settlement, which he could not pay. They went to court, and Louis got his life sentence. He took various jobs as a home improvement store manager. At one he met a twenty-six-year-old saleswoman named Janet. He was thirty-nine, but the age gap felt inconsequential. Louis described her as "assertive, confident, full of life." Janet hailed from Queens; she balanced sales work with her own jewelry-making business. In Delaware they cohabited for twenty-three happy, marriage-free years.

Janet developed a cardiac disorder that her doctors could not diagnose. Tragically, she died in her sleep at age forty-nine. It was 2017, and Louis found himself more or less alone. "My mother died when she was thirty-six from a miscarriage," he explained. "My father died when he was fifty-six from a stroke." Had he stuck with his original chemistry major, Louis might have found employment in a lab and made long-term friends. Retail was peripatetic; moving between stores, he had never built a community.

Louis now has severe arthritis. Since retail involves standing for eight to ten hours at a stretch, work is not feasible. Had his ex-wife not sued, life would be difficult. With life alimony it is grim. Falling between society's cracks is a real possibility.

Louis believes that Daniella should not have entered a sexual relationship. But he is not angry at her. He is incensed at the judge who ruled in their case. Louis also dislikes the term "spousal support:" "That's the new phrase, at least in Delaware. So, lots of people confuse alimony with child support."

For twenty-three years Louis has paid someone who was in his life for thirteen years. She may be unable to care for herself, but that should not make her upkeep his permanent job. Because he is her senior, it seems likely that Louis will predecease Daniella. At that point she will gain access to his Social Security. If his lover of twenty-three years was alive, she would lack this right.

Daniella marrying someone else would ameliorate Louis's situation. This is the most bizarre aspect of a congeries of macabre laws. Suspension of alimony rests on the recipient's remarriage. Payments cease, not if the collector earns a degree that opens professional doors, lands a job, or makes good investments. The payments stop upon remarriage. Again, matrimony is the legal benchmark.

With the late twentieth century's loosening of social restrictions, many alimony recipients have lovers whom they see openly. They have every reason to not remarry. They can enjoy themselves at the expense of retirees living on fixed incomes and force people in poor health to continue working. Americans live longer than they used to. Alimony payers are, therefore, caught in a time warp—oppressed by laws embodying 1950s attitudes, which force them to support people enjoying twenty-first century freedoms.

Prior to interviewing Louis, I did not know that Social Security could be garnished. But even cursory study of divorce law is illuminating. The Office of Child Support Enforcement defines alimony as follows: "Periodic payments of funds for the support and maintenance of a spouse or former spouse and, subject to and in accordance with State or local law, [it] includes, but is not limited to, separate maintenance, alimony pendente lite, maintenance, and spousal support."[3] Alimony also includes attorneys' fees, interest, and court costs, if they are mandated through a decree, order, or judgment.[4] Pensions, retirement benefits, federal employees' contributions to thrift savings funds, survivors' benefits, retirement contribution refunds, and monetary compensation for work-related injuries can all be tapped. SSI, a federally-funded supplement for disabled people, is technically invulnerable to alimony collection. However, in Tennessee SSI has been garnished for alimony payments.[5]

Alimony-reform organizations have sprung up in, among other states, Arkansas, Colorado, Connecticut, Florida, Georgia, Maryland, South Carolina, Tennessee, Vermont, and Virginia. Their work has had ripple effects. A 2013 bill to end durational alimony almost cleared the Florida legislature but was vetoed by Governor Rick Scott.[6] The push for modification continued in that state, led (unsuccessfully) by Congresswoman Colleen Burton.

Overall, alimony is an underreported subject. It flies beneath news junkies' radar screens. But no marital analysis is complete without a discussion of this practice. Mine is unusual in two ways. First, I do not understand alimony as a clash between the sexes. Instead, I view it within the context of nonmarital discrimination. Second, I see it as a practice rooted in marriage ideology. I believe that alimony shows this ideology's instability. The marital ideal can backfire at any moment. Americans who embrace conjugality and play by its rules secure expansive privileges. But marrieds who stray outside the prescribed boundaries or alter the script leave themselves vulnerable. Any spouse having a change of heart or developing new beliefs about relationships can face ferocious reprisals.

When Entitlement Gives Way to Oppression

Divorcing does not involve the central component that makes an action a crime: harming someone or society at large (in Latin, *causa*).[7] Nevertheless, those who end marriages are often treated as criminals. On the slippery terrain of American conjugality, love turns quickly into hate and privilege turns rapidly into persecution.

This makes no sense to the nonbeliever in marriage and perfect sense to anyone unwilling to dislodge wedlock from its culturally supreme position. American weddings exude veneration, projecting images of noblesse oblige. The bride tossing her bouquet from a balcony emphasizes her elevated status and willingness to share it with another aspiring wife. I have previously described such practices in terms of "the politics of marital entitlement."[8]

Adulation of wedded couples is not just naïve, ahistorical, and prejudicial toward nonmarrieds; it is hazardous to spouses. Think of the Silicon Valley executive hitched to a graduate student. He welcomes an amicable split . . . until speaking with a divorce consultant. He then successfully sues for half his wife's assets and alimony that ends after he his dissertation is completed. He's been "writing" for three years. The academic job market offers bleak prospects; he's just received an incentive to never finish. What does she do?

Consider the Virginia internist whose librarian wife works part-time. When they divorce she decides to sue rather than take a full-time position. Having just hit the twenty-year-marriage mark, she finagles life alimony. The doctor's friends are outraged, but they assure him he won't starve. Then a large health network buys the hospital that employs him. Its executives slash by 40 percent all doctors' salaries. He can't keep his ex in the style to which she's accustomed. Too bad; a nonmodification clause in his contract says he must. It seems he'll have to work double shifts . . . forever. To whom does he turn?

These examples come from research I conducted when first investigating alimony. Others too numerous to include come from alimony reform organizations I contacted. Alimony reform has always seemed shortsighted to me because it challenges the punishment rather than its root cause. But these loosely run associations, which often operate from people's basements, provide some resistance to ongoing miscarriages of justice.

I wrote to Virginia Alimony Reform in November 2017, hoping to find people who would share their stories. I heard back from Sam Brittingham, the group's Founder and Director: "There's a member currently contemplating suicide. If he goes through with this, he'll be the second member lost to suicide this year. With the holidays just around the corner, I'm worried . . . Please contact him."[9]

Reading this email, I felt any sense of writing for career advancement, or to impress my impressive friends, evaporate. I searched online for the doctor, whose name Sam had provided. His profile appeared: early forties, dark-skinned with inquisitive brown eyes . . . I grabbed my *Siddur* (prayer book) from the shelf, opened it, and started praying for him.

Paying 100 Percent of Your Salary to an Ex-Spouse (Yes, This is Really Happening)

The doctor is a forty-year-old pediatric anesthesiologist named Kamal. Like many people who pass through Virginia's family-court system, he is scared—of future reprisals from his ex, of a certified letter waiting in the mailbox. Alimony payers often fear speaking with writers. Kamal and I traded a few emails before he agreed to talk. On the phone his Pan Middle Eastern accent attested to an international upbringing. I sensed someone cosmopolitan and keenly intelligent.

Equally fluent in Arabic, French, and English, Kamal is a member of Egypt's Catholic community. He grew up wanting to be a doctor and attended medical school in the Middle East, proceeding to his residency at a hospital in Ohio, where he met a nurse. He was twenty-eight; she was thirty. Both were Egyptian; they shared memories of particular sights, scents, and tastes. Working in health care, they understood each other's professional stresses. Combined with strong physical chemistry, these commonalities seemed auspicious to Kamal. In a short time, they were engaged, with the caveat that she would convert from Islam to Catholicism. "I wanted to make sure we could be buried in the same cemetery," he explained.

A priest married them in Egypt. It was 2006; they returned to the United States in 2007.

I interrupted to ask, "How are you?"

"You never get used to being a slave."

"You mean, feeling like a slave?"

"No. I'm an actual slave. I pay 100 percent of my income to my ex-wife."

"How is that possible?"

"I don't know," Kamal said, in the flat voice of one who won't defend what he considers an unpardonable lapse in judgment. "I'm trying to figure out . . . First, I fell for her. She's attractive. She seemed ambitious. I saw her as an excellent fit for me. I was completely wrong."

Initially their relationship was enjoyable, despite her unpredictable temper; three children (two boys and a girl) came along. Eventually, however, the household became volatile. According to Kamal, her animosity toward his loved ones spurred frequent arguments. "It was irrational. My relatives posed no threat to her. Once I asked why she kept starting fights about them. She said, 'I'm pushing to see who you'll leave first, me or your family.'

"I'd sometimes mention starting the conversion. She'd say, in this hissing voice, 'I don't believe in your Christ.'"

In 2014 the hospital Kamal worked for purchased two neighboring facilities. Executives cleaned house, firing most of these hospitals' employees. During the twelve months it took to restaff, temporary workers were needed. Kamal took two additional monthly ICU shifts. This added ten thousand dollars per month to his salary.

"It seemed right," he said glumly. "We'd bought a home in Virginia. My wife was studying for a doctorate in nursing. I thought she should focus on her courses. The goal was for her to finish her degree and take a higher paying position. I would go back to normal hours, and we'd live comfortably.

"Meantime, my younger brother was finishing college in Cairo. He wanted to follow in my footsteps. My father had retired from corporate; my mom was working part-time in a convent, helping the sisters with bookkeeping and various things. Her salary was modest. They couldn't afford medical school tuition. I wanted to help. My ex was against it, which should have been a red flag . . . I'd say, 'He's a good kid; I have to help him.' She'd say, 'But it's our money.'

"Then she became preoccupied with buying a home in the Middle East. My best friend is a builder, and she asked him to scout investment properties for us."

"Why, do you think?"

"Well, Egyptian property has become quite valuable. A small house on the Mediterranean would have been a good investment for people who didn't have a mortgage, one spouse in graduate school, and three kids. I said what she knew; we couldn't afford it. She kept at me. Finally, I figured out the whole thing was a ploy to have someplace for her mother and aunt to live. She might as well have worn a sign around her neck saying, 'I'm using you.'"

Their relationship could not survive the conflicting agendas, and they agreed to divorce. In Egypt they filed papers in 2014. The hearing took place in December 2015; the final ruling came in April 2016.

An American divorce followed. Kamal's lawyers told him to expect mandatory child support, which he considered fair: "Of course I was going to support my children!" Virginia family court, however, was a shocking ordeal. He came with two attorneys and a psychologist prepared to testify about home dynamics, including his ex-wife's mood lability. A career consultant was ready to discuss nursing as a growth field.

The psychologist was not allowed to speak. "The judge permitted testimony from the career expert," Kamal explained. "But he ignored everything she said. He imputed no income to my ex, who had finished her degree."

Kamal began dating a physician's assistant named Lauren, whom he now refers to as his significant other: "My ex and I had no agreement about seeing or not seeing other people before the American divorce came through. It was never discussed."

Considering the marriage's duration and Kamal's ex's credentials, his lawyers prepared him for approximately seven years of alimony. He put his financials before the court; they showed a deceptively high salary. The judge surveyed those numbers and asked if he had slept with Lauren. Kamal said yes; he and his ex were living apart. Egyptian law considered the relationship finished. Virginia law did not consider it finished. Technically, he had committed adultery. Perhaps this is why the judge based Kamal's payments on an inflated figure and ordered life alimony.

"I had one male and one female attorney," Kamal said. "Both were floored . . . They said that in thirty years of practice they had never seen a judge come down on anyone like this."

The court ordered Kamal to pay $9,000 per month in permanent alimony and $2,308 per month in child support. He also had to cover his ex-wife's legal fees, which came to $1,200 a month in temporary payments. Excluding that amount, the combined alimony and child support equal what he earns at work. With his salary reduced to its usual level, Kamal writes monthly checks for his entire income.

I asked him to speculate about the judge's motives. "I was told he is full of himself—thinks of his courtroom as some temple where justice is parceled out," Kamal replied. "So maybe the fact that I first divorced in Egypt pissed him off. Sleeping with Lauren before the American divorce was final, before he gave me permission—that might have seemed like an insult. Whatever the case, I'm in bondage because of this man."

Kamal's lawyers want to wait until this judge retires before filing an appeal. Hopefully, the next one will be less vindictive. There is no way to know. While states are empowered to police families, Americans remain at the mercy of judges' predilections.

Since the children are small, it should be a while before child support ends and Kamal's payments come down. He now takes extra hospital shifts to survive. This means working from 6:00 a.m. to midnight. During one shift he collapsed in pain from what turned out to be a kidney stone. On other occasions his fingers have become numb. This could signal anxiety or the onset of something serious. When Kamal has symptoms, he can't complete his night shift. When he can't complete his night shift, he doesn't get paid.

Kamal's ex has moved back to Dayton. The drive from Herndon, Virginia, is seven hours. He makes it every month to see the children. I asked what might have motivated this move. "It wasn't a job," he said. "She's perpetually 'looking for work.' That's her line . . . I think . . . it's hard to say this, because I'm a good dad. But I think in her mind I became a negative influence on the kids. She wanted to put distance between us. This is bullshit. But I think it's bullshit she believes."

"I'm starting to separate postmarital extorters into two categories," I replied.

"You mean alimony recipients?"

"I use another term. I think there are money junkies and destroyers. The first are motivated by greed. With the second it's more complex. They weaponize alimony and use it to destroy an ex. Which kind is your ex-wife?"

"The first," he responded unhesitatingly. "I believe she set out to marry a doctor. Maybe her animosity toward my relatives came from seeing them as a monetary threat. If I helped my brother, I might eventually help my parents. That would take from her pot."

I asked if Kamal had advice to share. He said, "Don't get married."

Handcuffed and Ankle-Shackled After Maxing Out Her Credit Cards

In 2009, ABC News profiled Holly Chiancola, a fifty-two-year-old real estate agent whose income plummeted when the housing bubble burst. Under regular circumstances she could have managed. But she was divorcing her husband of nineteen years. He sued for alimony; a Massachusetts court ordered Chiancola to pay him $96,000 per year. It also awarded him sole possession of a property in Costa Rica that she had purchased. Speaking with reporters, Chiancola characterized her predicament as "obscene."[10]

When I talked with her, many years had passed. I called on a Sunday afternoon in the spring of 2019: "Ms. Chiancola, it's Jaclyn Geller."

"Call me Holly," she said warmly.

Over the next hour she shared a story whose basics I understood from news reports. In the 1980s, Holly was a bartender in Gloucestor, Massachusetts. A man came in whom she described as "charming;" he worked for a company that sold luxury boats. They hit it off and dated for almost a year. During this time he characterized himself as someone on a spiritual journey that involved healthy living.

When she found herself pregnant, they married and moved to another seaside Massachusetts town. It was 1985. She gave birth to a boy with cerebral palsy who now lives and works independently. One year later, she gave birth to a girl.

According to Holly, approximately two years after their wedding, her husband began drinking. He had trouble holding a job, and Holly found herself supporting the household. She would be punished for her resourcefulness; family courts routinely treat competence as a crime.

Holly began studying to earn her realtor's license: "At this point, my ex was looking for work: pulling himself together long enough to meet someone and convince them he was, let's say, a kitchen designer. He's so gorgeous and winning . . . people wanted to believe him. He'd say, 'I can transform your kitchen.' Then it would fall apart. He wasn't qualified."

"How did you manage the logistics of working, studying, and . . ."

"Having a special needs kid? You can say it. I have a daughter from a previous relationship. She was thirteen. She babysat, did laundry, heated dinners—while her friends were at parties. When I divorced, I said, 'If I have to pay someone ninety-six grand a year, let it be Sara!'"

Holly got her license and discovered that she loved showing homes. Between 2000 and 2006 her career took off. At this point the spouse was trying his luck as a model. "He's remarkably photogenic," Holly explained. "He'd book gigs. But sometimes he wouldn't show up when photographers were waiting. By this point, I was considering divorce. He didn't take it seriously. But I went to counseling and realized it was my only option. In 2004, I really decided, and I made sure he knew I meant it."

Proceedings began; they spent four routine days in court. A legal divorce was pronounced. Holly took a short vacation to Italy, came home, and returned to work. One month later, a call came from her attorney with news that he was requesting alimony in the amount of $96,000 a year. He accused Holly of misrepresenting her income during the divorce, and the presiding judge concurred. Holly fought back, but the result was a judgment in her ex's favor.

"It was like living in a nightmare," she recalled. "Aside from alimony I had to pay his lawyer's fees, which came to 25,000 bucks. We were ordered to split our assets. And I had to make these crushing monthly payments. I accumulated $75,000 of credit card debt paying alimony. I refinanced my home to keep sending checks."

When Holly fell behind he took her to court in Salem, where he was living. She learned that there was no legal defense for missing payments. Their judge noted the arrearages and sentenced her to thirty days in prison.

She recounted certain details: how time seemed to slow down, how the judge said, "Handcuff and ankle-shackle her," and the bailiff replied, "Judge, do I have to?" A few lawyers emerged from the back rows, offering free representation. Dazed, Holly was led out of court and transported to the local jail, where she remained for a few hours.

"Why didn't you do the thirty days?"

"A wonderful man I was dating came over and wrote a check for thirty thousand dollars to my ex. That got me out. But this shows something; alimony does not just affect the payer; it affects *everyone* in that person's circle."

Holly is not one to flounder. "I wasn't going to take this," she exclaimed. "Ninety-six thousand a year, for life? No. I kept fighting. I kept going back to court. In the end I had no money left for lawyers. For four years I represented myself. And I began getting reductions. The first one was thirty thousand a year. That made a real difference.

"I came before a lot of judges. One stands out. He said, 'If you can't meet your obligations to your ex-spouse, sell your house.' I almost shouted, 'I have a handicapped son. He needs a place to live. I cannot sell my house!'"

Ultimately, Holly made a cash offer, which her ex accepted. She liquidated her retirement fund and gave him approximately $60,000. It was 2015; she had paid alimony for ten years.

Holly is now back in Gloucester. She and her ex do not speak. "The market is alive again," she said. "I'm moving properties. Not the level of home I used to sell. But I'm not complaining. I'm grateful to be getting back on my feet."

When I asked how she survived, Holly said, "I had anxiety attacks the whole time. They talk about PTSD I think I had DTSD—During Traumatic Stress Disorder. Now I feel basically okay. What got me through? Two things: yoga and incredible friends."

I understood on both counts. When I asked if she had advice

to share, Holly paused, as if taking a deep yogic breath. Weighing her words, she replied, "I stayed ten years too long. We separated from 1991 to 1993. By then I knew he was not some spiritual giant. But I returned, with a deluded hope that it would work out. My advice to married people in this situation: You know, deep down, if it's unsalvageable. Don't bother with couples therapy. Don't kid yourself. Get out: the sooner the better."

Temporarily Married, Permanently Entitled

With gay men and lesbians filing papers and more straight men suing for alimony than ever before, the American divorce attorney's client base is expanding. In 2009 the United States Census Bureau reported that the number of men receiving alimony had risen from 7,000 in 1998 to 13,000 in 2008. It continues to climb. Nashville-based attorney Marlene Moses considers this a wondrous men's-rights revolution.[11] Male alimony receivers are less rapturous and more doctrinaire. California-based actor John Costellanos, who divorced television producer Rhonda Friedman in 2005, defends his $9,000 per month award as the right of a lower-earning spouse who was married for nine years. Friedman, who says she feels "financially raped," spits into the envelope she sends Costellanos each month. As bitter as these payments are, the fact of covering his legal fees is perhaps more wrenching.[12]

I prepared for this chapter by spreading the word about looking for alimony payers to interview. Three times out of four, I got the same response: "I know someone paying child support." My interlocutor would mentally translate the question into a more palatable one. Usually I had to reiterate, emphasizing the word, "alimony." Usually I heard, "That still exists?" An editor colleague queried,

"If access to a spouse's body entitles that person to maintenance upon divorce, doesn't that make every lower-earning spouse a whore?"

It's easy to believe that this practice is sputtering toward its final end. Yet, when I recently applied for a VISA card, the representative asked for my total annual household income, "including alimony paid." Clearly, she asks this of all applicants during a daily interview process. Alimony is alive.

Documentarian Joseph Storge believes this is because so many professionals benefit from divorce litigation: fifty billion dollars per year go from private households to those who superintend divorce.[13] These include judges, attorneys, mediators, custodial evaluators, divorce consultants, and psychologists serving as expert witnesses. Alimony has become an industry.

Materialist explanations don't sit entirely well with me. I think alimony's acceptance flows from interlockings beliefs: government has a major role in citizens' sex lives, spouses deserve special treatment, and law should discourage conjugal dissolution. I fear that until these ideas are extirpated, family court's reward-and-punishment modus operandi will continue. The practice will end only if matrimonial privilege goes first. This is not the position of alimony-reform groups. They seek modifications: limiting payment schedules, tweaking local laws. Such half measures will not fix a system that punishes those who choose nonmarriage.

Historically, alimony is rooted in coverture. Codified in eighteenth-century Britain and practiced in North America, this term meant that a married couple was one person: the husband. Upon marrying, females eschewed autonomy along with their names. They could not independently draft legal documents, sign contracts, or own property. A married woman's estate—even land inherited—belonged to her husband. If she worked, her earnings were his. Criminal proceedings did not treat wives as independent agents. Unless the charge was murder or treason, wives were presumed to be acting under a husband's "cover."[14] The word for absorption into a spouse's identity, taken from French, is *feme covert*. The legal term for this overall arrangement is *respondeat superior*: Latin for "let the master reply." It means that guardians are accountable for their charges' actions.[15]

Supporting his wife was a husband's legal duty. Seventeenth-century Suffolk County, Massachusetts court transcripts record instances of husbands mandated to provide "Suiteable meate drinke and apparrell" for their wives or give weekly allowances.[16] Southern courts awarded alimony to ex-wives found guilty of desertion, since they had relinquished their assets. Nancy Cott observes, "These grants kept in place the assumption that wives were dependents . . . husbands their supporters."[17]

Throughout the mid-nineteenth century, America's legislature expanded justifications for divorce to include excessive cruelty, invalid marriage contracts, neglect of matrimonial duties, and chronic inebriation. The requisite period of abandonment was reduced from five years to a year or two. Jeremiads appeared in newspapers. Self-appointed custodians of sexual morality generally sound the same; antebellum editorialists augur Marriage Movement didacts: society was becoming lax, rising divorce rates signaled moral decline, apocalypse lurked around the corner. In February 1854, a journalist writing for the *San Francisco Chronicle* objected that "marriage among us seems to be regarded as a pleasant farce."[18]

Actually, in spelling out the terms of marriage contracts and stipulating when they could be broken, government was moving deeper into Americans' private lives—laying more explicit groundrules for sexual behavior. Rather than tarnishing an ideal, "the states in allowing divorce were perfecting the script for marriage, instructing spouses to enact that script more exactly."[19] Wives' dependence on husbands was essential to this drama.

Twelve percent of married women were part of America's labor force in 1930. Matrimony was presumed to be a fulltime job. It was a full-time job in a world without clothes dryers, dry cleaners, self-cleaning ovens, self-defrosting refrigerators, and markets that sell prepared food. Ninety percent of house-wives living in cities devoted roughly thirty-five hours per week to domestic chores; in rural settings the number was higher. A sole (usually male) worker often supported one household. Upon marrying, a man assumed an obligation to maintain his wife, because she often lost or relinquished the ability to support herself. She mortgaged her future on one relationship—a deci-sion that probably felt less hazardous than it was, since the choice signaled normality. If a union ended, only the wife's death or remarriage to another man (similarly obliged) dissolved her erstwhile husband's obligation.

This system's flaws are retrospectively obvious; it presumed the health, luck, and competence of each man, the domesticity of each woman, and a universal desire to marry. But while the practice rested on terrible assumptions, at one time, systemati-cally granting divorced women support seemed logical.

By the mid-1930s coverture was eroding. States were imple-menting laws allowing wives to own property independently, inherit estates, initiate lawsuits, draft legal agreements, sign contracts, and compose wills. Functioning as businesspeople became an option for married women.[20] Still, postwar America's mental health advisors encouraged the male-breadwinner ethic by claiming that any man who avoided it was puerile. If providing for one's marriage-based family gave a man maturity, accepting his support gave a woman liberty. The postwar idea of female emancipation did not target education, career, or contraceptive access but homemaking aided by a battery of time-saving appliances and gizmos.

In 1969 California became the first state to make no-fault divorce available. Others followed suit throughout the 1970s. By 1985 all states had a version of this option. The party petitioning for divorce no longer had to show that a spouse had slept with someone else, left the marital abode, or otherwise deviated from governmentally framed norms. Now couples could split on the basis of "irretrievable breakdown." This change responded to a suggestion by the American Bar Association.[21]

States began granting settlements to divorced men. In 1977 a wealthy Floridian named Margaret Pfohl was enjoined to pay her spouse, Roger, $30,000 followed by $5,000 per month in alimony for eighteen months. After two years of marriage, Margaret had begun pressuring Roger to leave his job as a toy salesman. He capitulated. After nine years of what Jane Austen would call "conjugal felicity," Margaret ejected him from their home. Several lawsuits ended with *Pfhol v. Pfhol*, where an appellate court ruled that since Margaret had pressed him to abandon his career, Roger deserved compensation.[22]

In 1979 alimony became gender-neutral with a Supreme Court ruling that recurred to the Fourteenth Amendment's equal protection clause.[23] This decision fueled culture wars. Throughout the 1970s, lawyer Phyllis Schlafly (1924–2016) had campaigned against the Equal Rights Amendment. Her 1974 essay, "How ERA Will Hurt Divorced Women," posits that the amendment would imperil alimony paid by ex-husbands to ex-wives.[24]

While Schlafly effectively blocked the ERA, another attorney was straddling gender issues. As a Rutgers Law School professor from 1963 to 1972, Ruth Bader Ginsberg had campaigned for equal pay among male and female faculty. She left teaching to head the American Civil Liberties Union Women's Rights Project.

Her work led to cases like *Califano v. Goldfarb* (1977), where the Supreme Court ordered amended Social Security, so widowers could access survivors' benefits without proving financial dependence on their late wives. The Court accepted Bader Ginsburg's argument that Social Security denied female wage earners equal protection by impeding the ability to offer their husbands financial support.[25]

Bader Ginsburg never questioned the government's right to monitor sexual relationships or challenged the belief that one spouse should maintain the other. Taking America's overriding bias toward marriage into account, one sees that Schlafly and Bader Ginsburg occupied much common ground. Both envisioned married households as the basic modules of society. Neither acknowledged alternative social configurations. Schlafly and Bader Ginsburg each accepted connubiality; they just endorsed different versions of it.

New laws recognized women's increased acceptance in higher education and the workplace. But wedlock remained a *ménage à trois* between husband, wife, and state. A judge had to divide property and determine conditions of economic support before any divorce could be finalized. Too often the reactionary premises built into such laws go unnoticed. If wedlock is, as Focus on the Family claims, "the basic building block of human civilization," a man threatens civilization when he chooses divorce. If two people merge when they take vows, as Marriage Movement publicity insists, the woman who initiates separation leaves behind a fragmentary half self. She merits retribution. But if the amorous bond is one of many personal alliances, its truncation should be accessible and penalty free.

Penalizing Education, Punishing Work, Encouraging Unemployment

Like matrimony, divorce has a boilerplate narrative and frequently repeated pieties. It is often described as "traumatic" or "shattering." This histrionic language is misleading. Any household is only as loving, stable, and sane as the people in it. Shared experience over time can be wonderful or terrible, depending on who is involved. Some relationships are worth preserving; others are not. When they treat divorce as a social crisis, matrimaniacs fail to differentiate between form and function.

No one knows this better than Lynn Sebold, who grew up in Berkeley Heights, a New Jersey suburb. "We were middle class," she told me when we spoke on the phone in March 2019. "Dad was a stockbroker; mom was a part-time secretary. We were 'church every Sunday' people, and my four siblings and I attended a wonderful Catholic high school."

Lynn majored in business at Pennsylvania State University, planning to work in advertising. She found the starting salaries disappointing and accepted a field marketing assistant position at Eastman Chemical Products. She then tripled her salary by moving into sales. "My twenties were a blast," she recalled. "I shared an apartment in Jersey City with a girlfriend. We had parties and potluck dinners and trekked into the city every day for work."

Eventually Lynn began renting alone in the quieter town of Chatham. Through her landlady she met a contractor eleven years her senior who ran a wallpaper and painting business. They dated for six months before getting engaged.

"At some level I knew it was a mistake," Lynn admitted. "I couldn't pinpoint the problem. John was Catholic, handsome. He supervised his own crew and made good money . . . I confessed my vague doubts to a friend. She said, 'Cancel!' I said, 'I can't. I bought the dress.' Ridiculous, right?"

"Don't beat yourself up. I can't tell you how many times I've heard this."

After the wedding Lynn and John purchased a 130-year-old farmhouse in the town of Basking Ridge. A brook ran through the backyard. John landscaped the grounds, planting colorful flowers. The setting seemed perfect for children: "I got pregnant quickly both times. I thought this house was ideal for kids. I'd had an idyllic childhood. I wanted to duplicate it for my girls. My parents were nearby, and I wanted them involved."

Hardware sales became Lynn's professional niche; she succeeded at a number of companies. Except for two maternity leaves and three months of job hunting, there has never been a period since college that she did not work full-time. When the girls were small, she packed their lunches, got them to daycare, and drove to the office.

At IBM her strong sales record earned an award: a trip to Hawaii for two. When she told John he replied, "I'm not sitting on a plane for thirteen hours."

"That was typical," she explained. "Within a year of the wedding he became nasty and after that really nasty." His cruelty targeted Lynn's appearance. She discovered that John had a morbid obsession with body size. He began to tell her, regularly, that she was too large. "He'd say, 'you're fat.' I'd say, 'I'm pregnant!' After each pregnancy, he harangued me. He'd say, 'My customers have babies and get right back into shape.' Sure! He had a high-end clientele! Those women had full-time nannies and trainers. I was working, chauffeuring the kids. I had maybe fifteen extra pounds on me. He treated this as a crisis."

One year, Lynn's birthday fell on New Year's Eve. John offered to build a fire and cook dinner. When Lynn got home there was no fire and no set table. John asked when dinner would be ready. She expressed surprise, and he replied, "I'm not making dinner. Do you understand? Or do I have to kick it up your fucking ass? Bend over, so I can kick it up your ass."

"My oldest was in the room," Lynn recalled. "That was it. The relationship was over. We'd been married for eleven years. I saw no point wasting another eleven."

She instituted new sleeping arrangements: "The girls and I took the main bedroom. He took one of their rooms. I told him I wanted a divorce. He said, 'If you don't ask for child support, I won't ask for alimony.' I thought, 'He'd be embarrassed to ask for alimony,' and he was. He ended up getting it, but he would tell people, 'I don't want alimony, but I have to take it. It's the law.'"

In March Lynn had an attorney prepare the papers. She claimed that immediately after divorce proceedings commenced, John stopped working: "He was his own boss, so he could do this."

"How did he pass his days?"

"Sitting at home in his underpants. I was working partly out of my home office. When I passed by, he would say, 'Watch your back; I've got big guns that will take you out.'"

"Did he mean firearms?"

"I think he meant hotshot attorneys."

"What did he want?"

"In retrospect, I think he stopped working to get alimony and stayed because he wanted the house. He thought if I left the premises, he would get it de facto."

Lynn said that one night, John kicked her and immediately disappeared. He came back thirty minutes later, with "fake scratches" on his face and called the police, claiming she had attacked him: "They came, arrested me, took me to the county jail, fingerprinted me. I sat there for four hours. Then they let me go."

"Is this on your record when you apply for jobs?"

"I don't even know. I haven't had any problems."

"Do you think he was following a lawyer's advice?"

"Absolutely. It seemed staged. At that point I sent the girls to live with my parents, but I stayed. I wasn't going to get pushed out of that house. From the beginning we'd split every mortgage payment."

The divorce took two years and cost $80,000. The presiding judge ordered a forensic accountant to review both their financial profiles; this cost $60,000, which they split. John didn't agree with the findings and hired an accountant to rebut them. His rebuttal was used in court.

Lynn realized that this process could bankrupt her: "I finally moved in with my parents. I couldn't afford lawyers' fees plus a mortgage. He'd stopped paying the house bills when our divorce proceedings began, so I was covering gas, electric . . . We went to a mediator, which cost me $600. The 'mediation' centered around him wanting the engagement ring back. It was ludicrous.

"This was 2008; the housing market was starting to go bad. Our place was almost foreclosed on. We accepted a lowball offer and split the proceeds. But John had become quite weird. He insisted on staying there, even though the buyer was ready to paint and move in. I got a court order of eviction—another expense."

In a San Francisco airport Lynn got the call with his final offer. Ironically, she was en route to Hawaii, taking the trip she had postponed. "His attorney said, 'We'll settle if you agree to pay alimony: $60,000 a year.'

"I was actually prepared for a curveball. But John's brother and I were very close. I thought he would talk him out of whatever idea popped up. I immediately called his brother about the alimony. He was dead set against it and agreed to intervene. To this day, I believe he tried.

"Finally, we went to court. They requested life alimony. My lawyer told me I might as well take it because if my circumstances changed, I could apply for reductions. Not great advice. The judge said, 'He's a high school dropout with no income. You have a college degree and a corporate career. You're the payer.' So this woman is punishing me for finishing school and working hard!

"His side agreed to take his child support out of the alimony. So I was paying five hundred bucks a month for a while. But now, with the kids emancipated, it comes to $1,250 a month."

Lynn got an education and became financially independent. With a wonderful childhood behind her, a university degree, and a terrific personality for sales, she anticipated an excellent life. She made one mistake. I think she would say that was marrying the wrong person. Hearing her story, most people, including myself, would agree. But I would argue that something larger precipitated her decision; accepting marriage as part of the excellent life package. This is an easy error for anyone living in a marriage-centric society to make. I think it's especially common among people who grow up in households run by couples for whom the formula seems to have worked.

She was married for thirteen years. By 2009, when her divorce was finalized, she had paid legal fees, accountants' bills, mediators' charges, house costs, and moving expenses. Her bank account had dipped to four thousand dollars. Like Louis, Kamal, and Holly, she had discovered malevolence embedded in our legal system, which often targets those who think they can end marriages.

Lynn and her ex agreed on joint child custody: the girls would live with her. He would take them to dinner every Wednesday and have them at his home every other weekend. "He never did it," she told me. "Not the dinners, not the weekends."

I asked what the worst part has been. Lynn said that her sense of trust has been shattered: "I think back to that optimistic kid who hit the city after college. She's gone. I'm wary. I can't help thinking that everyone's out to screw me."

Still, Lynn hasn't stopped fighting: "I went to court last year to challenge the alimony. I heard the same old thing: 'You're educated, he's not. You have earning capacity.' I paid legal fees. But at least I was awarded $2,000 for my older daughter's community college tuition."

These days Lynn rents a townhouse in Pottersville, New Jersey. At Canon she has a good job. I observed that the alimony must make it tempting to do sloppy work. "It does," she replied. "But if I do sloppy work, I could lose my job. It's no-win."

After taxes and alimony are deducted from her paychecks, she has $3,300 per month to live on, which makes paying a $2,000 dollar rent hard. She recently took in a male tenant to help with expenses. To Lynn's knowledge her ex, who still lives in New Jersey, has not dated anyone since their relationship ended. With alimony recipients there's no way to tell. I believe that those who have romances often keep them quiet, afraid that any hint of imminent remarriage will threaten their income stream.

"I've had moments of desperation," Lynn admitted. "Suicide would end the payments."

"No. We end the payments by changing the laws."

I asked her for advice to people contemplating betrothal. She spoke carefully: "If you're going to marry, make sure you *really* study your state's marriage laws. At first what you learn will sound unreal. It's real. Remember, fifty percent of married Americans divorce. One day, their stories could be your story."

Supporting a Debtor for Life

Evan Lewis—E. to his friends—exudes warmth when he opens the door to his Stamford, Connecticut home. He sports a worsted-wool navy jacket paired with a pale grey shirt. Tall and broad-shouldered, Evan is in his early sixties. With silver-grey hair cropped close to the scalp and a warm smile, he looks like an older, heavier set version of the actor Taye Diggs.

Evan grew up in Clinton Hill, Brooklyn, before coffee bars and bistros filled that neighborhood. He lived in the projects, close to downtown Brooklyn, where the family courts remain.

"It was my mom, my sister, and me," he says, as we settle into a leather sofa. The floor is covered with shiny black tile; an oversized vase filled with white roses sits on the glass coffee table next to two goblets of sparkling water left by Evan's wife and my friend Denise, a corporate trainer. "My mom worked in a factory during the week and cleaned people's houses on the weekends," Evan explained. "My sister and I went to Brooklyn public schools. We took the subway. We were latchkey kids, but we didn't know it. We had our homework and our shows.

"Now, my mother was quite a woman. She was ambitious for me. She signed me up for singing lessons: jazz, opera. I worked hard and became this little singer. I ended up doing it professionally through my teens."

"Did you like it?"

"Well enough. I sang at Lincoln Center. I got into the High School of Performing Arts as a voice major. Performing Arts had good and great singers. I was good. I would always be good: never more. Many middle-of-the-road singers don't mind this. They keep going for sheer love of it. I guess I didn't have that. So I left after two years and finished at a mostly Jewish high school, Erasmus. Then Mom started pressuring me to do something. I don't know how she came up with data management, but that was her next idea. So I went into that. I worked at a hospital in Queens for a while before moving to Connecticut. I came up to New Haven and started working. I worked for the state for fifteen years."

"What does this involve?"

"All kinds of things, and it's changed radically. Every medical visit, test, and procedure has a paper trail. Doctors' offices used to overflow with boxes of records. Hospitals too. At one point it was a matter of transporting these records to warehouses and sending them out when requests came in. Now everything is digitalized. Practices and hospitals use electronic health records. Test results are burned onto CDs. People like me are responsible for digitalizing doctor's notes, patient contracts, and tests . . . keeping it all organized.

"At a certain point, I decided to go out on my own. I was in my thirties—very nervous. To leave the state was a big move. I was making $85,000 a year, which was something back then.

"My Ukrainian friend Phil was more financially established. We agreed to go into business together. We worked out of his house in Darien. There were a couple of other firms that did what we did. But they paid employees when they got paid. We decided to structure things differently; we'd give our employees a regular salary. They'd be independent contractors. But they'd get paid every two weeks.

"So, people wanted to work for us. Meantime, I went out among physicians, drumming up business. We got more clients, so we hired more staff. I guess we did a decent job. Now we have twenty specialists working for us. They have to keep their computer certifications up, and we do too. Anyway, my mom died in 2004. She got to see us succeed."

"Going back to Clinton Hill . . . "

"The old neighborhood. One thing I should mention: we were Baptists. Not growing up, but when we got into our teens, Mom thought it would be good for us to have something faith-based. Really, I think she wanted to keep us out of trouble.

"I met Rose, my first wife, at a Baptist convention in Manhattan.

She was sixteen. I was eighteen. She lived in the Bronx. I liked her. She was very pretty, and she was smart.

"When I moved, I was twenty-one. By then we were dating. I went back to the city every weekend. I did that for three years. Then we got married and had apartments in Norwalk. Eventually we bought a house there. She worked for an optometrist as an office manager. Then she decided to have a baby and stopped working."

"Taking care of a baby is work."

"No, she decided to have a baby. She didn't have one. She didn't get pregnant for ten years and didn't work all that time. By then I was making good money. In the eleventh year there was still no baby, and we decided to adopt. We adopted our daughter, Amber. Then we went to Puerto Rico, and when we got home, Rose was pregnant. She told me, but I didn't believe it until she started showing. That was Evan Jr.

"Rose never missed working. Her hobby was taking aerobics classes. When Phil and I started, money didn't come immediately. It was four years before we started turning a real profit. I asked her to get a job and help out. She refused. By then I had learned that her whole family is like this. They're simply not driven to be more than they are. If someone will shoulder the burden, that's fine with them.

"Once she interviewed with a startup pediatrician's office. Two practitioners. She has good skills, and they hired her. She quit after one day. She said the bathroom was nasty."

"Were you resentful?"

"It sounds that way now, but no. I was reasonably content. It doesn't take a lot to make me happy. But it turned out that Rose needed a lot; she wanted to go on lavish vacations. After I started doing well, we went to Thailand, then France. We flew first class. She was living the life.

"Then came the first big fight. One winter we went down to Naples, Florida. On the coast I saw a nice piece of property and said I would buy it and build a house one day. She was like, 'You can't.' She wouldn't even get out of the car. I bought it anyway. A year later I bought more land there. She was antagonistic. We argued about that land nonstop, but it wasn't the real issue. There was underlying stuff . . . that she wouldn't work, that she spent money like crazy when I started earning.

"By then I *was* unhappy, and I'd go out alone. Women can sense frustration. Other women would give me understanding I wasn't getting at home. I started seeing someone, and she got pregnant. That's Shirley, my youngest.

"What was Rose like with the kids?"

"Affectionate, but they came second. She came first. She had the ability to spend money when she felt like it and do whatever she wanted. That was her thing.

"I moved out, somewhere around 1996. I continued to support the household. My plan was to get back with Rose. She and I talked most days. We were raising the children Baptist. Our church frowns on divorce and urges separated couples to reconcile.

"I thought we agreed, but one day a subpoena arrived. I was confused. We had dinner every week. Suddenly, I was hiring a lawyer, and she already had one.

"So the case started: two years of going back and forth to court. A lot of money and time. I settled, eventually. I shouldn't have, but I got sick of the whole thing. Family court makes you feel dirty. Anyway, I learned that with any marriage twenty-five years or longer in Connecticut, the earner pays life alimony."

"Was your lawyer effective?"

"Probably at one time. I didn't know at the time, but he was having health problems—serious ones. Overall, he didn't do a great job. The first thing they wanted was 75,000 bucks before I walked out of the courtroom, so she would sign off on the business, plus $10,000 every year for five years to buy her out of the business. He didn't fight this."

"Had she contributed to the business?"

"No. Phil's girlfriend contributed. She did secretarial work before we could afford office staff. Rose gave no time, no money. Yet by law half of everything I had was hers. This didn't include alimony and child support.

"She got the house, which had $20,000 left on the mortgage. Her lawyer told her to pay it off. Instead she kept refinancing it, and then there was nothing left to refinance. She lost it. The settlement gave her one of the Florida properties—worth $250,000. She sold it. Where did that money go? She's a debtor. The business payments are over, and with the kids grown, child support is over. So I'm paying $3,000 a month in alimony for what? She's travelled and bought designer clothes. Now she's in a one-bedroom apartment by the airport. It's like I've been throwing cash down a black hole."

"Does she work?"

"She pretends to. Her card says she's a personal shopper. I don't recommend her. Look, Jackie, she grew up in the South Bronx. In the Brooklyn projects we did better. Basically, we were okay. Maybe she's always felt deprived. I don't know. But I keep paying . . ."

"Do you two talk?"

"Not much. I did talk to a lawyer recently. He said to fight the life alimony *I* would need a negative change in financial circumstances."

"So, you're rewarded if you do less well?"

"Basically. The Connecticut guideline is the payer's situation. The recipient's track record isn't scrutinized. And Rose used to go around bragging that she'd never remarry because if she did, she'd lose her alimony.

"We were married twenty-five years, including the separation. If I had left earlier, I wouldn't have gotten life. But after the divorce I said to myself, 'I'm not going to let someone like her pull me down.' You can't let people crush you because they have the upper hand. My cousin said, 'Think about Job. At the end he got twice as much back as he lost.' If Job can do it, I can. I've been with Denise for fifteen years. We met on an elevator of all places. She's an amazing woman."

"I know it. Hey, E., you must have faced racism at some point. Was that worse than family court?"

"Growing up I never got beat up or stopped by the cops. Then I came up here and worked in an all white world. Only three black folks employed in the first building back then. But I felt acceptance."

"I'm not talking about people burning crosses on your lawn. Subtler stuff?"

"Sorry to disappoint you, kid, but no. I'll tell you one thing, though. Whatever your color, sex, religion, when you walk into family court, if you're successful, and you've been married long enough, you're in trouble."

"That leads to my final question. What advice would you give people based on your experience?"

"Life is too short to be bitter. Originally I was. The alimony floored me. Six months after the divorce I was struggling to make payments. I had coffee with someone and was a real asshole. I picked a fight, and she hadn't done anything. That night I said to myself, 'I don't like who I'm becoming.' I stayed away from dating until I got my head straight. That's something I would suggest. Also, if you're paying alimony, keep fighting. Don't lose hope. I did not get a fair shake in court. Still, today I have a great life."

* * *

The accounts presented here are too brief to encompass relationships in their full complexity. These interviewees struck me as credible. (Those who did not were excluded.) During our conversations I listened carefully as each speaker attempted to remain objective and accurate. Still, only one side was presented, and details surely fell out. Every narrative is selective; personal stories may be the most partial accounts of all.

Gap ridden as they may be, these interviews are anchored in fact. They show postmarital extortion's devastating effects. How the interviewees annoyed their spouses doesn't really matter. In light of such horrendous outcomes, I don't need to know who left the toilet seat up or misplaced car keys. No one in any romantic relationship is blame free. I assume that these people made mistakes they did not share with me.

It is not my place to readjudicate separations. Rather, I hope to show what part divorce plays in the marriage system. It seems to have a major role. In family court there is a "he said, she said" (now "he said, he said" and "she said, she said") drama where one person's story contradicts the other's, and truth becomes elusive. With minimal documentation, family court judges must assign events meaning. Religious, atheist, or agnostic; Republican or Democrat, such judges tend to be friends of marriage. Most privilege monogamy. These magistrates can dole out punishments based on interpretations of state law. The process is capricious; much of a divorcing person's fate depends on what state they married in or which judge decides the case. Here I found overt abuses: disallowances for changing circumstances, unforgiving formulae based on past salaries, and punitive administration of the law based on narrow-minded bias.

Louis, whose life is a struggle to survive, does not qualify as the Social Security beneficiary of a women he lived with for twenty-three years. Kamal, whose life is a struggle to survive, rubbed a judge the wrong way. Holly wanted to repay the adolescent who ran her household during hard times; she couldn't because they weren't married. Friends sustained her through a horrendous ordeal, providing emotional support and money. If she had to, she could not claim testimonial privileges with them. Lynn has situational depression. Evan is a self-made man—a maverick—who embodies the American dream. His reward is writing checks to someone whose financial track record will not come under judicial scrutiny.

While these stories don't hit big news circuits, alimony has received random criticism. Boston-based attorney Wendy Murphy worries that it encourages victims of domestic violence to stay married with hopes of receiving larger awards.[26] Journalist Elizabeth Benedict argues that permanent alimony fuels feelings of entitlement with "a presumption that the person who receives the alimony never has any obligation to take care of him or herself—even if they are educated and have a work history."[27] Pharmaceutical manager Linda Zampino observes that spousal support seems designed for abuse: "Women and men play the system," she asserts. Zampino was married for nineteen years to a mechanic who stopped working after losing his job. When they divorced, her success earned penalties: $120,000 in legal expenses, a life-insurance policy in her ex's name, and $36,000 a year in durational alimony. Zampino, who refinanced her Sparta, New Jersey home to make payments, declares, "He took everything the state would give him, and they were very generous with MY HARD-EARNED MONEY."[28]

No wedding officiant will mention the truth nested in such stories: marriage is a poor organizing principle for any society. The cleric or judge uniting individuals in wedlock proclaims that couples are fused by (private) love, licensed by a (public) office, and graced with the (mysterious) gift of prophecy. Bride and groom *know* that their feelings for each other will never change, until death parts them. This is companionate matrimony's seductive rhetoric. Marriage propagandists want Americans to believe it and gaze admiringly at diamond rings, lace dresses, and wedding canopies.

I want Americans to scrutinize miscarriages of justice that contemporary marriage engenders. I want them to ask whether politicians should be crafting policy around notions of licit and illicit sex, relationship value, and financial responsibility between lovers. Until more media outlets expose postmarital extortion, nonmarital people must get the word out. Let's do that.

(Endnotes)

1   "Virginia Needs to Reform Alimony Rules," *The Progress Index*, May 5, 2017, http://www.progress-index.com/news/20170505/virginia-needs-to-reform-alimony-rules.

2   Jennifer Ludden, "Alimony Till Death Do Us Part? Nay, Say Some Ex-Spouses," NPR, May 28, 2013, https://www.npr.org/2013/05/28/186784580/alimony-till-death-do-us-part-nay-say-some-ex-spouses.

3   Office of Child Support Enforcement, https://www.acf.hhs.gov/css/resource/processing-garnishment-orders-for-child-support-and-or-alimony.

4   Ibid.

5   Ibid.

6   Gary Fineout, "Amid Emotional Outcry, Governor Rick Scott Vetoes Alimony Bill," *The Washington Times*, April 15, 2016, https://www.washingtontimes.com/news/2016/apr/15/florida-gov-vetoes-alimony.

7   Witte, Jr., *The Sins*, 6.

8   *Here Comes the Bride*, 151–73.

9   Email message to author, November 13, 2017.

10 Alice Gomstyn and the ABC News Business Unit, "Role Reversal: Ex-Wives Angry Over Paying Alimony," ABC News, September 30, 2009, https://abcnews.go.com/Business/role-reversal-wives-angry-paying-alimony.

11 Paul Wallin, "Ex-Wives Angry Over Paying Alimony," Wallin & Klarich Family Law Attorneys, October 28, 2009: https://www.wkfamilylaw.com/ex-wives-angry-over-paying-alimony.

12 Anita Raghaven, "Men Receiving Alimony Want a Little Respect," *Wall Street Journal*, April 1, 2008, https://www.wsj.com/articles.

13 *Divorce Corp.*, (Divorce Films LLC, 2014).

14 These laws were codified in 1765 by the British jurist William Blackstone. See *Blackstone's Commentaries on the Laws of England Book the First: "Chapter the Fifteenth: Of Husband and Wife,"* http://avalon.law.yale.edu/18th_century/blackstone_bk1ch15.asp.

15 Witte, Jr., *The Sins*, 7.

16 Morgan, *The Puritan Family*, 40.

17 *Public Vows*, 49.

18 Quoted in Roger W. Lotchin, *San Francisco, 1846–1856* (New York: Oxford University Press, 1974), 308.

19 Cott, *Public Vows*, 52.

20 Ibid., 168.
21 Alison Lefkowitz, *Strange Bedfellows: Marriage in the Age of Women's Liberation* (Philadelphia: University of Pennsylvania Press, 2018), 23–4.
22 Ibid., 22–3.
23 Ibid., 23.
24 "The Phyllis Schlafly Report" 7, no. 6 (1974): https://www.phyllisschlafly.com/Company_Images/PDF.
25 Lefkowitz, *Strange Bedfellows*, 23–4.
26 Yamiche Alcindor, "Should Alimony Laws be Changed?", *USA Today*, December 16, 2011, https://yamichealcindor.com/2012/01/19/should-alimony-laws-be-changed.
27 Ibid.
28 Ibid. Jeffrey Dobkin, ed., *Shattered Lives: The Personal Horror Stories of Marriage and Divorce* in New Jersey, https://doczz.net/doc/215120/shattered-lives---new-jersey-alimony-reform.

6

The Politics of Postmarital Entitlement

---

*"'Why if I ever did fall off—which there's no chance of—but
if I did—'" Here he pursed his lips and looked so solemn and
so grand that Alice could hardly help laughing. 'If I did fall,' he
went on, 'The king has promised me—ah, you may turn pale if
you like! You didn't think I was going to say that, did you? The
king has promised me—with his very own mouth—to—to—'*

*'To send all his horses and all his men,' Alice interrupted,
rather unwisely."*

—LEWIS CARROLL, *THROUGH THE LOOKING-GLASS,
AND WHAT ALICE FOUND THERE*

In March 2010 a sixty-year-old housewife named Cynthia Shack-elford sued forty-nine-year-old college administrator Anne Lundquist for alienation of affection. Shackelford was married to an attorney who provided legal services to Guilford College in Greensboro, North Carolina, where he met Lundquist. He began seeing her and ended things with his wife, insisting that Lundquist was not the reason. Prolonged unhappiness had provoked three separate forays into couples counseling, to no avail. It was time to separate.

Mrs. Shackelford saw things differently. She portrayed herself as a family-values standard-bearer and Lundquist as a nefarious lady in black. "She set her sights on him," Shackelford snarled. "You don't go after married men and break up families." A North

Carolina judge concurred and ordered Lundquist to pay Mrs. Shackelford nine million dollars. ABC News reported, "The large dollar figures surrounding the Shackelford case are unusual, but the lawsuit itself is not."[1]

An amount few venture capitalists could manage, the figure was so far beyond a college dean's reach that it was almost funny. What had Lundquist done to invite this cannonade? She met another adult and spent time with him. She expressed her feelings for him through physical touching, and vice versa. Their bond motivated him to do what he would have anyway: terminate a pre-existing relationship. Probably it accelerated that process.

For this, the North Carolina judicial system delivered an annihilative penalty. It couldn't wring money from a stone. It could ruin Lundquist's credit rating, prevent her from maintaining bank accounts, and threaten future job prospects. North Carolina's family court could turn a professional into a beggar—payback for Lundquist enjoying a man's company. Allan Shackelford was viewed as someone's asset. Lundquist got retribution for purloining this choice piece of property. The ruling was clearly intended to deter anyone considering intimacy with a married person.

When two people truncating a long-term relationship stand in court, they each present a social mask. Even the most intuitive jurist cannot fully know their backstory. Judges also recur to what Carrie Jenkins calls "the 'justice' argument: the notion that romantic partners are a kind of resource akin to wealth or private property." Jenkins reminds readers that the idea of sexual partners as property stems from ancient laws that controlled female sexuality. She describes these laws as "horrifying."[2] I agree. Historical residue of Bronze Age attitudes remains in American law that treats sexually transgressive women as villains and male marriage renegades as criminals.

In my experience, Americans don't just tut-tut at relationships between married and unmarried people; they condemn the "single" participant. I've found this attitude among people in whom I would least expect it: scholars who study marriage as a social construct and therapists who are supposed to help, not prejudge. Educated adults who consider themselves open-minded still recoil from the idea of wedded people conducting open relationships, often viewing the nonmarital participant as a toxic interloper. Somehow, the married one fell into their snares. The Lundquist outcome shows this view taken to an extreme. Marital supremacism, which has no place in American courtrooms, drives such rulings.

Here I must remind myself that betrothed people, newlyweds, and spouses celebrating silver anniversaries do not consider themselves prideful. They don't see marital supremacism as problematic because wedlock is generally presented as a social adhesive that lets spouses pursue a path of sexual righteousness and mature citizenship. Even today, when dissenting voices are more common, the media generally enshrines wedlock as a sanctuary where mutual fondness blossoms, children thrive, and adults take shelter from professional tensions.

Many truncated unions show how specious these assumptions are. No benign way of life could turn so quickly into blood sport. Marriage provides no haven from animosities. Indeed, it is often dead center in the most heated conflicts. Marriage refugees are commonly shellshocked by a family court system in which no one is what they seem, and rules don't correlate with justice. American taxpayers support this superstructure, which throws people's lives into chaos that can last months or years. Divorcing people mandated to pay long-term settlements often feel misrepresented, misheard, and deprived of agency. The consequences for their loved ones, who often provide financial and emotional sustenance, are overlooked. As long as the marriage system remains in place, this mode of ending relationships will stay entrenched.

A Divorced Man Learns that He's More Dangerous Than a Terrorist

Those who watched journalist Lisa Ling's November 2018 "This is Life" broadcast know of Carlos Rivera, a Long Island-based pediatrician who has generated media buzz over the last few years. Dr. Rivera was ordered to pay his ex-wife $160,000 per year when they divorced. Because he could not produce this sum (which combined life alimony and child support), Dr. Rivera was found to be in contempt of court in May 2013. He served six months in a medium-maximum security prison in Suffolk County.[3]

Dr. Rivera's case shows how events can snowball for those who end marriages. While incarcerated, he could not practice medicine. This left him unable to pay his malpractice insurance. Missed payments sent the premiums sky high. By the time he was released, they had more than tripled. To pay them required working overtime, which he wanted to do. But he learned that an ex-convict pediatrician does not present the most appealing profile. While some patients remained loyal, many went elsewhere.

With his practice tanking, Dr. Rivera again faced imprisonment for failing to pay his ex-wife, a credentialed special education teacher. She began openly dating a former police officer. They did not marry, and prima facie, one can guess why. New York law enabled the former Mrs. Rivera to extract large portions of another adult's income and use that money as she saw fit.

"I speak about this because I'm not the only person," Dr. Rivera told interviewer Gary Jacobs in July 2016. "I went from not wanting to talk because it's so humiliating, to . . . the truth is, people need to see what happens in the system."[4] Two years later, Ling interviewed Dr. Rivera, who had filed for bankruptcy and was living on $100 per month. "I'm currently at $680,000 in arrears, at nine percent interest," he told Ling. "I will never be able to get out of this hole."[5]

I spoke with Dr. Rivera by telephone on a Thursday afternoon in the spring of 2021. From television and YouTube interviews, a Change.org petition, a GoFundMe page, and numerous rallies on his behalf, Dr. Rivera's information is accessible. But I wanted to hear from him. On the phone he was warm and outgoing. Underlying his friendly demeanor, however, was the melancholy of an optimist who has lost hope. My first question was, "How are you?", to which he replied, "Okay."

"Really? I . . . would not be okay in your situation."

"For a long time I wasn't."

"What changed?"

"First, I realized I would never get justice from the family court system. Second, I stopped expecting things to make any degree of sense. With that came acceptance—and a certain calm."

Dr. Rivera told me that he had grown up on Long Island: "My dad was a custodian. My mom was a licensed professional nurse. So I got exposure to the medical field, which always interested me."

Dr. Rivera put himself through SUNY Stonybrook by working as a house-framer. He continued at Stonybrook's medical school and did a residency there, focusing on pediatrics. At age twenty-seven he married the second girl he had ever dated: "I was the proverbial late bloomer," he admitted. "I had very little confidence with women. I met someone I liked, and we hung out as buddies. Eventually I learned the attraction was reciprocal. It seemed like a great stroke of luck.

"During my medical training my mother got terminal cancer. She said a wedding before she died would give her joy. So, I got engaged. But the relationship never had a strong foundation. I was inexperienced, and we were both responding to a moribund parent's wish. Look, I thought twenty-seven was middle-aged. Now I look back and see how young that is."

"Did she work?"

"Yes, as a teacher. She stopped when the kids came along: three girls and one boy."

"How long did the relationship last?

"We were together for twenty-two years and married for fifteen."

"How would you characterize it, overall?"

"Our kids became the focus. Children need so many things, and from a doctor, patients need so much . . . I was very into being a provider; a lot of my self-image came from that. Since divorcing, I've actually become a better dad. Anyway, busyness can mask estrangement for a long time. Then, ultimately, it can't.

"We divorced in 2011. The court date was 2013. I was asked to pay $160,000 per year. This combined alimony and child support, but it was mainly alimony. For a solo practitioner like myself, this was unfeasible."

"How was the sum calculated?"

"Bizarrely. The judge said my ex was 'not working,' as if this was a permanent existential state. Then, she looked at my practice's gross revenue before expenses. She ignored malpractice insurance, equipment purchases, phone, electricity, gas, and rent bills. She didn't take my medical school loans into account."

"After you had worked your way through college framing houses?"

"Yes. Her audit produced a sum I wasn't earning. Now, there's an assumption that a nonworking spouse should enjoy the lifestyle he or she had during the marriage."

"I know."

"So, my attorney came back with an offer of $80,000 per year, which was rejected."

"Then?"

"A judgment. And jail."

"Tell me."

"It's a medium/maximum facility called Riverhead, on Long Island. I did six months in 2013. At first it was terrifying to be confined with felons. Luckily, some of the corrections officers knew me. I had taken care of their kids. They transferred me out of the cell block into someplace called 'the dormitory.' I did landscaping outside. The inmates left me alone. They knew the guards had their eyes on me. They also saw me as someone with medical training who could help them if necessary. I was scared of getting sick—contracting hepatitis or something—but not so much of being attacked.

"I have memories that are actually funny. I wanted to keep my career alive, so I applied for jobs. I couldn't go on interviews, so one physician came to me. This nice Chinese woman and I are discussing pediatric technique. I'm sitting at a table, wearing a yellow jumpsuit that says, 'Inmate.'"

"Does one moment stand out as the worst?"

"Oh, yes. Prisoners get their personal items from a commissary. This comes out of an account your job pays for. My landscaping salary was garnished because of a judgment, and it all went to my ex. I went to get underwear one day and learned that I didn't have enough in my account to cover it. I had lost the ability to buy underwear. That was my nadir."

"What did you do?"

"A crackhead gave me some underwear."

"It's hard to know what to ask after that . . . "

"I know. The story doesn't get rosier. I'd always struggled with anxiety. After I got out, facing these bills, with the escalating interest, and her attorney's fees, I broke down. In 2015 I was hospitalized for a week."

"What was the diagnosis?"

"PTSD. After my release, I realized that I wouldn't practice medicine again. Who would use a pediatrician that has been jailed and hospitalized? Even if I re-establish myself, if I earn more than $1,100, most of it would be garnished. The Child Enforcement Agency demands that I pay $9,000 a month in child support and alimony. Two thirds of that is alimony. There's an additional $4,500 for arrearages. That comes to $13,000 per month. As a working doctor I could not have afforded that. At this point, I would lose the disability I live on, two thirds of which goes to my ex. This leaves me surviving on $770 a month. Our house went into foreclosure. The court deemed it an asset, so, with that judgment, my Medicaid benefits were cut."

"Dr. Rivera—"

"Carlos."

"Dr. Rivera, when I ask people why they're getting married they say they're in love. They slide quickly from marriage—an institution—to personal feelings. Now, I want you to tell these lovebirds something you wish you had known."

"Oh, there are so many things no one tells you . . . Here's one: default on alimony, and you lose your driver's license. I now have a restricted license that lets me drive to and from a job. Of course, this makes it ten times harder to get a job, but . . . I'll never have a driver's license again. I can't travel internationally. People on a terrorist watch list can fly overseas. Americans with alimony judgments can't."

"Insane."

"Absolutely insane, but as I said, I accept the insanity. Many of my former patients have given me clothes and furniture. Some drive me to appointments. My friend Ira opened the GoFundMe account. I'm grateful to all of them. My girlfriend Jamie is a nurse. She's stuck by me. We hang out, have meals at home."

"If you could advise anyone considering betrothal, what would you say?"

"If you were considering starting a business, and you learned that fifty percent of these kinds of businesses failed, would you go ahead? That's exactly what you're doing with marriage."

"There's an 'it won't happen to me' mentality."

"I know. For someone utterly determined, please hear this: if you're on a professional track, get your licensure before the wedding. I married when I was training, so my ex owns half my license. This gives her a lot of power. So if you're training to be a doctor, an attorney . . . whatever . . . at least protect yourself in this area."

The Rape Discount

"Sexual Assault Victim Ordered to Pay Alimony to Attacker Fights to Change California Law," a 2012 headline reads.[6] The article is one of many that tell Crystal Harris's story. She grew up in a San Diego beach town and attended California Polytechnic State University in San Luis Obispo. Waitressing during college, she met Shawn Harris. She was twenty; he was twenty-one. They married in 1996 and bought a home. Two kids, both boys, followed. Shawn was their primary caretaker; Crystal built a career in financial services. In 2008, Crystal hit the "record" button on a tape recorder in her dresser drawer before Shawn approached and, she reports, raped her. Though muffled, the recording emits her pleas: "I don't want to be raped," and "You're hurting my neck." It records her saying "no" over fifty times." [7]

They went to divorce court while Shawn was simultaneously prosecuted for rape. Crystal was earning $120,000 a year. Shawn had no income. She was ordered to pay alimony, despite the pending rape verdict. He was convicted of forcing Crystal to perform oral sex on him. The other two charges, spousal rape by force and sodomy, got a hung jury. Shawn was sentenced to six years in jail. Crystal then worked with the California State Assembly, lobbying for a policy that Californians convicted of sexual assault cannot receive alimony from their alleged victims.

Through email, we agreed to speak, and I found Crystal at home on a Friday afternoon in April 2021. We hit it off, quickly establishing a verbal rhythm. Crystal described her childhood positively: "My dad owned an electrical contracting company; my mom was a homemaker. They supported my dreams. Maybe this is why I grew up with minimal self-doubt. Truthfully, I think I was born confident. I planned to make it in financial services, marry young, and have two kids. I ended up doing all that—at a price."

Regarding Shawn, she admitted, "I had a crush on him from the start. He had more hustle than anyone in that restaurant. He was smart, especially with computers. After five months as coworkers we got together. It was wonderful."

"Any wrinkles?"

"One. He had what I call 'kick the bucket' syndrome. He had a baseball scholarship at Christ College Irvine but never graduated. Did well as a math major and dropped out a few credits shy . . . I majored in finance and got job offers out of the gate. In my field the hours are long. I thought it would be great to have a stay-at-home parent, so the kids wouldn't be in daycare. Given his knack with computers, I figured he'd eventually get a decent job. Lots of companies will hire someone who can code, with or without the degree."

"When did things change?"

"Really, inch by inch. At first we got along. Neither of us slept with anyone else. We had our health. I made enough money. Then, two years into the marriage, he hit me.

"I told you I'm a planner. Abuse was not in the plan. I didn't fuck around; I had him arrested. We separated, and I got a restraining order on him. He was instructed to attend anger management sessions for fifty-two weeks. It was 1998, and we reconciled. I believed he'd improve with the therapy."

"Did he?

"Not really. He continued going downhill. But there were good times. Four years later my oldest came along. Shawn had been selling cars part time. With our first son he became a full-time dad. He was good at it."

"When did things really go sideways?"

"Well, Shawn had an idealized version of his father. This was someone he would never disappoint. With our first son, he was very loving. Then his dad passed away two years later, and the second baby came. I swear, some kind of switch went off in Shawn. He didn't bond with the new child. At this point the market was tanking. I'm a portfolio manager, and I don't do 'buy and hold.' Anyone can invest that way. I'm tactical. When the market goes bad I tell some clients, 'go to cash;' for others that's inappropriate. But I was watching indicators and analyzing each client's situation under crisis conditions. Meantime, Shawn wasn't taking care of the baby properly. This became a source of contention between us. Then he started getting verbally abusive. Still, I stayed."

"How come?"

"I was somewhat old fashioned. I thought you stayed together for the kids. Each time he apologized and we made up, I thought he had learned his lesson. Honestly . . . I also thought 'single mother' sounded pathetic. It seemed like the saddest thing you could be. If I've learned anything from this experience it's to think less simplistically.

"Anyway, at a certain point I realized that Shawn loved and hated the same things about me. I was energetic, hardworking, and involved in our community. Life was not especially hard for me. I'm not anxiety prone. But this 'can do' quality also infuriated him. And he was getting nastier.

"I had to consider leaving. I started bringing it up, and when I did Shawn would threaten me with violence. Then he started threatening to kill me if I left. By this point I wanted out. I was scared, but I didn't panic. I got a permit and a handgun and put a tape recorder in my dresser drawer. Later, people would ask why I recorded him. This is why. I thought one death threat on tape would be my ticket out. I could play it to a judge as proof and get some lasting safety—not someplace where he could drive by anytime."

"Do you think some of his rage came from self-consciousness about being the primary caretaker?"

"He said no. He said his friends were jealous of the flexible schedule and the opportunity to spend quality time with his kids. But when he raped me, I knew, at some level, I was being put in my place. I called 911. I told the boys, 'Daddy hurt mommy.' They didn't need details. And they didn't want to see him. They haven't since I called 911 that night.

"I got excellent legal representation. When the judge heard the tape in court, he acknowledged it had recorded a rape. But he didn't seem to take marital rape very seriously. He had this computer he kept fiddling with. He made some entries. It spat out the number three thousand dollars per month. He lowered that to one thousand per month in alimony. I call that 'the rape discount.'"

"What happened next?"

"Shawn was convicted. I paid a grand a month until he went to jail. Then, I drafted a proposal. Here, my community volunteerism really helped. People knew me. I worked with my assemblywoman and local politicians, Democrat and Republican. The proposal went through different committees; ultimately we got the law changed. It's AB1522, and it was changed in 2012—not just for San Diego but for the whole State of California. I just got a grateful email from a gal who said, 'I don't have to pay alimony because of what you did.'"

"May I ask what your ultimate financial damage was?"

"I had to pay his attorney's fees, which were $47,000. Including the trips to court since he's gotten out, I've lost about $400,000. He continues to sue for custody of the kids. At my new job I got a good bonus. He sued for part of that, unsuccessfully. But you don't want to start someplace being served with papers. It's embarrassing."

"Might I suggest, that's why he did it?"

"Might I suggest you're probably right? Anyway, each time I have to hire lawyers. That's expensive."

"Anything you wish you had done differently early on?"

"Yes. I shouldn't have overlooked that puzzling thing about Shawn because he fit my calendar: job in finance, house six months after graduation, marriage . . . I was too much of an organizer. Now, for the first time in a while, I'm seeing someone and getting to know him slowly. There's no rush to the finish line. My mom said, 'it's wonderful to see you fall in love at your own pace.'"

"Your story is so remarkable. Do you have advice for people contemplating marriage?"

"I try not to give unsolicited advice."

"I'm soliciting."

"Well, I now have mixed feelings about marriage as an institution. I guess I'd say, if you marry, be cautious. If you separate, your relationship won't necessarily end. It's hard, but try to imagine this person as your legal adversary. How would they behave? Remember, family court judges have enormous discretion. And the decisions they make are basically subjective."

Better Alternatives

Marriage offers extraordinary benefits, protections, and status that make sexual conformity attractive. But many tantalized Americans marry only to learn that wedlock is not for them. Or, as my earlier work shows, they wed in a tongue-in-cheek fashion, as if playing a conjugal game rather than fortifying matrimonial structures. They flip marriage the bird while enjoying every entitlement. That mockery ends when they become vulnerable to retribution.

An underlying belief that once married, people become better, is essential to the practice of shaking down an ex-spouse. A few mental pivots are required; the person needs to feel ever-married. This is different from being never married. Ever-married people grasped the brass ring, albeit temporarily, and still feel entitled. Law and custom encourage this feeling; the man who marries for citizenship and divorces fifteen years later does not lose his right to live here. When she divorces three years after her wedding, the woman whose home is filled with housewares ordered at a bridal registry does not return them. The passionless wedded couple without biological children maintains spousal immunity privileges. The sexually active duo next door, who care for four children, can't access that benefit. It is no small leap for any ex-spouse to feel like part of a superior caste.

In the United States, where celebrity divorces make daily headlines, legal drama has an air of unavoidability. One hears it discussed as the inevitable outcome of marriage, rather than a sign that the institution is flawed. Sometimes things get ugly, is how the line goes. And when things between spouses get ugly, they get litigious. It's a real shame, but . . . it's life.

It doesn't have to be. Postmarital extortion is not a cosmic imperative. Better alternatives exist for maintaining erotic relationships and, when necessary, terminating them. The Na or Mosuo people, a community of perhaps 56,000 Buddhists, live in southeast China between the Yunnan and Sichuan provinces. Among them sexual partners do not marry; individuals reside with their extended biological families and enjoy evenings together: *nansese*, which means, "to visit furtively." A male guest arrives at night and departs the next morning. Some prefer "conspicuous visiting," in which men come earlier, socialize—even have a meal. Here too, the lovers remain obligation free.[8] Children produced by either kind of visit grow up in their biomoms' homes: intergenerational collectives that provide multiple caregivers of both sexes. Men may take a hand in raising their biokids but don't have to.

There is no Musuo word for husband or wife. Long-term lovers use the noun, *adhu* (friend).[9] These pairings are not, as some anthropologists claim, "walking marriages" (i.e., marriage-like partnerships in which principals reside separately). They entail no public oaths, licensure, or asset transmission. Sexual exclusivity is not an issue; as lovers don't share property, they are not considered each other's property. Both parties can sleep with other people, a right considered respectful of individual autonomy.

As the Mosuo have no birth outside marriage, their culture has no concept of "illegitimacy." *Cha mu cha zo* refers to a child whose biological father is unknown. Such children are not swathed in ignominy; kids with identifiable genitors are not exalted.[10] Divorce and alimony don't exist, because assets are not institutionalized within the romantic couple. "All Musuo women are essentially single," explains Choo WaiHong, a Singapore-based corporate lawyer who lives with the Na for part of each year.[11]

A flurry of articles about this tribe depict it as a culture where women rule.[12] This is inaccurate. If Na women excel in politics, men manage business affairs, fish, and farm. Na culture highly esteems monks. Women have a saying: "A woman, no matter how strong she is, would never be able to have a baby without knowing a man."[13] Men are expected to help raise children that live in their households.

Nonmarriage is an organizing principle of Na culture. This distressed Chinese occupiers, who mounted a promatrimony campaign when they seized control of the region in 1956. It included lectures against sexual freedom and marriage-propagandizing films. Communist China halted deliveries of foodstuffs, determined to starve the Na into conjugal bliss. The initiative failed. Some Mosuo agreed to sham weddings, but older customs prevailed, as they had for more than eighteen centuries. Indeed, for those who continue to insist that matrimony is the sole means of raising children, sharing resources, and ensuring asset transmissions to future generations, the Na stand as a corrective. They show how nonmarital people can lead stable, meaningful lives in societies that do not organize everything around and through wedlock.

Other cultures sustain relationships that go by the name of matrimony but depart from modern western understandings of that word. Northern Alaska's Eskimo culture, for instance, includes something anthropologists call "comarriage:" an agreement between two couples in which each person has sex with the other's partner. Because this practice horrified nineteenth-century missionaries, the indigenous population learned discretion (i.e., secrecy), so statistical evidence on comarriage is scarce. But experts suggest that it is widespread, having perhaps extended to the majority of Northern Alaska's married population.[14] Prior to Alaska's Americanization, expressing jealousy about a spouse's lover was considered uncouth. Stephanie Coontz observes this setup's advantages. Cospouses' offspring have a special connection; they are considered siblings. The discouragement of jealousy, possessiveness, and cupidity makes separations smoother when they occur.[15]

Eastern Paraguay's Aché are hunter-gatherers who believe in partible paternity; among a child's dads is the *miare* ("father who put it in") and the *bykuare* ("fathers who provided the child's essence"). Christopher Ryan and Cacilda Jethá observe, "Rather than being shunned as 'bastards' . . . children of multiple fathers benefit from having more than one man who takes a special interest in them."[16] They believe that such practices reflect our prehistoric forebears' values.[17] The Paleolithic world was inhospitable. For survival, human beings had to form hunting-gathering bands that migrated seasonally between encampments. The band-level society, not the couple, took responsibility for food gathering, defense, and childcare. Indeed, no two people could have performed this work exclusively without expecting to die. Accordingly, "No Stone Age lovers would have imagined in their wildest dreams that they could or should be 'everything' to each other."[18] Merging resources is necessary in a hunting-gathering society, where yields vary from day to day. Band-level societies "put extraordinary time and energy into establishing norms of sharing."[19] Erotic sharing would seem natural in such environments.

Better Alternatives Closer to Home

It is not necessary to mine other cultures for better ways of terminating amorous relationships. Some American subcultures are instructive; among them is the gay community, pre-*Obergefell v. Hodges*. I base one fictional couple on many actual partnerships I have witnessed.

Raphael is a distinguished, greying fifty-six-year-old psychiatrist. He grew up bilingual in Williston Township, Pennsylvania. After high school, he earned an undergraduate degree in biology from Yale. He attended medical school at New York University and did his residency at Northwestern. A specialist in the treatment of anxiety and depression with concomitant mental illness, he built a private practice while working part-time at New York Presbyterian Hospital. Upon turning forty-eight, Raphael inherited two million dollars, which he invested well. A modern art lover, he has amassed a small but impressive collection of paintings. At age fifty Raphael attended an opening and met Robert, one of its two bartenders. They began dating.

Robert is twenty-nine-years old; he grew up in Queens. A third-generation Chinese American, he knows some Cantonese but never really mastered the language. He has a high school diploma. He spent one semester at Queens College, learned that significant reading was required, and dropped out. He works part time in two restaurants, sometimes assisting the chefs, sometimes tending bar. Simultaneously, he pursues a career as an actor. Multiple tattoos enhance his muscular physique. He enjoys weight lifting and positive thinking.

These two live together in a one-bedroom coop on Central Park West and a house in Rhinebeck, New York. They travel between Manhattan and the Hudson Valley in a Mercedes Benz. Both properties are held exclusively in Raphael's name, as is the car. Raphael supports the households. He also pays for Robert's clothing, gym membership, acting lessons, haircuts, and tattoos. Robert makes craft cocktails for Raphael's friends. When he tells them about the process of getting into character before an audition, they fall tactfully silent.

Both partners, as they call themselves, understand the nature of this relationship. Neither expects fidelity. Their policy is, "don't ask, don't tell," so long as measures are taken to protect against sexually transmitted disease. Raphael believes that constraints imposed in an attempt to control extracurricular sex fail; sexologist Alfred Kinsey said this in the postwar years.[20]

Until recently, gay men in such arrangements had an understanding: the upkeep continues as long as the relationship lasts. When it's over, money stops flowing. Neither expects that Raphael will owe Robert anything when they break up. Gay culture has told people like Robert the opposite: living this well is a privilege, not a right. It's been six years; there may be another six, and there may not. But if it ends, Robert will fend for himself. To expect ownership of an apartment or house for which he paid nothing and paintings he does not like would be absurd. Even more bizarre would be the demand of long-term support from someone who is no longer his boyfriend.

No one tells Robert that he's in a structurally weak position, with less earning potential than Raphael. Robert dropped out of school, forsook vocational training, and pursued acting. No one treats this as "society's" fault; no one sees it as anyone's fault. This choice may not have been profitable, but it was Robert's. To suggest otherwise would be paternalistic.

Robert genuinely likes Raphael. Breaking up in a public venue with outcomes determined by judges seems strange to him. If that time comes, he expects a private goodbye. He knows Raphael will set him up in a rental with some getting-started money. Down the road, if he needs a loan, he can turn to his ex-lover. And if Raphael starts to have health problems, Robert will help—no questions asked. As author S. Bear Bergman writes, "among lesbian, gay, bi, and queer people there are many stories of ex-lovers who have become close, intimate partners over time."[21]

Experience has taught me that economic security, or its illusion, is a major marriage propellor. When mature wives coach young spinsters, the gloves come off. "Aren't you worried about not having any security?" and "When are you getting a ring?" were questions I fielded regularly before entering academia. They came from relatives but also from coworkers and realtors—

people who did not know me particularly well. Fallacious, married-knows-best logic liberates such spouses to pry as they corral dissenters toward wedlock. If American society set out to raise a new generation of cowed, dependent, underachieving, women—and now men—it could not devise a better method. This one encourages duplicitous self-interest; each lover becomes a potential source of revenue. So, if Americans wish to facilitate helplessness and cunning, the current marriage system, alimony included, should be preserved. If the goal is nurturing independence, strength, confidence, ethical seriousness, and candor in the next generation, a different approach is required.

When considering how to dismantle the alimony machine, pre-*Obergefell v. Hodges* gay relationships provide a reality check. There is no reason heterosexuals cannot adopt gay men and lesbians' traditionally private, *laissez-faire* methods. Rather than grafting heterosexual assumptions onto homosexual relationships, we could use some timeworn gay strategies to encourage more appropriate responses to romantic breakups.

Attorney Paula Ettelbrick exemplified these practices. Director of the Stonewall Foundation, she remarked tartly, "I do not want to be known as Mrs.-Attached-to-Somebody-Else. Nor do I want to give the state the power to regulate my primary relationship." Ettelbrick presumably meant civil rights lawyer Suzanne Goldberg. When they split, Ettelbrick got involved with television producer Marianne Haggerty. They divided their time between Manhattan and Yonkers, New York. Vacations included Ettelbrick, Haggerty, Goldberg, and her partner. Also in tow were Adam and Julia, the children from Ettelbrick and Goldberg's relationship. Goldberg assumed their custody when Ettelbrick died from peritoneal cancer in 2011.[22]

Actress Jane Lynch fared less well. She divorced psychologist Lara Embry after four years of marriage. These turned out to be four expensive years. A Los Angeles court awarded Embry $1.2 million and half of Lynch's television residuals. Adding insult to injury, the ruling judge gave Embry half of several bank accounts, totaling $847,485, and 50 percent of Lynch's 401K: $315,079.[23]

You want marriage? We'll give you marriage. You want normal? Here it is.

For the most part, marriage evangelists' attempts to prevent Americans from exiting wedlock have not worked. In the face of feverish warnings, an enormous population seeks divorce. This reveals something unrelated to civilization's decline. As a locus of intimacy, financial betterment, and family, marriage does not serve. A lifelong romance/best friendship/financial alliance/domestic partnership/family anchor represents an inflated ideal. But no compulsory one-size-fits-all model would suffice.

Postmarital extortion victims' experiences show the American legal system at its worst. Why is such brutality permitted—even condoned? I suspect that divorced people often become scapegoats who bear the brunt of general anxiety about high marital-separation rates. They pay the price (literally) for an obvious truth: matrimony cannot sustain the ideological burden placed upon it. It must give way to more workable forms, in which demagoguery has no place, as government has no place in American adults' bedrooms.

(Endnotes)

1   Alice Gomstyn, "Wife Wins $9 Million from Husband's Alleged Mistress," ABC News, March 22, 2010, https://abcnews.go.com/Business/wife-wins-million-husbands-alleged-mistress.

2   *What Love Is and What It Could Be* (New York: Basic Books, 2017), 161.

3   "Dr. Carlos Rivera," Ira Scott, Go Fund Me, https://www.gofundme.com/dr-carlos-rivera-md.

4   *Long Island Backstory*. YouTube, July 16, 2016.

5   Quoted in Thom Patterson, "Divorce and Child Custody: Men Cry Foul," CNN, November 7, 2018, https://www.cnn.com/2018/11/05/us/divorce-child-custody-tips-lisa-ling-this-is-life/index. For the Ling interview visit https://cnn.com/videos/tv/2018/11/07/this-is-the-life-lisa-ling-season-5-episode-7-ron-3.cnn.

6   Juju Chang and Alyssa Litoff, ABC News, April 4, 2012, https://abcnews.go.com/US/sexual-assault-victim-ordered-pay-alimony-attacker-fights.

7   Paul Thompson, "Husband is in Prison for Sexually Assaulting Wife . . . Now She Has to Pay Him $1,000 a month in Alimony After the Divorce," *Daily Mail*, December 5, 2011, https://www.dailymail.co.uk/news/article-2069879/Shawn-Harris-sexually-assaulted-wife-Crystal-pay-HIM-1k-month-alimony.

8   Coontz, *Marriage*, 33.

9   Cai Hua, *A Society Without Fathers or Husbands: The Na of China*, trans. Asti Hustvedt (New York: Zone Books, 2008), 495.

10   Ibid., 228–9.

11   Hannah Booth, "The Kingdom of Women: The Society Where a Man is Never the Boss," *The Guardian*, April 1, 2017, https://www.theguardian.com/lifeandstyle/2017/apr/01/the-kingdom-of-women-the-tibetan-tribe-where-a-man-is-never-the-boss.

12   See for instance Sharyn Shufiyan, "Not All Societies Practice Male Dominance," *Star*, October 26, 2014, https://www.thestar.com.my/lifestyle/viewpoints/tapestry/2014/10/26/not-all-societies-practice-male-dominance-those-that-do-should-check-how-women-are-bullied.

13   Hua, *A Society Without Fathers*, 226.

14   Ernest S. Burch, Jr., "Marriage and Divorce Among the North Alaskan Eskimos," *Anthropology for the Nineties: Introductory Readings*, ed. Johnetta B. Cole (New York: The Free Press, 1998), 161.

15 Coontz, *Marriage*, 22.

16 *Sex at Dawn*, 92.

17 Ibid., 6.

18 Coontz, *Marriage*, 38.

19 Ibid., 39-40.

20 Alfred Kinsey, et al., *Sexual Behavior in the Human Female* (Philadelphia: Saunders, 1953), 415.

21 "From Exes to Friends: The Lasting Bonds of Many LGBTQ Relationships," *The Globe and Mail*, Februrary 22, 2017, https://www.theglobeandmail.com/life/relationships/from-exes-to-friends-the-lasting-bonds-of-many-lgbtq-relationships.

22 David Dunlap, "Paula Ettelbrick, Legal Rights Expert in Gay Rights Movement, Dies At 56," *New York Times*, October 8, 2011, https://www.nytimes.com/2011/10/09/nyregion/paula-l-ettelbrick-legal-expert-in-gay-rights-movement-dies-at-56.

23 Rebecca Macatee and Baker Machado, "Jane Lynch Divorced Finalized, Ex Lara Embry Gets $1.2 million Over Two Years," ENews, October 29, 2014, https://www.eonline.com/news/592936/jane-lynch-divorce-finalized-ex-lara-embry-gets-1-2-million.

7

Why Same-Sex Weddings Are Not the Solution[1]

*"If there is no marriage
then no one can be unfairly denied access to it."*

— CLARE CHAMBERS,
"THE LIMITS OF CONTRACT: REGULATING PERSONAL
RELATIONSHIPS IN A MARRIAGE-FREE STATE"

The Jubilee

"I have always said that everyone has the right to love who they love," exclaimed actress/singer Liza Minnelli. "And today, with the historic decision from the Supreme Court, I am so happy it is now the law of the land."[2] The 2015 *Obergefell v. Hodges* ruling evoked many such declarations.

If the Court had protected a "right to love," effusions like Minnelli's might make sense. But *Obergefell v. Hodges* did no such thing. It extended matrimonial benefits to another group of people. One can't entirely fault Minnelli and her Hollywood associates for missing the difference. In America the marital fallacy remains ubiquitous. Popular psychology's pervasive literature, commercial films, and political debates often equate wedlock with love. Conversely, the absence of legal marriage is misrepresented as a paucity of attachment.

Thunderous accolades for *Obergefell v. Hodges* drowned skeptical voices out. These voices persist. Michael Warner argues that same-sex marriage strengthens something that is already too powerful and authorizes the state to make one favored lifestyle even more privileged. He denounces such "blind majoritarianism, armed not only with an impressive battery of prohibitions and punishments, but with an equally impressive battery of economistic incentives and disincentives."[3] In other words, a verdict that expands wedlock's influence does so at the expense of nonmarital Americans, whatever their erotic preferences. Warner notes that married people are "taken more seriously than unmarried people; they are more likely to be invited to dinner parties, offered jobs, and elected to public office. In short, they have status."[4] Qualifying another class of couples for that status does nothing for those who cannot or will not lay claim to it.

It's not just a matter of making matrimony more prestigious. Doubters have concerns about family diversity, which exploded in the late twentieth and early twenty-first centuries. Bella DePaulo explains, "Most of the people who are living in the innovative ways that are changing the face of the nation do not see themselves as agents of change . . . they are just people who are navigating their lives."[5] By navigating nonmaritally, however, many are redefining family. Gay intellectuals have long encouraged this process. In 1980 John Boswell noted that "pair-bonding of various sorts is manifestly advantageous to most human societies."[6] He considered the overvaluation of child-producing marriages extremist, since various bonds strengthen communities with reciprocal supports and modes of sustaining those who can't care for themselves.

Katherine Franke observes that gay marriage advocates base

relationship licensure on government criteria for authentic family status. Instead of thinking "gay" or "straight," this lesbian scholar thinks "married" or "unmarried." She finds the latter category becoming increasingly disadvantaged. Our analyses gel: homophobic intolerance stems partly from the dread of nonmarital people that has plagued modernity. Gay people may well have been vilified, not only because of their erotic preferences but since marriage did not suit them. Many, like England's King James I (1566–1625), married.[7] But many did not. When the post-Reformation marriage-mystique intensified, the idea of people who implicitly challenged conjugal norms helped to create a category of sexual outlaws. When they started marrying each other, they become sexual insiders: normals. Such acceptance can be addictive. As Franke drily observes, "Not very long ago lesbians and gay men found themselves harshly regulated by criminal law, subject to long prison terms for having sex with other persons of the same sex. Now we clamor to have the state regulate our romantic lives . . . You'd think that we might have wanted a bit of a break from the state."[8]

America's founders held that matrimony created optimal citizens by encouraging virtue and civic stability. Accordingly, the United States made coupledom foundational.[9] This does not mean that the founding parents held romantic views of wedlock—just that they ranked it highly and considered it sui generis. In ensuing centuries, the principle of erotic fidelity permeated states as a form of common sense. Holy matrimony and the government's right to enforce it represented beliefs so widespread that they required no proof.

Each generation passed marriage-centrism to the next one. Today, adultery is a crime in twenty-five states. Five of these, including Idaho, Massachusetts, and Michigan, make it a felony. In the others it's a misdemeanor—no trifling matter. In Arizona, a married person who has sex with someone other than their spouse can go to prison for thirty days. Both the experimenting spouse and the lover are prosecutable.[10] While these laws are generally moribund, they remain on the books. Police officers can use them to harass individuals they find unsavory. An angry spouse can access them to launch personal vendettas. *Obergefell v. Hodges* has increased the number of people vulnerable to prosecution for consensual adult sex.

The opinion contains distressingly familiar language: "Without the recognition, stability, and predictability that marriage offers, children suffer the stigma of knowing their families are somehow lesser."[11] There it is again: the belief that nonmarital children are inferior to kids born within wedlock.

Gay people have a list of serious historical grievances. But skeptics wonder if wedlock was the platform from which to demand justice, since it brings incentivization into relationships. Gay men and women now have hundreds of enticements to wed—health insurance being the most salient. Lesbian author Yasmin Nair objects: "Health care is an economic matter and something that should go to everyone, regardless of marital status."[12] Linking insurance and other entitlements to marriage reproduces a straight dilemma. When a man proposes to his boyfriend, is he feigning emotion to get benefits? When a woman accepts a proposal, is she in love with her partner or the opportunity to plan a self-dramatizing gala?

Wedlock's personal components cannot be disaggregated from its perks. Because spouses can spot each other through periods of unemployment, married women are less likely than unmarried ones to accrue debt. Nonmarital partners can also support each other through transitions but not with marriage's joint benefits. And they can't shake popular misconceptions that equate matrimony with responsible living. Financial journalist Kerri Anne Renzulli cautions, "Insurers and lenders may see married couples with two incomes as more reliable than singles and thus might offer lower premium or repayment rates, making it easier to sock away for home buying or retirement savings." She reports that after taking marriage vows, a woman's wealth increases by 16 percent per annum.[13] Economist Jay Zagorsky concurs. His longitudinal studies show that after roughly ten years, married people have approximately four times as much wealth as unmarrieds. Zagorsky states flatly, "The best thing you can do to increase your wealth is to get married."[14]

Gay women cannot be expected to ignore such advice. Nor is lesbian love so pure that it will eschew 50 percent of a partner's assets if the relationship ends. An angry Nevadan who feels mistreated by her girlfriend is—a pissed-off girlfriend. Once married, she can treat slights as monetizable demands. Did she wed to secure stronger financial footing? Even if her wedding vows sound sincere—even if they are sincere—the oaths may be tools for self-advancement. Or perhaps married strikes her as a nice middle-class thing to be. What Warner calls "the lure of the normal" may be the strongest of motivators.[15]

Many now fear losing vital benefits. Author Lynn Lamstein has health coverage through her girlfriend of over twenty years, Sandra Haggard, who teaches biology at the University of Maine. "I don't believe economic benefits should go exclusively to married people," Haggard told the *New York Times* in June 2015. Nonmarital cohabitants Andrew Parks and Ashlea Halpern, coeditors of the website, Cartogramme, concur. Parks also addressed the *Times*: "No American should be denied benefits by their employer or otherwise penalized for choosing to opt out of a religiously and societally mandated but historically problematic institution."[16]

Now, one frequently hears that all Americans in relationships stand equally before the law. This is incorrect. A never-married professional, I cannot leave any of my life partners Social Security benefits. Neither can my never-married colleagues, whatever their sexual orientation. Indeed, Americans who cannot wed and stay consistent with our own values have cause for alarm. By the time *Obergefell v. Hodges* was decided, thirty-six states and the District of Columbia had legalized same-sex marriage. Simultaneously, employers had begun yanking domestic partnership benefits with the "everyone can marry" argument. These included large corporations: Verizon, Delta Airlines, Corning. For untold numbers of employees, the new policies made betrothal virtually mandatory.

Universities throughout the country altered their policies. Columbia gave employees with partners included on the school's health plan one year to marry before the latter lost coverage. Franke and other faculty protested. The administration responded incoherently: same-sex lovers could receive domestic partnership privileges. Those in mixed-sex amorous relationships could not. For both groups, only sexual partners qualified.

California's 2003 Rights and Responsibilities Act made domestic partnership the legal equivalent of marriage. Same-sex marriage campaigners lauded this overhaul, which ran roughshod over anyone who preferred a union that could be truncated on its participants' terms.[17] California domestic partnership had not forced people to share property or required those breaking up to divorce. Ending a relationship required informing the other person in writing. Many preferred this option to court-supervised breakups, splitting resources under community property laws, and paying spousal support. Too bad. With chilling efficacy, the law converted straight and gay domestic partnerships into marriages. One could only avoid marital assimilation by truncating the relationship. This often meant losing essential rights, including state employee health insurance.

Accordingly, legal scholar Kaiponanea T. Matsumura does not see same-sex marriage as reformist. He posits that reconfiguring partnerships without individuals' affirmation is unconstitutional, violating a fundamental freedom: *the right to not marry*. New policies offer a "default to marriage or lose everything" choice, which is no choice. They also create quagmires. State agencies inform people of their imminent marriages through hard mail. Some discard unsolicited mail without opening it. Others read the announcements and passively accept wedlock without researching its history or legal risks. Yet others lack money to consult experts or time to consider alternatives.[18] Californians who read notifications late, in the midst of health or other crises, are shunted into marriages.

In June 2016, Maryland's Montgomery County Council repealed laws mandating domestic partnership benefits. The 1999 law enforcing entitlements for heterosexual partners, like the 2010 regulation requiring them for homosexual lovers, applied to contractors and county workers, so limited numbers of people were affected. But the symbolism was potent and the rhetoric chilling. Married council member George Leventhal chirped, "Marriage . . . entitles its participants to certain tax benefits, certain insurance benefits, certain classifications under the law."[19] He did not say why this is the case.

Connecticut had long given adults in civil unions health insurance entitlements. The state abolished this policy in 2008, after same-sex marriage kicked in. My boyfriend Jim became seriously ill in 2018. I called my university's human resources department and learned that our eight years together meant nothing. So what if he had taken care of me during an abdominal surgery? His unflagging devotion to my family was irrelevant. An HR representative marriagesplained the situation: "He can get on your plan as your husband." I countered that the university had hired me *because* I write critically about matrimony; my work on marriage satire got me the job. "But you *can* get married. Now everyone can," she replied, seeming pleased to offer me the opportunity to better myself.

"Yesterday there was one dogma," gay journalist Douglas Murray writes. "Now there is another."[20] Indeed, strange laws are emerging abroad. Germany legalized same-sex marriage in 2017. Almost immediately, believing in same-sex wedlock became requisite for citizenship in the state of Baden-Württemberg. This measure emulated regimes that punished citizens for what went through their minds. England's 1673 Test Act, for example, mandated that all civil servants reject transubstantiation (the belief that Eucharistic bread and wine become Christ's body and blood). This act went beyond prosecuting observant Catholics; it penalized people because of what they thought.

What does Baden-Württemberg do with people who don't believe in marriage, period?

For some, nonmarriage is a considered, ethical choice. Others want to protect assets or keep their sex lives private. Yet others enjoy being someone's companion and don't want to be that person's spouse. Domestic partnerships and civil unions give such people limited legal benefits. Neither solve the problem of romantic exceptionalism. They invest amorous relationships with special status. However, they represent a beginning: a sense that certain nonmarital bonds merit respect, and some adults whose lives don't fit matrimonial contours deserve fundamental benefits. A legal ruling that undermines this modest recognition of non-marriage should give pause.

Some Overlooked History

Gay lawyer Nancy D. Polikoff provides a helpful overview of sociopolitical forces that predate *Obergefell v. Hodges*. Her mono-graph, *Beyond (Straight and Gay) Marriage*, describes the 1960s and 1970s as watershed decades. Gays, women, and nonmarital

Americans made strides together. In February 1969, the Women's International Terrorist Conspiracy from Hell (WITCH) disrupted a bridal bazaar at New York's Madison Square Garden by setting loose hordes of mice. That June, a raid on Manhattan's Stonewall Inn met resistance. When three patrol cars arrived and police officers attempted to shut this West Village bar down, a crowd of butch lesbians, drag queens, young gay activists, and others fought back, throwing bricks and bottles. Skirmishes continued for several days. From this event the Gay Liberation Front emerged. Within a year it had established twelve consciousness-raising groups, three collective living quarters, and the newspaper, *Come Out!*[21]

That same year, *The Village Voice* applauded never-married author Shulamith Firestone and her cohorts.[22] In March 1970, between 100 and 200 women staged a sit-in at the *Ladies Home Journal's* Manhattan offices. They demanded an end to the "Can This Marriage Be Saved?" column and suggested replacement articles: "How to Get a Divorce" and "How to Have an Orgasm." Famously, Firestone stood on editor-in-chief John Mack Carter's desk and tore copies of the magazine to shreds.

Discontent was splintering postwar matrimony's facade. "Always a Bride, Never a Person," one slogan declared. Researchers revisited studies that affirmed biological motherhood within marriage. Harvard psychologist Rudolph Schaffer argued that babies bond to consistent, emotionally invested adults; sex is irrelevant; no biological tie is required.[23] Findings like this helped pave the way for nonmarital childrearing arrangements.

Definitions of one born outside wedlock as *filius nullius* ended with *Weber v. Aetna Cas. & Surety Co.* (1972), where the Supreme Court found unconstitutional a Louisiana program awarding workers' compensation benefits to an employee's four marital children while withholding payments from his two nonmarital kids. *New Jersey Welfare Rights Organization v. Cahill* (1973) limited the government's ability to withhold benefits from unwed natal parents.[24]

Increasing acceptance of sex outside marriage provided the backdrop for these decisions. With *Eisenstadt v. Baird* (1972) the Supreme Court protected unwed adults' right to purchase contraceptives. Holding that reproductive functions were private, this ruling chipped away at the belief that states should police eroticism.[25] *Roe v. Wade* (1973) protected a woman's right to terminate a pregnancy during the first trimester. According to the Court, this right stemmed from constitutionally implicit penumbras of privacy.

In 1973, some thirty black women gathered in New York City to discuss their shared experiences. The National Black Feminist Organization was founded a few months later; 400 women attended its first conference. NBFO's mission statement detailed the deleterious effects of marriage on Antebellum black women: "We were seen as breeders by the master; despised and historically polarized from/by the master's wife."[26]

Simultaneously, the American Home Economics Association defined family according to shared beliefs, common objectives, and pooled resources—not wedding vows.[27] Public policy appeared to be moving in this direction. To the relief of some and the horror of others, it must have seemed that matrimony would teeter until it toppled from its high horse. In this spirit, gay-liberation activists joined other civil liberties groups working to broaden definitions of family. In 1972, the National Coalition of Gay Organizations (NCGO) called for extending wedlock's legal benefits to all cohabiting people. NCGO spokespeople also demanded the abolition of "tax inequities victimizing single persons and same-sex couples."[28]

A robust debate interrogated two cultural mandates: heterosexuality and marriage. Many rejected the latter in favor of unregulated sexual citizenship. According to historian Alison Lefkowitz, "most homophile activists did not want to embrace a repressive insitution that heterosexuals astutely seemed to be rejecting."[29] Journalist Jim Kepner characterized wedlock as a "straightjacket."[30] At the 1987 Gay and Lesbian March on Washington, a large sign read, "Love makes a family—nothing more, nothing less."[31] Stonewall, the British gay rights NGO founded in 1989, did not originally favor same-sex marriage.

At the 1973 Annual Meeting for the Society of Friends in Baltimore, Quaker leaders pledged to "put new energy into the struggle to end the oppression, often unconscious, that is imposed on people because of their sex or their sexual orientation."[32] That year, members of the American Psychiatric Association concurred that there was no scientific basis for considering homosexuailty an ailment. One year later, homosexuality was deleted from ithe DSM-II's list of mental disorders.[33] (The World Health Organization would follow suit in 1992.)[34] In 1977, Harvey Milk joined the San Francisco Board of Supervisors.[35] The never-married Milk was California's first openly homosexual elected official. He had run against three out gay candidates.

Numerous activists worked to push government out of American bedrooms rather than earn licensure for certain genital acts. Feminism focused on health and sexuality. New York City's branch of the National Organization for Women held a 1974 conference that featured erotic workshops and instructive sexual films.[36] In Free and Female (1972), women's health bellwether Barbara Seaman urged readers to question gynecologists who pushed regimens without explanation. She argued that this condescension dovetailed with marriage ideology: "To my mind, the most offensive antiwoman propaganda of all is probably contained in the pages of the marriage and family texts that young women (and men, of course) are forced to read in college," that "continually use 'happy' and 'durable' interchangeably."[37]

Cinematic plots were changing. Director/choreographer Bob Fosse's 1972 musical, *Cabaret*, stars Liza Minnelli as Sally Bowles, an American performer living in Weimar Berlin. She chases film roles and sings at the Kit Kat Club, which is overseen by a sexually ambiguous host (Joel Grey). Taken from never-married British writer Christopher Isherwood's short story collection, *Goodbye to Berlin* (1939), via John Van Druten's play, *I Am a Camera* (1951), *Cabaret* centers on Sally's relationship with Brian Roberts (Michael York), a graduate student who teaches English. They commence a love affair and she gets pregnant by him—probably. They've both been quietly seeing the same wealthy aristocrat, Maximilian (Helmut Griem), who quickly exits their lives. Sally accepts Brian's marriage proposal, reconsiders, and terminates the pregnancy; he returns to academic life at Cambridge. The film ends with Brian and Sally's separation marked by a handshake and warm smiles, which imply permanent friendship. Winning eight Academy Awards, *Cabaret* was the movie of its year.

By 1978, only one-quarter of Americans interviewed said that people who chose to remain unwed were maladjusted or morally suspect. By 1979, three-quarters of the population thought it was fine for unmarried adults to raise children.[38] Demographer Judith Blake wrote that increasing nonmarital birth represented a "quiet revolution;" Americans were less convinced that marital fathers validated children and set conditions for their futures.[39] In 1985, anthropologist Wade C. Mackey, who studied "thousands of public child-adult interactions in eighteen societies," published his findings, which state that men and women basically engage with children the same way. Apparently, females have no corner on nurturance.[40]

In 1981 the Center for Disease Control reported five men with a pneumonia seen only in the immunocompromised. These were the first acknowledged cases of AIDS. Ten years later, 230,000 Americans had been diagnosed with the disease. Approximately 150,000 had died. As the HIV virus ravaged America's gay community, people who had never relied on marriage for social support formed networks.[41] In New York City, therapists counseled patients pro bono; hotline volunteers disseminated information about safe sex. Attorneys waived their fees to help patients navigate complex health insurance forms. Chelsea restaurateurs hosted fundraisers. Buyers' clubs like the People with AIDS Health Group made pirated versions of new drugs and alternative therapies available.

Throughout the country, gay men committed to buddy systems. Volunteers escorted AIDS patients to doctors and read to those who had lost their eyesight. ACT-UP activists captured public attention with street theater, ultimately getting government agencies to make experimental medications more quickly available.[42] Among the people AIDS took was a never-married, decorated Vietnam War Veteran named Paul Popham. Founder of the Gay Men's Health Crisis, Popham summed it up: "Although we're paying a terrible price, we're finding in ourselves much greater strength than we dreamed we had."[43]

A 1980s Los Angeles task force suggested awarding domestic partnership to cohabitating Americans who shared immersion in the "common necessities of life."[44] In the 1989 *Braschi v. Stahl Associates Co.* case, a New York State appeals court ruled that beauty salon manager Miguel Braschi could remain in the apartment he had shared for eleven years with Leslie Blanchard. The salon's owner, Blanchard, had died of AIDS. He held the lease on this rent-controlled Midtown Manhattan unit. The court did not protect Braschi from eviction as a renter or Blanchard's lover, though he was both. It safeguarded him as someone in a family:

a group whose crux feature was the "totality of relationship as evidenced by the dedication, caring, and self-sacrifice of the parties."[45] Judges deduced, quite reasonably, that if anyone met these criteria it was Braschi, who had cared for Blanchard during his illness.

Some married people demonstrate mutual dedication; others don't. But no one could plausibly argue that dedication and self-sacrifice exist only within marriage. The court ruled accordingly. Attorney Thomas Stoddard observed, "It's an issue about the right of each individual to enter into a nontraditional, non-orthodox relationship and be protected by law."[46] In this spirit, never-married Boston city councilman David Scondrus prioritized "gaining recognition for an 'extended concept of family.'"[47]

The Obsession

In the 1980s, however, gay rights leaders began inviting government into their bedrooms. It seemed beneficial to do so because matrimony offered so many privileges and gave its adherents such a powerful sense of belonging. As wedlock became a concrete goal for many activists, gay leaders stopped fighting for non-governmental involvement in erotic relationships between adults. In so doing, they distanced themselves from a brilliant legacy of activism.

AIDS is frequently cited as the cause of this shift. Perhaps a deadly, sexually transmitted virus made marriage, and the fidelity it promised, attractive. Others explain gay matrimania as part of something vaster: assimilation into American society that occurred over thirty years and involved relinquishing drag, camp, and other distinct features of homosexual subculture.[48] I find the latter explanation convincing because it gels with accounts of other minority groups' assimilation.[49] As well, the AIDS crisis does not explain wedlock's strong appeal to lesbian women.

Whatever its etiology, the marriage initiative could not launch without rationales. Three basic ideas emerged. The first invoked marital superiority; matrimony had always been the highest commitment anyone could make. So, excluding LGBTQ+ people from wedlock meant denying them the opportunity to scale its sublime peaks. The second argument involved dignity. It said that marriage imbues spouses with noble excellence, so withholding it from homosexuals kept them in a state of degradation. Finally, proponents reasoned that if America wanted to cinch marriage as *the* superior lifestyle it should sanction same-sex wedlock, which would produce more married couples and leave fewer unwed weirdos.

Andrew Sullivan stepped forward as same-sex wedlock's ambassador. He applauded conformity as an excellent development in the gay world: "A need to rebel has quietly ceded to a desire to belong."[50] Sullivan made marriage the source of infinite richness that stood as a reproof to nonmarital life, which he saw as drab, tawdry, and juvenile. In his view, each individual's maturity could be assessed by their propinquity to wedlock.

My closest male friend called Andrew Sullivan "a remarkably boring person." This scholar of medieval literature was in his mid-thirties when he taught me at Oberlin College. He was not waiting for someone to arrive and grant him a reciprocal identity. Never-married anarchist Voltairine de Cleyre's (1866–1912) description of "an all-around person, with both productive and preservative capacities, a being pivoted within," suited him.[51] Lecturing on hagiography or Norse saga, speaking about his books in progress, and visiting multilingual friends, he seemed more immersed in life than most spouses I knew.

We both understood that marriage was the prescribed model.

He ignored the prescribed model, as if it did not apply to him. I had never seen anyone do this with a powerful norm. He seemed never to wonder if being unwed made him less-than. Unusual self-sufficiency partly explains this attitude; I also credit his being gay. During graduate school at Harvard and a teaching stint in Holland, he had had boyfriends. But among his group there was no pressure on amorous pairs to change their names, merge finances, and enact ceremonies in which two people "reduce to one."[52]

This is the person who most powerfully nudged me toward maturity. From our first coffee together, I started to make a connection; if the best professor on campus did not feel like a half-self, awaiting completion in a spouse, I should never view myself that way or crave social constructs to ratify my relationships.

This man gave me my first methods for evaluating literature: close reading and text-based analysis. He showed me how to research across disciplines and warned me that intellectual life would not provide popularity: "No one likes having myths upon which they base their lives questioned." These tools are the best gift anyone has ever given me; I would not trade them for anything.

"Practically every adult who experienced unnecessary suffering in childhood has a story to tell about someone whose kindness, tenderness, and concern restored their sense of hope," writes social theorist bell hooks.[53] "Tenderness" is not the word that leaps to mind regarding my friend. But the time he devoted to my undergraduate self can only be interpreted as concern. If this professor had been married, he could not have created such a wide space in his life for me. And my mental travels would be less rich, my reading less ambitious, my spirit less animated, my family less interesting, and my life less meaningful.

I hope that one day a name exists for this relationship. Among the challenges of constructing "queer" families, anthropologist Kath Weston lists "consistently asserting the importance of relationships that lack social status or even the vocabulary to describe them."[54] Nonmarital people face the same difficulty. As stiff as it sounds, "significant formative relationship" is the best I can do for this bond. *Obergefell v. Hodges* does not honor this designation or protect my friend, who came out before doing so was fashionable and took physical abuse for it in the backwater country where he grew up. If anyone deserves protection by civil rights organizations, he does, but that support cannot rest on marriage. He does not have or want a husband. If he gets sick, he will need assistance. Despite years of mutual devotion, we do not qualify for paid leave under the Family and Medical Leave Act. Yet I could take this leave to nurse someone I barely knew if we were married.

Countless straight people like myself have benefitted from such mentors. Yet Sullivan argued that married people had monopolies on family, love, and maturity because matrimony was a static constant. It never changed. It also changed continuously for the better. Marriage moved from a pragmatic model to a companionate one in the eighteenth century and granted women greater equality in the twentieth century. Its absorption of same-sex pairs would christen this march forward. Such thinkers view wedlock as fixed and mutable without noticing the inconsistency. In this way Sullivan resembled demagogues like William Bennett, Ronald Reagan's Secretary of Education who, at the 1992 Republican Convention in Houston barked, "Some ways of living are better than others."[55]

Same-sex marriage fever energized a powerful normalization initiative. Hunter Madsen and Marshall Kirk's *After the Ball: How America Will Conquer its Fear and Hatred of Gays in the '90s* (1989) was its public-relations handbook. It told LGBTQ+ people to clean up their image; a conventional façade would disarm opponents while helping homosexuals better themselves.

Emerging as same-sex marriage's ambitious young Turk, Evan Wolfson agreed. He published, "Why We Should Fight for the Freedom to Marry" in an academic journal. Because this piece is frequently quoted and anthologized, it bears examination.

Problems appear in the title, which presents marriage as a "freedom." This word denotes liberty and an absence of restrictions. Matrimony has historically provided the opposite: social regulation and circumscribed options. A Canadian musician who needs American citizenship for tax reasons is anything but liberated when he trudges to city hall with his boyfriend. Marriage will lighten his financial burdens while enlisting him as the benefactor of an institution he does not respect. Tax law leaves him minimal freedom and no real choice.

When we consider an actual person's circumstances, matrimony looks like a dubious right. But Wolfson proceeds with a rights-based analysis. He compares gay people's plight to that of interracial couples prior to 1967, when *Loving v. Virginia* struck down bans on mixed-race marriage. This argument is seductive. Any reasonable person knows that white and black people are equal, as straight and LGTBQ+ people are equal. Wolfson leapfrogs from these truths to the claim that marriage best expresses equality. This swift rhetorical move is easily missed. He prophecies that same-sex marriage will level out societal inequities, as *Loving v. Virginia* did.[56]

Actually, when the Supreme Court rendered Virginia's antimiscegenation laws unconstitutional, justices affirmed marriage as "fundamental to our very existence and survival" as a species.[57] This reinforced nonmarital Americans' lesser status. Construction worker Richard Loving's bond with his wife, Mildred, remained a three-way compact between two adults and Virginia. At first the contract rendered them criminals; then they became noncriminals who could be recriminalized for numerous private behaviors.

The Lovings transgressed a reprehensible law: Virginia's Racial Integrity Act. Its ugliness obscured an approach their American Civil Liberties Union lawyers might have taken: challenging as unconstitutional government surveillance of sexual relationships. A precedent-setting result would have enabled the Lovings to stay together as lovers freed from state-imposed constraints—racist or otherwise.

Wolfson didn't mind that *Loving v. Virginia* missed a major point: the state has no place qualifying adults' emotional bonds. He knew that if LGBTQ+ people accepted *Loving* as a beacon they would de facto affirm wedlock as "fundamental." This would mean viewing America's nonmarital alliances as pale facsimiles of the real thing and devaluing that which they helped to create: inspiring conjugal alternatives.

The strangest part of Wolfson's argument, however, is its statement that marriage's provision of benefits makes it a civil right. This claim begs the question. It says, marriage is a right because it confers rights. Reinforcing premises that underlie his case, Wolfson distracts from the real question: why should wedlock provide a single right?

Wolfson, who founded the Respect for Marriage Coalition in 2017, changed course in a July 2011 blog: "Americans understand that marriage is not about rights and benefits. It's about love. And that's the funny thing about love. It belongs to everybody."[58] This assertion flies in the face of his claim: love belongs to everybody who marries or plans to marry. Marriers possess what Wolfson elsewhere identifies as connubial dignity.[59] He assumes that dignity comes from an identification with collective practices and a sense of approval from the larger group, with whose members one marches in lockstep. Wolfson also contends that a license grants dignity.

He is wrong. Dignity stems from regular self-criticism and

admitting one's mistakes. It comes from failing and continuing to try, succeeding but not allowing success to inflate one's self-image. Dignity means taking responsibility for one's life, doing the right thing when no one is looking, championing a worthy but unpopular idea, saying no when saying yes is easy. These behaviors braid with what is resourceful, inventive, and unique in each person. Dignity cannot derive from a piece of paper.

Wolfson's seminal article asks, if interracial couples wouldn't accept second-class citizenship, "why should people facing discrimination based on their gender or sexual orientation, or the gender and sexual orientation of the person they love most, have to accept it either?"[60] I want him to tell me why people facing discrimination based on the nature of our relationships with those we most love should accept second-class status.

Many who did not share Wolfson's perspective remained silent. Challenging same-sex marriage, a nascent cause célèbre, was not for the fainthearted; one could be tagged as a monster. However, some spoke up. Gay gender studies scholar John D'Emilio argued that same-sex wedlock ran counter to contemporary life; matrimony was becoming less central—partly because record numbers of people were coming out.[61] "Why are gay people so anxious to get married?" asked English actress and self-described "dyke," Miriam Margolyes, who lives with Indonesian studies scholar Heather Sutherland: "The thought of referring to one another as 'wife' makes me feel sick."[62] British actor Rupert Everett agreed: "I loathe heterosexual weddings. The wedding cake, the party, the champagne, the inevitable divorce two years later . . . I find it personally beyond tragic that we want to ape this institution that is so clearly a disaster."[63] Historian Martin Duberman remarked sardonically that gay liberation had narrowed its focus to "the loving couple, the tight-knit family—that positions the movement squarely within the framework of a Norman Rockwell painting . . . "[64] These critics understood that wedlock's detrimental features included obsessive hostility to same-sex eroticism. They suggested that repealing marriage as a status-conferrring institution was the best path toward equity; ensconcing gay people within matrimony's system of reward and punishment seemed like a half-hearted measure—a misdirected attack.

Blogger Andrew Sullivan condescending to Professors John D'Emilio and Martin Duberman was a dismaying spectacle. But, any same-sex marriage skeptic risked ostracization on the charge of "ruining marriage for everyone."[65] Farmer Christopher Williams faces this accusation. He lives outside Winston-Salem, North Carolina with two boyfriends. Williams does not believe in wedlock, which would exclude his "threeo." Political commentator Rachel Maddow, who lives in Manhattan with artist Susan Mikula, recently explained, "I feel that gay people not being able to get married for generations . . . meant that we came up with alternative ways of recognizing relationships. And I like gay culture."[66]

Such critiques impugn marriage's channeling of love and sex into nuclear family units. Lambda's Marriage Project and like-minded organizations threw their weight behind this practice, seeking protections for married homosexuals while spiffing up their community's profile in a country where wedlock is an image-enhancer. Understandably, LGBTQ+-marriage activists rebutted the claim that homosexual people could not form healthy families. Unfortunately, they accepted matrimony as the chief indicator of mental health and the sole version of family.

Nonmarital Americans did not meet this juggernaut by asserting ourselves. Most never-married men and women, nonmarital youth, marriage renegades, and marriage refugees stayed silent. Some did not know the biases against nonmarriage embedded in American law. Others knew but found the situation tolerable.

Never-married adults were not, after all, lynched. Nonmarital children were not sent to labor camps. Matrimony disadvantaged millions, but it did not turn their lives into a waking nightmare. When inequities feel livable, acquiesence is easy.

In retrospect, I see a larger problem. Nonmarital history's patterns were invisible to experts, let alone lay people, so non-marriage as a source of strength was hard to see. Contraception was available and sex outside marriage common. But nonmarital relationships were tolerated, married ones enshrined. Putting up with a social phenonmenon (nonmarital life) is one thing; desig-nating it the superior option, as I do here, is quite another.

Obsolescence

During the late twentieth century, increasing numbers of people began building nonmarital lives. Some countries' public policy accommodated them. Since the late 1960s, Sweden has deployed legal neutrality toward significant loving relationships. (Inter-estingly, Swedish children living with unwed caretakers are less likely to experience household interruption than American kids living with bioparents.)[67] In 1979, the European Court of Human Rights issued an opinion protecting nonmarital children in inheri-tance cases. It contended that unequal treatment of marital and nonmarital children might violate the European Convention.[68] Between 1979 and 1996, the number of British lovers cohabiting outside marriage catapulted from one-third of a million to 1.56 million.[69] The 1980s saw the most intense surge in nonmarital births in British history. Thirteen percent of children had been born nonmaritally in 1981; by 1991 the figure was 30 percent.[70] British law made some concessions; as of 1992, cohabiting lovers could receive state compensation if one died in a criminal assault.[71]

At this point more than 300,000 people above the age of sixty-five cohabit nonmaritally in England and Wales—a figure up one third from 2002.[72]

In 1989, the United Nations Convention on the Rights of the Child produced an entitlement program for all children, which disregarded marital birth status.[73] European urban planners began accommodating nonmarital populations. Vienna's Women-Work-City I was designed in 1993. With playgrounds and a doctor's office on site, this 360-apartment complex caters to unpartnered women who care for children.[74]

In 2002, the *New York Times* reported that more than one-third of unwed Italian men between the ages of thirty and thirty-five lived at home. These derisively labeled *mammoni* (mama's boys) were not, as a rule, uneducated or unskilled. They just liked living in houses where they had grown up.[75] More than 70 percent of Iceland's children born in 2018 were nonmarital.[76] More than 60 percent of Japanese men and almost 50 percent of Japanese women between eighteen and thirty-four are not involved in an amorous relationship. And "according to the Japanese magazine, *Joshi Spa!*, 33.5 percent of Japanese people polled believe that marriage is 'pointless.'"[77]

In the 1950s, married couples occupied 80 percent of American Households. By the outset of the twenty-first century, marrieds represented less than 51 percent of all households. The number of homes occupied by marriage-free romantic cohabitants increased by ten times between 1960 and 1998. This growth rate was more than five times the number of overall domestic arrangements. In 1960, one American child in twenty was born outside wedlock; by the century's end the number was one child in three.[78] Between 1966 and 1979 the rate of divorce more than doubled.[79]

Adults residing alone composed one fourth of the nation's households in 1998. The number of people who opted to not marry increased between 1972 and 1998, from 15 to 23 percent. Almost a quarter of America's population was turning away from marriage.[80]

In 1980, the American Census Bureau listed 3.3 million households of dwellers unrelated by blood. By the early twenty-first century this figure had increased to 6.5 million. Between 1980 and 2018, the number of amorous pairs residing nonmaritally increased from 1.6 million to 8.5 million.[81] In 2002, the American Academy of Pediatrics recommended allowing unwed adults to adopt their same-sex lovers' biochildren.[82] In 2017 the Pew Research Center reported that 42 percent of American adults lived without a spouse or lover.[83]

In 2003, the Supreme Court declared unconstitutional Texas's Homosexual Conduct Law, which criminalized oral and anal sex between men. In *Lawrence v. Texas,* justices found Texas to be in violation of Americans' right to privacy, guaranteed by the Fourteenth Amendment. Antisodomy laws in twelve other states were overturned. By this year, practically 40 percent of cohabiting unwed lovers housed children under the age of eighteen. In 2005, Stephanie Coontz could assert that for many Americans, "living together has become an alternative to marriage."[84] In 2011, the Census Bureau affirmed that married couples no longer made up the majority of American households.[85]

The Ontario Court of Appeal ruled, in 2007, that a child could have three legal parents. In this instance it was a boy's biological mother, her girlfriend, and the man who had donated sperm. "This ruling concerns us," said David Quist, executive director of the Institute of Marriage and the Family Canada, an offshoot of Focus on the Family. Of course it did. Any constellation of adults building a nonmarital home raises questions about marital supremacy. Toward this end, the mesh-like families created by LGBTQ+ people have long threatened notions of wedlock as a superior way of life.[86]

"Millennials are not showing many signs of interest in getting hitched as they get older," *Washington Post* journalist Brigid Schulte reported in 2015. "And as a result, the marriage rate is expected to fall by next year to its lowest level to date." Many millennials did (and do) marry, but a 2015 Gallup report showed a parallel tendency: avoiding romantic cohabitation. Only 16 percent of all millennials were married; 14 percent of those between the age of eighteen and twenty-nine described themselves as living with a romantic partner. In the United States, 27 percent of white women were unmarried when they gave birth to children; 75 percent of black women were unwed.[87]

Matrimony was no longer America's default lifestyle. Media imagery of coupling remained potent, but numbers told another story. That most enshrined abode—a home with married parents and natal children—accounted for a fifth of all American households. A haloed institution was turning out to not be many people's first choice. A once coveted license was becoming expendable. Not quite obsolete, marriage was starting to look obsolescent: potent but on its way out.

Literary critic Donald R. Howard believes that at such junctures, preservationists emerge. They set about enshrining a past that is not quite past, in an effort "to forestall what is to come."[88] Indeed, at the point when matrimony seemed imperilled, a cadre of enthusiasts—same-sex marriage proponents—began shoring it up.

Because wedlock had long vilified same-sex eroticism, it was an ironic platform for LGBTQ+ self-identification. At one level, though, a natural connection existed; gay men were a mainstay of America's wedding industry, fueling its ranks with gown designers, florists, makeup artists, and event coordinators. Gay lifestyle gurus like Preston Bailey and Colin Cowie authored books such as *Fantasy Weddings* (2004) and *Wedding Chic: 1001 Ideas for Every Moment of Your Celebration* (2008).

David Tutera's 2010 wedding primer starts with a bang: "You're engaged! *Congratulations!* Finally, you're en route to the day you've been waiting for *your entire* life . . . "[89] Tutera seems to believe that every woman frantically anticipates her wedding. He appears unaware that many marry to secure an inheritance, qualify for subsidized housing, or mollify an insistent boyfriend. These motivations influenced the married women in my circle, none of whom exhaled in relief when a diamond ring materialized.

America's ranks of never-married women now include celebrities. The most prominent is Oprah Winfrey, whose humble origins (in Kosciusko, Mississippi) are well known. She left Tennessee State University before graduating when her broadcasting career took off. In 1984 she was asked to steward a flagging Chicago program on WLS-TV. This became *The Oprah Winfrey Show*, which ran for twenty-four seasons. A nonmaritally born powerhouse, Winfrey lobbied for the National Child Protection Act, which was signed into law in 1993. It mandated establishing a national database containing indictments and convictions for child abuse.

Winfrey lives in Chicago, Montecito, and Maui with businessman Stedman Graham. She has publicly stated that they will not marry and is famously loyal to her best friend, broadcaster Gayle King. Winfrey celebrates their bond and weighs it equally with her romantic partnership.

According to Winfrey, the best day of her life wasn't a wedding. It happened in 2002, when she brought presents to impoverished children in South Africa. At one point, 183 kids opened their gifts simultaneously: "The joy in the room was so thick, you could physically feel it." Winfrey relayed the experience to a *TV Guide* interviewer, who seemed confused: Didn't she worry that Graham would stray without marriage's constraints? Did Winfrey and King really wear matching diamond rings to honor their friendship? "Why not have it all?" the journalist prodded. "If I were a wife and a mother, I wouldn't be open to this experience," Winfrey replied. "I wouldn't have had the space in my life to embrace the world's children, because I would be taking care of my own children."[90]

Winfrey has discarded every component of the modern marital equation: togetherness is not institutionalized; relationships are chosen; licensure doesn't impinge; blood doesn't matter; female independence prevails. Retrograde cornballs like Tutera forgot Winfrey as they presented blueprints for *pièce-de-résistance* nuptials; same-sex marriage advocates conveniently overlooked her.

In 1993, Hawaii's supreme court found that that state's ban on same-sex marriage might be discriminatory. Its opinion defined marriage as "a state-conferred legal partnership status, the existence of which gives rise to a multiplicity of rights and benefits reserved for that particular relation."[91] Organizations like Lambda's Marriage Project circulated petitions and enlisted Hollywood power players, with whom their agenda became popular.[92] "One sign of obsolescence is nostalgia," writes Howard. "Another is renewal. Nostalgia produces all kinds of efforts to force renewal upon obsolescent things."[93] With its strenuous Victorian aesthetic (lace gowns, tiered cakes, tuxedo-clad gentlemen), nothing could be more nostalgic than the blockbuster wedding.

Then came the preemptive Defense of Marriage Act (1996). It defined matrimony as heterosexual and released each state from honoring same-sex marriages performed in other states. The bill's endorsers made hysterical slippery slope arguments about what would follow same-sex wedlock: adults would date toddlers, men would romance poodles, women would marry dolphins ... Missouri Congressman James M. Talent sentimentalized the marriage-based family as a bastion of "ordered liberty." North Carolina senator Jesse Helms reminded everyone how "sacred" wedlock was.[94] (By extension, nonmarriage was spiritually bereft.) Ironically, LGBTQ+-marriage advocates shared these beliefs. Both camps used identical marriage-idealizing language. As Nancy F. Cott writes, same-sex wedlock proponents were giving marriage "renewed honor."[95]

The Bandwagon

By the twenty-first century, same-sex marriage advocacy was *de rigueur,* as evinced by a media trend: profiles in which gay couples rake leaves, toss salads, and read children bedtime stories, usurping the relationship style of heterosexual culture, which Sullivan and Wolfson deemed superior. *Elle Décor's* February 2010 issue features photos of fashion designers Mark Badgley and James Mischka's Lexington, Kentucky, farmhouse. Two pillow shams monogrammed with the designers' respective names sit side by side on the main bed.[96]

Articles that showed gay husbands doing yard work, cohosting cocktail parties, and handing out Halloween treats were not just advertisements for same-sex marriage. They were advertisements for marriage. None came with the disclaimer, *Nonmarital Americans don't have the same rights as married ones!* No counterbalancing puff pieces dramatized nonmarital American's lives. Glossy magazines portrayed same-sex matrimony as an undeniable good. *Obergefell v. Hodges* exemplifies the power of our nation's media—particularly venues that do not report hard news.

In a recent television interview author Dan Savage explained how movement leaders realized that the term "same-sex marriage" was causing strategic problems. Though "sex" did not denote sexual activity, the term evoked images of men sodomizing men and women performing cunnilingus on women. Age, upbringing, or religion prevented some Americans from comfortably considering such acts. "Same-sex marriage" was therefore replaced with "marriage equality."[97] Paradoxically, this sanitizing move denuded homosexuality and lesbianism of sex. The new phrase was insidious in other ways: say "marriage equality" fast enough, and it sounds inclusive. The noun "equality" connotes identical rights and opportunities for all. Activists were not making this demand. They wanted privileges for LGBTQ+ marrieds only.

Theodore Olson and David Boies were commissioned in 2009 to push same-sex wedlock forward in California, where a ban stood. This bipartisan legal duo showed marriage's ideological entrenchment among Republicans and Democrats. Serial marriers with seven wives between them, they rode the "dignity of marriage" horse from California's district court to the Supreme Court.[98] They did not call Sommers Point, New Jersey, carpenter Frank DiPasquale and ask how dignified he felt being "strip searched, handed a bright orange jumpsuit, and thrown in county jail for loss of employment and not having the ability to pay his support." Pasquale, who was ordered to pay life alimony to a registered nurse, says he lives on $118.76 biweekly, after his wages are garnished.[99] Olson and Boies were too busy venerating wedlock to worry about its casualties. They stated that withholding matrimony from gay people "labels their families as second rate," affixing to them a "badge of inferiority."[100]

Shortly thereafter, same-sex marriage became a fait accompli with the *United States v. Windsor* (2013) case. Here the Supreme Court found unconstitutional restricting words like "spouse" to opposite-sex couples. IBM technology manager Edith Windsor lived in Manhattan with psychologist Thea Spyer. They had married in Canada. Spyer died at age seventy-seven. As her legatee, Windsor was charged $363,000 in estate taxes. She claimed the marital exemption that would eliminate this tax. The Internal

Revenue Service turned her down. The Supreme Court backed her up in an opinion that rested on the Fifth Amendment's Due Process Clause.[101]

This clause preserves the ideal of even-handedly administering justice. *United States v. Windsor* betrayed this principle by preserving tax privilege for married Americans and leaving the rest to deal with sometimes staggering bills. The response should have been a public debate centered on the question: "How can federal law discriminate blatantly against nonmarital Americans of all sexual orientations?" But same-sex marriage proponents were busy celebrating. *Time* magazine's staff was busy short-listing Windsor for its Person of the Year Award. Nonmarital people lacked a leader prominent enough to make this query heard. We had no one like Hillary Clinton or Barack Obama, both of whom somersaulted from the anti-LGBTQ+ marriage faction to the marriage-equality camp.[102] America's most influential policymakers were joining the same-sex wedlock march. None even mentioned nonmarital rights.

While politicians like San Diego mayor Kevin Faulconer probably started supporting same-sex wedlock to stay current, they must have seen how it fit on the American politician's list of compulsory fixations: nuclear family, privatized dependence, and sexual respectability. In 2014, writer Eli Lehrer praised same-sex marriage for bringing down the number of "illegitimate" births in America.[103] As Polikoff laments, "marriage-equality supporters . . . invoke the specter of illegitimacy and quote marriage movement rhetoric about child well-being."[104]

Clergy who guide young people often share this tendency. Daniel Alder, the rabbi of a Conservative synagogue in Manhattan's Gramercy Park neighborhood, conducted fashion editor Ariel Foxman and high school principal Brandon Cardet Hernandez's upscale 2013 wedding.[105] Here's a sample of Alder's philosophy, an essay based on Arthur Schopenhauer's parable in which porcupines can't get close to each other without pricks from their quills:

> We have learned in our society to keep a distance from each other . . . And now we are lonely but the human being, unlike the porcupine, can rationalize and make a virtue out of even this loneliness and call this loneliness "independence." I am independent, I am an individual, I am not a joiner, I am a nonconformist, I am self-sufficient. And so successful is this independence, this exalted notion of imperial self that social psychologists note that there is isolation even from family that may live in the same home.[106]

I am temperamentally independent. I am not a joiner. I am a nonconformist. None of this makes me an isolate. I have a beautiful nonmarital family. I am close to some people I grew up in the same home with and not others. I don't harbor the illusion that people thrust together through biological accident will experience lifelong intimacy. A marriage license creates no obligation on the part of a couple's offspring to remain entwined.

I've read and thought enough to make these claims. I fear for young grooms who hear that deviating from conjugal norms is grandiose. They probably know relatively little about wedlock's history. In terms of judging its value, their rabbi serves as a guide. If he admires conventionalism, as Alder does, the dominant view is not just what they will hear; it is all they will hear. It is probably all they want to hear; weddings now earn LGBTQ+ people brownie points with important people in their lives.

I wonder if Alder's students know how harshly the Talmud, Judaism's compendium of religious law assembled between the third and eighth centuries, condemns nonmarriage: "Any Jew who does not have a wife is not a man";[107] "A man who is twenty years old and has not yet wed is spending all his days in sin."[108] Indeed, I sometimes envy my nonmarital brothers and sisters who practice Catholicism, Buddhism, and other faiths with vibrant nonmarital traditions. Rich as it is, Judaism offers little in this respect. It considers wedlock the relationship par excellence. Classical Hebrew lacked a term to denote a never-married woman, as if such a creature boggled the mind. Weddings remain a central part of Jewish life, with seven special blessings uttered for brides and grooms. These include thanking God for granting them the happiness Adam and Eve knew in Eden. Adam and Eve were not married. Nevertheless, Jewish nuptials advertise matrimony as a return to paradise.

Foxman and Cardet Hernandez surely know that *Lawrence v. Texas* decriminalized homosexuality. Its origins may be unfamiliar to them: Robert Eubanks and his sometimes boyfriend, Tyron Garner, visited a medical technologist named John Lawrence, Jr. at his apartment outside Houston. Garner and Lawrence hit it off, angering a drunk Eubanks. He left, called the Harris County police, and lied, claiming that Garner was brandishing a gun. Officers appeared at Lawrence's home; what they found involved no firearms. They charged Lawrence and Garner with deviate sexual intercourse. Their case eventually reached the Supreme Court with a positive outcome, but it began with an irate lover's fabrications.[109] Chapters 5 and 6 show straight people deploying law maliciously. *Lawrence v. Texas's* backstory suggest that a percentage of LGBTQ+ marrieds will do the same. This alone calls into question an institution that polices Americans' private lives.

Nonmarital people need public forums that question matrimony. This is a tough case to make when marital triumphalism dominates highbrow media. On June 27, 2017, the *New Yorker* nodded to *Obergefell v. Hodges's* one-year anniversary with a cover illustration in which two men kiss, with Manhattan's skyline as a backdrop. This cover sends a message: all is well.

For the Good of the Children: "Experts" Weigh In

Statisticians attached to the theory that marriage is great and LGBTQ+ marriage greater are making news. A recent *USA Today* headline reads, "Fewer US Teens Attempted Suicide in States Where Same-Sex Marriage was Legal in the Years Leading up to the 2015 Supreme Court Ruling Upholding Gay Marriage, According to a New Study."[110]

Here's what happened: four researchers got together. The lead, Julia Raifman, came from Johns Hopkins's Bloomberg School of Public Health. Another represented Harvard's Department of Global Health Population. Between 1999 and 2015, this team disseminated a survey among 700,000 adolescents from forty-seven states; 231,413 respondents defined themselves as gay, lesbian, or bisexual. The researchers masticated results and purported to find a 7 percent decrease in suicide attempts among high schoolers in the thirty-two states that had legalized same-sex marriage.[111]

The survey relied on self-reporting. One can imagine young respondents mistaking suicidal ideation (a common phenomenon) for an actual suicide plan. The researchers could have handled this problem by using documented rates of teen suicide. They chose to ignore this information, explaining that it was not worth considering since teen suicide is rare. Yet two years earlier the journal that published their study warned that teenage suicide was "one of the three top causes of death for US teens."[112]

Scientists optimally avail themselves of the most reliable evidence: here, recorded suicide deaths, which constitute an undeniable data point. These researchers chose the least reliable evidence. They shaped a study around the topic of LGBTQ+ marriage, asking—perhaps prodding—respondents to see its connection to suicide. Intermittently depressed teens filling out the document could conclude that same-sex marriage—why not?—had prevented them from trying to take their lives.

Surveys are complicated by a "nonresponse bias." How do researchers interpret the number of people who don't return their mailings? Each nonresponder represents an unkown. En masse, however, nonrespondents reveal a lot. If the majority of recipients discard a survey, it means they don't care about its subject.

These researchers have withheld state-by-state response rates of teens who got their quiz. Only five states targeted may have reached the 50 percent level of response, which is when a survey becomes statistically significant. This omission alone makes it impossible to determine their work's validity.

The statisticians also tampered with their numbers in a method called "weighting." It could more accurately be called "bullshitting." Weighting involves inferences based on existing results. Here, the team inferred, from states with reasonably high response rates, what other subjects would probably have said had they replied. Simply put, the researchers made things up. They also ignored crux determinants: subjects' socioeconomic status, religious affiliation, and location. The self-reported nonsuicidal group could have been affluent. The purportedly suicidal group might have been dominated by kids living below the poverty line. Clearly, poverty has an enormous effect on mental health, as does region. Denizens of Ithaca, New York, feel different during February than residents of Miami, Florida. Sub-zero temperatures exacerbate depression, whether lesbians are thowing bridal showers or not.

One could find many components that associate with the study's findings. Fewer car accidents and better school attendance might coincide with LGBTQ+ marriage's legalization. But no one could prove that same-sex betrothals caused these positives. A "make news" study like this was designed to show causation between pro-marriage legislation and suicide attempts, when it fails to prove any association. A nonstatistician can see the problem with yoking one complex phenomenon (self-inflicted death among teenagers) to another (state legislation of same-sex wedlock). One might note a suicide drop in states where recreational marijuana laws are passed or college tuitions lowered. In each case it would be tempting to shape a cause-and-effect narrative about dipping teen suicide rates. This temptation would have to be resisted, because a policy change's quantifiable psycho-social impact cannot be proven.

"Gay Marriages Are Less Likely to Break Up Than Straight Ones, Study Reveals," a 2018 article proclaims.[113] UCLA Law School's Williams Institute sponsored the project this British headline alludes to. Researchers tracked 515 Vermont-based couples and concluded that gay male spouses were likelier to stay hitched than lesbian or straight pairs. A tiny sample group of people living in one state probably can't show much about any social initiative. And the headline distorts researchers' findings through omission. It also substitutes a simplistic question for a complex one: should two men pledge to love each other for sixty years, promise to eschew sex with anyone else, and ask state permission to be a family?

A media trend like this will strengthen prejudices against nonmarital people of all sexual orientations. It will imply that we are depressives who pull the culture down. Accordingly, divorced people are duds who took the marriage test and failed—not brave souls who ended mediocre relationships. Fancily educated researchers will give these misconceptions prestige. Journalists' ears will perk up, and headline-addicted Americans will read dumbed-down accounts of flawed experiments.

Reporters who interview me often mention "hundreds of studies" that prove marriage's benefits. There are not hundreds of such studies. In a post *Obergefell v. Hodges* climate, I fear successive waves of "research" that show matrimony delivering every variety of miracle. Armed with the right questions, we can deflate such reports.

(Endnotes)

1   I use the acronym "LGBTQ+" with trepidation. In my experience, transgender people contend that their status is unrelated to sexual attraction, and their leaders concur. In 2015, former Olympic-decathlon medalist Caitlyn Jenner told journalist Diane Sawyer that erotic attraction and sexual identity were like "apples and oranges." I therefore don't understand why "T" is clustered with "L,""G,"and "B." If these identities are unrelated, why should the same term encompass them? The modifier "queer" is imprecise. In academia it can mean gay, hardcore gay, bisexual, erotically transgressive, or resistant to belief systems tangentially connected with sexuality. What the plus sign indicates has been explained to me in different ways. These confusions may be my own, but I feel obliged to note them. When referring to specific people, I use the language they apply to themselves. German Lopez, "Myth #2: Sexual Orientation is Linked to Gender," *Vox*, November 14, 2018, https://www.vox.com/identities/2016/5/13/17938096/trans-gender-people-sexual-orientation-gender-identity.

2   Mikael Wood, "Same-Sex Marriage Ruling: Pop Stars React (and Mostly Rejoice) on Twitter," *Los Angeles Times*, June 26, 2015, http://www.latimes.com/nation/la-et-ms-same-sex-marriage-pop-react-20150626-story.

3   *The Trouble with Normal*, 112.

4   Ibid., 109.

5   *How We Live Now*: *Redefining Home and Family in the 21st Century* (New York: Artia Books, 2015), 249.

6   Boswell, *Christianity, Social Tolerance*, 10.

7   See Allan Massie for an account of James I's erotic tastes and relationship with George Villiers, the Duke of Buckingham (1592–1628). *The Royal Stuarts: A History of the Family That Shaped Britain*. New York: Thomas Dunne Books, 2010, 174–5.

8   *Wedlocked*, 9.

9   Cott, *Public Vows*, 24.

10 Christina Oehler lauds anti-adultery laws in her repellent article, "16 States Where You Can Get That Cheating Jerk Thrown in Jail," *Woman's Day*, June 23, 2016, http://www.womansday.com/relation-ships/dating-marriage/a50994/adultery-laws.

11 "Obergefell et al v. Hodges, Director, Ohio Department of Health, et al. https://www.supremecourt.gov/opinions/14pdf/14-556_3204.pdf.

12 "Gay Marriage Hurts My Breasts," *Yasmin Nair: Writer, Academic,*

Activist, Commentator. http://www.yasminnair.net. June 25, 2015.

13 "Single? Married? Broken Up? Your Relationship Status Affects Your Wealth. Here's What You Need to Know," *Glamour*, February 2018, 74.

14 Ibid., 72.

15 *The Trouble With Normal*, 61.

16 Tara Siegel Bernard, "Fate of Domestic Partner Benefits in Question After Marriage Ruling," *New York Times*, June 28, 2015, https://www.nytimes.com/2015/06/29/your-money/fate-of-domestic-partner-benefits-in-question-after-marriage-ruling.

17 Franke, *The Perils of Marriage Equality*, 145–6.

18 "A Right Not to Marry," *Fordham Law Review* 84, no. 4 (2016): 1549.

19 Aaron Kraut, "County Council Repeals Employee Benefits for Domestic Partners,"*Bethesda Magazine*, June 29, 2016: http://www.bethesdamagazine.com/Bethesda-Beat/Web-2016/County-Council-Repeals-Employee-Benefits-for-Domestic-Partners.

20 *The Madness of Crowds: Gender, Race, and Identity* (London: Bloomsbury Continuum, 2019), 19.

21 Michael Bronski, *A Queer History of the United States* (Boston: Beacon Press, 2011), 209–11.

22 Vivian Gornick, "The Next Great Moment in History is Theirs," *The Village Voice*, November 27, 1969, 11.

23 *Mothering* (Cambridge: Harvard University Press, 1977), 103–4.

24 Polikoff, *Beyond (Straight and Gay)*, 26–9.

25 Ibid., 30–3.

26 "National Black Feminist's Organization's Statement of Purpose," *Feminism in Our Time: The Essential Writings, World War II to the Present*, ed. Miriam Schneir (New York: Vintage Books, 1994), 173.

27 Ibid., 33.

28 Quoted in Warner, *The Trouble With Normal*, 90.

29 *Strange Bedfellows*, 36.

30 "Not for Us All, the Wedding Ring," *The Advocate*, October 14, 1970, 2, 7.

31 Kath Weston, *Families We Choose: Lesbians, Gays, and Kinship* (New York: Columbia University Press, 1991), 107.

32 Jim Downs, *Stand by Me: The Forgotten History of Gay Liberation* (New York: Basic Books, 2016), 53.

33 Lillian Faderman, *The Gay Revolution: The Story of a Struggle* (New York: Simon & Schuster, 2015), 297.

34 Murray, *The Madness*, 295.

35 Tim Fitzsimons, "Forty Years After His Death, Harvey Milk's Legacy

Still Lives On," NBC.com, November 27, 2018, https://www.nbcnews.com/feature/nbc-out/forty-years-after-his-death-harvey-milk-s-legacy-still.

36   Jane Gerhard, *Desiring Revolution: Second-Wave Feminism and the Rewriting of American Sexual Thought, 1920–1982* (New York: Columbia University Press, 2001), 49.

37   *Free and Female* (Greenwich, Connecticut: Fawcett Publications, Inc., 1972), 224.

38   Coontz, *Marriage*, 258.

39   "Structural Differentiation and the Family: A Quiet Revolution," *Societal Growth*, ed. Amos Hawley (New York: Free Press, 1979), 191–4.

40   Lewellyn Hendrix, *Illegitimacy and Social Structures: Cross-Cultural Perspectives* (Westport, Connecticut: Bergin & Garvey, 1996), 5.

41   Charles Kaiser, *The Gay Metropolis: The Landmark History of Gay Life in America* (New York: Grove, 1997), 330.

42   Rory Dicker, *A History of U.S. Feminisms* (Berkeley: The Seal Press, 2016), 115.

43   Kaiser, *The Gay Metropolis*, 325.

44   Ibid., 55.

45   Polikoff, *Beyond (Straight and Gay)*, 57.

46   Robert Bellafiore, "Gay 'Widower' Challenges Definition of Family Member in NY Rent Control Laws," *Los Angeles Times*, April 9, 1989, http://articles.latimes.com/1989-04-09/news/mn-1715_1_rent-control-laws-miguel-braschi-leslie-blanchard.

47   Weston, *Families*, 1.

48   Daniel Harris makes this argument in *The Rise and Fall of Gay Culture* (New York: Hyperion, 1997).

49   Two books that align with Harris's analysis are *Fighting to Become Americans: Jews, Gender, and the Anxiety of Assimilation*, Riv-Ellen Prell (Boston: Beacon Press, 1999) and *Translating America: An Ethnic Press Visualizes American Popular Culture*, Peter Conolly Smith (Washington, DC: Smithsonian Press, 2004).

50   "Here Comes the Groom: A (Conservative) Case for Gay Marriage," *The New Republic*, August 28, 2009, https://newrepublic.com/article/79054/here-comes-the-groom.

51   "They Who Marry Do Ill," *The Voltairine de Cleyre Reader*, ed. A. J. Brigati (Oakland, AK Press, 2004), 17.

52   "Equality and Non-hierarchy in Marriage: What Do Feminists Really Want?", *After Marriage*, ed. Elizabeth Brake, 120.

53   *All About Love: New Visions* (New York: Harper Perennial, 2001), 132.

54 *Families*, 212.

55 "Remarks by William Bennett, Former Secretary of Education, at the Republican Party Convention's Nomination of Dan Quayle for US Vice President," Forerunner.com, August 19, 1992, http://forerunner.com/forerunner/X0407_Remarks_by_William_B.

56 "Why We Should Fight for the Right to Marry," *Journal of Gay, Lesbian, and Bisexual Identity* 1, no. 1 (1996), 79–89.

57 Quoted in Coontz, *Marriage*, 256.

58 "Why Marriage Matters: Let's Start the Conversation," *The Huffington Report* (blog), February 9, 2011, https://www.huffingtonpost.com/evan-wolfson/why-marriage-matters.

59 *Why Marriage Matters: America, Equality, and Gay People's Right to Marry* (New York: Simon & Schuster, 2004), 194.

60 "Why We Should Fight."

61 John D'Emilio, "The Marriage Fight is Setting Us Back," *The Gay and Lesbian Review* 13, no. 6 (2006), http://mjohnso9.myweb.usf.edu/2007%20Research/demilio-article.pdf.

62 "Margolyes: 'Why Are Gay People So Anxious to Get Married?'", *Jewish News*, June 19, 2016, https://jewishnews.timesofisrael.com/margolyes-why-are-gay-people-so-anxious-to-get-married.

63 Quoted in Tom Heyden and Lucy Townsend, "The People Who Oppose Gay Marriage Law," BBC News, March 26, 2014. https://www.bbc.com/news/magazine-26634214.

64 *Has the Gay Movement Failed?* (Berkeley: University of California Press, 2018), 163.

65 Victor M. Feraru, "Will Polygamy Have Its Day in the Sun?", *HuffPost* Queer Voices (blog), July 23, 2013. http://www.huffingtonpost.com/victor-lopez/will-polygamy-have--its-day-in-the-sun_b_3629785.

66 Marisa Guthrie, "Rachel Maddow: How This Wonky-Tonk Woman Won TV," *The Hollywood Reporter*, October 5, 2011, https://www.hollywoodreporter.com/news/rachel-maddow-msnbc-243775.

67 Traister, *All the Single Ladies*, 239.

68 International Justice Resource Center, Children's Rights, https://ijrcenter.org/thematic-research-guides/childrens-rights/#Birth_out_of_Wedlock_and_Adoption.

69 Probert, *The Changing Legal Regulation*, 226.

70 Ibid., 230.

71 Ibid., 239.

72 *Sun* Reporter, "TAX BLOW: Rise in Number of Older Couples Living Together Unmarried Could Lead Them to Miss Out on Tax Pension Benefits," *The Sun*, May 34, 2017. https://www.thesun.co.uk/

money/3635282/rise-in-number-of-older-couples-living-together-unmarried-could-lead-them-to-miss-out-on-tax-and-pension-benefits.

73   United States Treaty Collection, Chapter IV, Human Rights, Convention on the Rights of the Child, New York: November 1989.

74   Odette Chalaby, "How Vienna Designed a City for Women," *Apolitical*, August 13, 2017, https://apolitical.co/solution_article/vienna-designed-city-women.

75   Alan Riding, "Italian Court Rules That Son Knows Best About Leaving Home," *New York Times*, April 6, 2002, https://www.nytimes.com/2002/04/06/world/italian-court-rules-that-son-knows-best-about-leaving-home.

76   Manvir Singh, "Is Marriage Over?" *Aeon*, March 31, 2020, https://aeon.co/essays/marriage-is-dead-long-live-marriage-how-will-we-couple-up.

77   Traister, *All the Single Ladies*, 238.

78   Coontz, *Marriage*, 264.

79   Ibid., 261.

80   Cott, *Public Vows*, 203.

81   Singh, "Is Marriage Over?"

82   Coontz, *Marriage*, 272.

83   Rhaina Cohen, "What if Friendship, Not Marriage Was at the Center of Life?", *The Atlantic*, October 20, 2020, https://www.theatlantic.com/family/archive/2020/10/people-who-prioritize-friendship-over-romance.

84   Coontz, *Marriage*, 272.

85   Sabrina Tavernise, "Married Couples Are No Longer a Majority, the Census Finds," *New York Times*, May 26, 2011, https://www.nytimes.com/2011/05/26/us/26marry.

86   Tim Lai, "Court Rules Boy Has Dad and 2 Moms," *Toronto Star*, January 3, 2007, https://www.thestar.com/news/2007/01/03/court_rules_boy_has_dad_and_2_moms.

87   Franke, *Wedlocked*, 86.

88   *The Idea of the Canterbury Tales* (Berkeley: University of California Press, 1976), 90.

89   *The Big White Book of Weddings: A How-to Guide for the Savvy, Stylish Bride* (New York: St. Martin's Griffin, 2010), 1.

90   Michael Logan, "The Power of One," *TV Guide*, October 4, 2003. Quoted in DePaulo, *Singled Out*, 261.

91   Hawai'i Supreme Court, *Baehr v. Lewin*, May 5, 1993, http://gaymarriage.procon.org/sourcefiles/baehr-v.-lewin-gay-marriage-case-hawaii.pdf.

92   Polikoff, *Beyond (Straight and Gay)*, 91.

93   Howard, *The Idea*, 92.

94   Quoted in Cott, *Public Vows*, 221.

95   Ibid., 225.

96   Julia Reed, "At Home with Badgley Mischka: The Design Teams *[sic]* Getaway is Where Thoroughbred Horses and High Style meet," *Elle Décor*, February 27, 2010, http://www.elledecor.com/design-decorate/house-interiors/g170/at-home-badgley-mischka.

97   *Real Time with Bill Maher*, HBO, July 4, 2017.

98   Lionel Barber, "VF Portrait: David Boies and Theodore Olson," *Vanity Fair*, June 17, 2014, https://www.vanityfair.com/news/politics/2014/07/david-boies-theodore-olson-marriage-equality.

99   Jeffrey Dobkin, ed., *Shattered Lives*.

100 *Hollingsworth v. Perry*, Brief for Respondents on Writ of Certiorari to the United States Court of Appeals for the Ninth Circuit, https://www.afer.org/wp-content/uploads/2013/02/2013-02-Plaintiffs -Brief.pdf.

101 Brigit Katz, "What to Know About Iconic Gay Rights Activist Edith Windsor," *Smithsonian Magazine*, September 13, 2017, https://www.smithsonianmag.com/smart-news/iconic-lgbt-activist-edith-windsor-has-died.

102 Amy Sherman, "Hillary Clinton's Changing Position on Same-Sex Marriage," *Politifact*, June 17, 2015, http://www.politifact.com/truth-o-meter/statements/2015/jun/17/hillary-clinton/hillary-clinton-change-position-same-sex-marriage. Phil Gast, "Obama Announces He Supports Same-Sex Marriage," CNN, May 9, 2012, https://www.cnn.com/2012/05/09/politics/obama-same-sex-marriage.

103 Gay Marriage: Good; Polyamory: Bad," *HuffPost*, January 21, 2014, https://www.huffpost.com/entry/gay-marriage-good-polyamo_b_4165423.

104 *Beyond (Straight and Gay)*, 102.

105 Bob Morris, "A Relationship with Style and Substance," the *New York Times*, December 26, 2014, https://www.nytimes.com/2014/12/28/fashion/weddings/a-relationship-with-style-and-substance.

106 "Introducing the Havurah to the Brotherhood Synagogue," *Brotherhood Synagogue Newsletter*, October 2017, http://brotherhoodsynagogue.org.

107 BT, *Yebamot*, 63a. I refer to William Davidson's digital edition of the Koren Noé Talmud, Commentary by Rabbi Adin Even Israel Steinsalz, https://www.sefaria.org/new-home.

108 Ibid., Kiddushin, 29b.

109 Dahlia Lithwick, "Extreme Makeover: *The Story Behind the Story of*

Lawrence v. Texas," the *New Yorker*, March 12, 2012, https://www.newyorker.com/magazine/2012/03/12/extreme-makeover-dahlia-lithwick.

110 Steph Solis, *USA Today*, February 20, 2017, https://www.usatoday.com/story/news/nation/2017/02/20/teen-suicide-down-as-same-sex-marriage-legalized-study.

111 Julia Raifman, Ellen Moscoe, S. Bryn Austin, et al, "Difference-in-Differences Analysis of the Association Between State Same-Sex Marriage Policies and Adolescent Suicide Attempts," *JAMA Pediatrics* 171, no. 4 (April 2016): 350–5.

112 Megan Moreno, "Preventing Adolescent Suicide," *JAMA Pediatrics* 170, no. 10 (October 2016): 1032, https://jamanetwork.com/journals/jamapediatrics/fullarticle.

113 Josh Jackman, *Pink News*, March 25, 2018, https://www.pinknews.co.uk/2018/03/25/gay-marriages-are-less-likely-to-break-up-than-straight-ones-study-reveals.

8

Toward an Ethic of Nonmarital Life

"Whatever is attempted without previous certainty of success, may now be considered as a project, and amongst narrow minds may, therefore, expose its author to censure and contempt; and if the liberty of laughing be once indulged, every man will laugh at what he does not understand, every project will be considered as madness, and every great or new design will be censured as a project. Men unaccustomed to reason and researches think every enterprise impracticable, which is extended beyond common effects or comprises many intermediate operations."

—SAMUEL JOHNSON, ADVENTURER 99

Relationship-Status Discrimination: The Problem That Has Never Had a Name

No one group is solely responsible for America's devaluation of nonmarital life. Stereotypes of stunted bachelors, bitter spinsters, and deviant nonmarital children trace to numerous sources. Prejudices about nonmonogamous people being unstable, celibate adults being emotionally delayed, and marriage renegades being selfish are multifactorial. Seventeenth-century treatises of preachers like William Gouge, twentieth-century primers of "experts" like Sidonie Gruenberg, and contemporary diatribes of pundits like Andrew Sullivan have sold wedlock as the basis of a meaningful life. Twentieth-century abstinence-only education programs distinguished sharply between licit (marital) and illicit (nonmarital) sex, revitalizing Puritan settlers' *idée fixe*. Current fashion magazines contain photospreads featuring designer bridal attire accentuated by captions like, "Head Over Heels" and "Save the Date."[1]

I ask readers to imagine a hypothetical Connecticut couple: Jonathan and Alexandra. After dating for a year, they became engaged because it was the normal step. Alexandra reflexively enrolled in a bridal registry to get household necessities. She vaguely recalled learning, in her college American history class, that Connecticut's Puritan elders graced newlyweds with gifts of land, cash, and "houssehould stuff."[2] But the memory seemed disconnected from her registration. The registry seemed sweet: an older generation's way of helping the next one get its footing.

Furniture, dishes, and housewares from the registry fill Jonathan and Alexandra's Litchfield home. These gifts enabled them to start a healthy savings account. Jonathan works from their attic as a freelance journalist. The media company where Alexandra is an editor covers his health insurance. He may switch plans when he starts writing full time for a new magazine that does restaurant and bar reviews. If the periodical folds he can re-enroll on Alexandra's plan. Jonathan and Alexandra pay lower homeowner's and car insurance than their nonmarital friends do. If Jonathan needs a surgery, Alexandra can take paid time from work to care for him. They are each other's Social Security beneficiaries, so each payment into that system buttresses another savings account. They just celebrated their ten-year anniversary. If they divorce, one can still lay claim to those monies.

Their neighbors, Paul and Isabella, have identical careers. After dating for a year, they decided not to wed, since marriage long constrained women by erasing their legal identities and now traps myriad Americans in unhappy relationships through fear of an abusive family court system.

This decision left them buying their own household necessities and saving less money. Paul cannot freelance; Isabella's company won't put him on her health plan. At the magazine that employs him he earns less than his married colleagues for the same work. Paul and Isabella pay higher insurance bills than their wedded neighbors do; the American Family Leave Act won't let her take time from work if his health fails. They have been together for ten years, yet if one dies their Social Security payments go back into the system. Sometimes, Isabella's coworkers ask when they'll marry. When she says, "Never" and explains why, they stare silently at her, as people do when hearing something they consider extremist.

A journalist named Joshua lives across the street with Jane, his best friend of ten years. Joshua spends weekends with his boyfriend, Philip, who resides in Manhattan. Jane identifies as asexual. She derives deep satisfaction from her publishing career and friends. The legal biases that hurt Paul and Isabella disadvantage Joshua and Jane. They are each other's medical emergency contacts but can't take paid leave if a health crisis arises. When purchasing their home, they got less advantageous mortgage options than a married could would have. Though they co-own, Joshua and Jane can't provide each other with health insurance. Social Security won't let them name each other as beneficiaries.

Jane recently became an executive editor. Coworkers know she deserves the promotion but find it sad. They see her as a workaholic who won't let a man into her life. They don't notice that she has a man in her life. Among themselves they wonder what happened in Jane's childhood that made her this way. They theorize about "early attachment" and "trust issues," locutions learned in therapy. Joshua and Jane have approached two agencies about adopting children. Both advised him to marry Philip (who doesn't like kids) and move forward as a couple, without Jane on the application; her presence would create confusion.

The six neighbors consider themselves educated, middle class, and enlightened. When they dine together, these imbalances are not discussed.

A marriage-free nation would treat these three relationships as equal. This would discourage norm-governed liaisons based on flattery. In 1814, Jane Austen described marriage as "of all transactions, the one in which people expect most from others and are least honest themselves."[3] As matters still stand, one or both parties can gush endearments, have third-date sex, and propose while feeling nothing. Matrimony's privileged status makes such performances inevitable. It encourages marital opportunism by ranking erotic relationships highest, demanding that they entail an organic, spontaneous process of romantic bewitchment, and heaping benefits with the issuance of a license.

Shifting the focus from relationship form to relationship function has ameliorative potential. This does not involve iconoclasm or provocation for their own sake. Relationship-status discrimination should engage everyone concerned with equality, because it is overpoweringly real. It can be explained in plain language, through clear examples, without the opaque jargon often used by academics pursuing popular justice agendas, whose words seem somewhat detached from their initial denotations. Widowers' tax exemptions provide a good example. In Florida, any homeowner whose spouse dies gets a $500 rebate on property tax. A cohabiting nonmarital homeowner cannot claim the exemption. This is unfair.

Another academic truism states that individuals (or, rather, "subjects") act without agency. Products of group enculturation, they behave in ways that benefit their collective identities, maintaining dynamics of oppression. They cannot do otherwise, and the worst error a well-intentioned subject can make involves trying to effect change. This will create a repetition of the old pattern in disguised form.

I don't believe this. I think that lobbying to change marriage law and creating new nonmarital customs can produce significant, positive change. In any case, I cannot sit politely, lips pursed, as nonmarital Americans lose rights, organizations that vilify us proliferate, journalists denigrate nonmarriage with baseless claims, and the few nonprofits that represent our concerns shut down. In this atmosphere, nonmarital people had better hang together, or we will dangle separately. Hanging together means acknowledging ourselves as a force, recognizing nonmarital contributions to history, and making those achievements known.

Our diversity makes this difficult. Nonmarital people lack instant recognition. We represent such different groups that our experience resists depiction in a single narrative. Most don't know the extent of our historical disadvantaging. Viewing history through a nonmarital lens will complicate rather than simplify matters. This is a good thing. Identity politics' reductionisms can produce collectivist, one-note thinking. The argument for nonmarital equality encompasses such a multifaceted population that crude sloganeering seems unlikely.

Marriage-free individuals experience our status differently. The best aspects of my life are relationships with people who love, support, and challenge me intellectually. After that come reading and writing. I trace these endowments to being never-married, so this identity, above all others, expresses (if not contains) who I am. Reading alone and practicing yoga with three women unconnected to me by marital or blood ties, bear the stamp of nonmarriage.

For others the absence of matrimony is one blessing among many. Different ways of feeling nonmarital contribute to our richness as a group.

Incomplete historical evidence presents additional challenges. Medievalist Sharon Farmer suspects that fourteenth-century Paris housed many unwed working women living outside religious communities. She is unsure, since this period's French tax records don't list wage earners. French medievals often had regional or work-related monikers. Distinguishing between wives, widows, and never-married women is difficult.[4] Author Saidiya Hartman describes how "state surveillance and police power acted to shape intimate life" during the Harlem Renaissance.[5] In 1922, singer Trixie Smith (1895–1943) recorded the song, "My Man Rocks Me with One Steady Roll." (It may be the source of the term "rock and roll.") The song's sexual content led to Smith's arrest for renting part of her Harlem apartment to a prostitute. The "prostitute," stage-and-screen actress Nettie Berry, roomed with Smith. Criminal charges were dropped. How many nonmarital Harlem Renaissance households were similarly harassed remains unclear.

Hendrickje Stoffels (1626–1663) was a domestic in the Amsterdam home of Holland's greatest painter, Rembrandt Van Rijn (1606–1669). Twenty years her senior, Rembrandt was famous when they met—acclaimed for his realism, achieved through the interplay of color, shadow and light. He was also financially incompetent. When he and Stoffels got together, Rembrandt was subsisting on a legacy from his widow and remained subject to her will, which truncated support if he remarried. He managed to have the document nullified but did not wed Stoffels. In 1654, the local church council summoned Stoffels, told her she was a whore, and banned her from taking communion. She continued to live with Rembrandt, setting up a shop from which to sell his work, commandeering the sales process, and giving birth to a girl. She took her thoughts about nonmarriage to the grave when she died, probably from bubonic plague. Rembrandt's painting of her as the biblical Bathsheba has been praised as a "deeply moving tribute to his concubine."[6] Actually, Stoffels was not Rembrandt's concubine but his boss. She oversaw the commercial aspect of his career, dispensing monies to him. Sensibly, they both recognized this as the best arrangement.

Many artists' biographers and curators ignore their subjects' relationship status. Pittsburgh's Warhol Museum chronicles its subject's humble West Pennsylvania origins. It omits Warhol's bachelorhood and collaborative methods. In the early 1980s, he and never-married painter Jean-Michel Basquiat did a sequence of canvases and the sculpture, "Ten Punching Bags (Last Supper)." "The Last Supper," by never-married sixteenth-century painter Leonardo da Vinci, who was born out of wedlock (to a notary and a Florentine peasant), inspired this painting.[7]

Warhol's collaborative Union Square "factory" was not the first of its kind. Joshua Reynolds (1723–1792) ran a similar operation in London. The never-married Reynolds excelled at portraits. He honed his talent by studying Rembrandt's portraiture and applying what he learned in his Leicester Square studio. A 1780 self-portrait alludes to Rembrandt's "Aristotle Contemplating a Bust of Homer." Admiring a bust of the never-married Michelangelo, Reynolds stands draped in academic regalia from Oxford University, which had awarded him an honorary doctorate.[8]

Reynolds, who had sporadic dalliances with women, lived with his biological sister Frances (1729–1807) for roughly twenty years. Another superb never-married portrait painter, Frances Reynolds worked full time in her Queen Square home after Reynolds died. No one in their circle expressed anxiety that these two were imperiling civilization. Indeed, contemporaries saw their contributions to the visual arts as invaluable.

Surveying these talents, one sees a matrix of nonmarital influence linked across genders and occupations. The individuals may not have perceived their participation in nonmarital history, but to retrospective observers, nonmarriage, originality, and community emerge as constants.

Knowing Our History

Our nation is largely shaped by and for the married. Daily, our interests are sacrificed to what collective wisdom considers a greater good. This happens when a spinster's taxes subsidize the NIH, which restricts travel monies to patients' spouses, or when a bachelor covers at work for his colleague on subsidized leave to care for her postoperative wife. Never-married contenders for university positions self-abnegate when they step aside for faculty-spouse applicants, as professorial hiring committees expect them to. Cultural consensus holds that penalizing and excluding nonmarital people is not an offense. Critical constructivism—in common parlance, Critical Social Justice Theory or "woke" politics—concur. They represent oppression on a spectrum. The most downtrodden are situated at a juncture of numerous identities (e.g., differently abled, female, indigenous). At the continuum's other end are those with intersections of privilege, such as able-bodied male descendants of people who colonized a particular region hundreds of years ago. Everyone has a place on this gamut but nonmarital people, whose disenfranchisement is historically undeniable. This fact casts a glaring light on current campus politics and their preoccupation with rectifying historical imbalances. Unwilling as it is to consider over 1,000 laws and countless customs that marginalize nonmarital people, academia's selective redress project appears inauthentic.

Everywhere, Americans enjoy mocking excessively wealthy people for their supersized homes, bevvies of underlings, and zany purchases. The married person's status does not come from being rich or socially prominent. So, marital/nonmarital inequality is hard to detect for those who take offense at unrestrained displays of privilege. Wedlock does not trip the alarms elicited by corporate moguls, titanic athletes, and movie stars. When nonmarital

Americans help to shift our culture's focus from a few wealthy oligarchs to countless beneficiaries of marital supremacism, a severe imbalance will become obvious.

Matrimaniacs will resist this process by accusing us of immaturity. Andrew Sullivan hurls this *ad hominem* at any LGBTQ+ person resistant to wedlock. It was levelled at me years ago, by an occupational safety consultant named Robin Gillespie over a group dinner in Connecticut. She explained that I was experiencing a phase. She herself had been conjugally critical before getting mature and married. Passing on exciting jobs to remain by her husband's side was the evidence of hardcore maturity. I asked if Robin, a Marxist, thought bestowing exclusive financial benefits on marrieds was fair. She shrugged: "Married couples get support because we have the babies. It will always be that way."

I've since kicked myself for not asking why babyless married couples get the same benefits. But this wouldn't have mattered. Matrimaniacs' pseudoreligion of normalcy provides confidence that sends them soaring above the facts.

To change the misprision that disenfranchising nonmarital people is acceptable, we must start objecting to it. How do we respond to accusations of callowness? I wrote a book. For most nonmarital people this is unrealistic. Becoming conversant in our history is not. There are things we should all know. First: nonmarriage is not a modern phenomenon akin to some terrifying new disease. It is integral to civilization. A few examples should suffice.

Going Forward: Nonmarriage as a Path to the Sacred

Prince Siddhattha Gotama of India's Shakya Republic may be the world's most famous marriage renegade. Heir to a minor Himalayan kingdom, he likely grew up in the sixth century BCE, near what is now the border between India and Nepal. Buddhist lore describes three early excursions outside his home, a splendid royal palace. During these outings he encountered, in succession, a tired old laborer, a leper, and a deteriorating corpse.[9] After apprehending hard work, illness, and death, Gotama found the sheltered life of a royal oppressive.[10] Circa 538 BCE he left his home in Kapilavashtu, 100 miles north of the city, Benares. Gotama was not sui generis. During his lifetime, thousands of people were leaving home to wander through forests near the Ganges River in search of *brachmacariya* (holy life).

This meant rejecting classical Indian religion, with its Brahmin-controlled sacrifices to multiple deities. It also meant renouncing conjugality. Married householders of India's eastern Gangetic region made babies, maintained houses, and supported the religious superstructure with their taxes. Ganges ascetics saw this as entrapment within *samsara*: the cycle of birth and rebirth linked to materialism. Children necessitated households. Upkeep fostered attachment to their interiors and grounds. This compelled work: time exchanged for money. Additional children necessitated larger living quarters and longer work hours, reinforcing conjugality's circular routine. Perhaps this is why Gotama referred to the boy he had fathered as "Little Fetter." This child bound him to an existence dominated by the earthbound and the quotidian.

Sixth-century BCE Indian mendicants typically participated in a *Pabbajja* ("Going Forth") ceremony, which involved shaving one's head and donning a beggar's yellow robes. This clothing signaled one's embrace of a beautiful shimmering state of homelessness. Participants swallowed fire, which symbolized rejection of all they were leaving behind, including social caste.

These peripatetics were not seen as deadbeat spouses or half-cocked fools. Indian culture accorded them respect for relinquishing familiarity, and in cases like Gotama's, power enhanced by delectation. Severing ties to home and hearth, spiritual seekers could seize truth where they found it. Urban and rural dwellers competed for the honor of feeding these mendicants, who carried begging bowls.[11] With his bowl and colorful robes, Gotama must have blended in with others traversing the countryside during a period of religious ferment.

Gotama is said to have spent six years studying with different gurus. The first, Alara Kalama, preached that the self was not a set of sensory impressions, memories, or moods. It was synonymous with a force called *purusa*. One reached *purusa* by discarding emotional debris and refining the intellect. But before commencing yogic exercises and meditation, initiates took vows, promising not to steal, lie, act violently, use intoxicants, or have sex. Tradition holds that Gotama embraced these prohibitions. He also deprived himself of water and endured prolonged exposure to cold. Gotama rapidly mastered yogic positions that took others years to learn. These practices were supposed to give practitioners access to consciousness aware only of itself: an uplifting sense of absence, a liberating nothingness. Gotama may have started to experience what his teacher promised. However, he rejected the invitation to colead Kalama's community.[12]

His next teacher, Uddaka Ramaputta, taught Gotama to enter a trancelike state. But after each period of immersion Gotama would return to his cravings, anxieties, and worldly preoccupations. He concluded that yoga gave practitioners respites from earthly, desire-based existence but offered no permanent relief.[13]

Gotama joined a group of forest monks in Uruveli near the Neranjari River. They wore hemp clothing and slept outside on gelid nights. In spite or because of these austerities, Gotama remained sharply aware of his own desires.

A childhood memory is said to have triggered his intuition that physical self-harm does not produce enlightenment. Sitting alone beneath a rose apple tree and watching local workers plow in preparation for the coming crop, he had felt compassion for dying insects and their ova. Sorrow for blades of torn-up grass overtook him. A surge of joy followed. The young Gotama crossed his legs and sat erect in the posture of a yogi: something he should not have known how to do.

Spontaneous compassion had generated ecstasy. Years later, sitting in the woods, under a Bo tree, Gotama re-experienced this event. He concluded that *Nibbana* could be reached by working with human nature, not against it. Contemplating this possibility, Gotama became so engaged with ratiocination that he dissolved into it, attaining selflessness. He achieved *Nibbana*. Free from the cycle of birth and rebirth, he was now Buddha, "the Enlightened One."[14]

The event said to auger Gotama's transformation was private. Caressed by solitude, he knew sudden empathy for all living things. Years later, sitting cross-legged in what is now called the Bodh Gaya Grove, he had his epiphany. The thread of continuity between seminal moments is aloneness. Having a spouse in tow would have prevented the metamorphosis. Gotama's focus would have been external, as the social world tugged him to meet its needs.

Like most ancient histories, Buddhist sources demonstrate less concern with accuracy than the delivery of a message: in this case, that enlightenment is achievable. One adjunct belief is clear; Buddha's awakening could not have occurred had he remained married. Wandering, study, and religious experimentation required nonmarriage. Before Gotama received revelation, preceded by a *jhana* (yogic trance), he is said to have known universal benevolence. This feeling contravened preferential kinship attachment. The conjugal household was dominated by emotional, sexual, and logistical interaction. *Nibbana*, a silent center, was its opposite.

Gotama—now Buddha—restored himself to health after years of asceticism. He found his cohorts and converted them to a "Middle Way," which rejects hedonism and austerity. Buddha developed a yoga in which participants watch their psyches' operations from an imposed distance. He maintained his vows of abstinence. Sex was not sinful; it just wasted time and energy better spent on meditation. Concupiscence also epitomized craving for its own sake, which trapped people in *samsara*.

Ultimately, Buddha articulated his Four Noble Truths: that suffering infects human life, that suffering stems from desire, that *Nibbana* is an exit from desire, and that he knew a way toward it. He advanced a three-fold method: moral living through right speaking, action, and work; mindful meditation; and wisdom focused on comprehending *Dhamma*, the essential condition of all things. Buddha insisted that this schema was not his. Rather, he had found the ancient practice of previous Buddhas.[15]

Buddhist writing recommends looking past desire and rational understanding to become fully realized human beings.[16] Optimally, this process entails forgoing sex, procreation, and matrimony. Buddha's nonmarital path to threefold action is woven into history's fabric. Marriage propagandists who view contemporary disenchantment with wedlock as newfangled might acquaint themselves with this tradition.

Many—perhaps most—religions stress humility. Buddha went farther. He did not seek to constrain the self but denied its existence. At the core of each person lay a set of fluctuating mental frameworks rather than an identity. Moderns preoccupied with personality find this baffling. The sixth century BCE was more receptive. An old merchant who heard Buddha's beliefs reportedly likened the experience to a lamp being held up in darkness.[17]

Buddha spent forty-five years travelling through India, preaching his message that all existence is *dukkha* (suffering), with release possible through the threefold plan, a path available to people of all sexes, races, and classes. In lieu of the hierarchy that granted him privilege as a royal from India's second highest rank, he built a *sangha* (community of disciples). Its collectivism was intended to help members reduce selfishness and develop compassion.

If Buddha did not invent monasticism, he was one of its earliest architects. *Sanghas* are among the most ancient living arrangements on earth. That they survive to this day shows nonmarriage as an excellent foundation for durable social structures. The *sangha* does not pit individuals against each other in a race to find spouses. Rather than growing inheritances, members bequeath what they have, including themselves. "After our wedding, /my husband and I put on robes together/and soon went our separate ways," proclaims a Buddhist nun included in the *Therigata*, a collection of female-authored poems. She continues,

True love doesn't throw a curtain
over the whole world
and imprison whoever it cares about most on an empty stage.

When the mind is free,
it's free of expecting
more than is reasonable
from any one person.[18]

What of Yasodhara, whom Buddha had married at age sixteen? Did she try to capture or punish Gotama for abandonment? No. She emulated him. At first she relinquished her jewelry and took an austere diet. When Buddha visited her, she requested ordination and was told to wait. Eventually, disgusted with her role of queen, she left the palace with 1,000 other women and found Rahula

("Little Fetter"), who was grown and immersed in Buddha's *Sangha*. Having become a marriage renegade, Yasodhara entered the Order of Monks and Nuns and became an ordained Buddhist monastic.[19]

At age eighty, travelling through Vesali, a city in Bihar, Buddha elected to die. He reminded his retinue of *bikkhus* (disciples) to follow the threefold plan and then entered what some erroneously imagine as a dark abyss. Buddhists see it as existence without rebirth into a pain-dominated life. Buddha would never define *Nibbana*. Tibet's never-married spiritual leader, the Dalai Lama, offers synonyms: "*destruction* of ignorance . . . *deathless[ness]* . . . *excellence.*"[20] One comparative religion scholar calls it a rebirth to "freedom, bliss, and nonconditionality."[21]

Buddha's final message echoed his teaching; while universal compassion benefitted each practitioner, it could ultimately uplift the world.[22] Toward this end Buddhism gives its devotees practical advantages. People who jettison regional and familial affiliations become mobile. Without parochial obligations, they can move freely in the world. This liberty enabled Buddhists to travel, disseminate their beliefs, and translate seminal texts into various languages.[23] Buddha's reputation spread throughout Southeast Asia; his iconography became established. Early numbers of converts are hard to quantify, but in 2012 the Pew Research Center estimated 488 million Buddhists worldwide, with practitioners concentrated in China, Japan, South Korea, Vietnam, Tibet, Thailand, Sir Lanka, and Cambodia.[24] This religion, or as some call it, philosophy, which views marriage in an unflattering light, is hardly a lunatic fringe.

Buddhist monastics of the Axial Age (c. 800–200 BCE) required nonmarital conditions: expanses of solitary time and discrete space for meditation. That conjugal life conflicted with the purest spiritual experiences seems to have been so obvious to

Buddha that it was not worth discussing. Then, as now, marrieds content to practice a modified Buddhism could become periodically celibate and give charity to monastic communities.[25] But the superior option entailed abandoning marriage to pursue *Nibbana*, thereby emulating Buddha himself.

Going Forward: Nonmarriage as a Path to the Eternal

People who have never cracked a Bible know of Jesus Christ from the staggering amount of legend surrounding his life. This includes several noncanonical gospels, myriad historical biographies, and countless scholarly articles—not to mention special magazine issues, biopics, documentaries, and musicals. Whatever the venue, accounts are hard to interpret because when Jesus's interlocuters ask what his presence means, he hedges.

The official story comes from four canonical gospels, none of which details his childhood. Only those attributed to the apostles Matthew and Luke represent Jesus's birth. Matthew situates it in Bethlehem, depicting a visit from gift-bearing wise men and a journey to Egypt, where Jesus is concealed. Luke has Augustus's implausible census decree, which brings Joseph and Mary to Bethlehem; the crowded inn; Jesus's birth in a manger; and visiting shepherds. It then portrays twelve-year-old Jesus sitting in the temple among learned teachers during an annual visit to Jerusalem. Then Luke, like Matthew, fast-forwards to Jesus the adult.

Bible scholar John Dominic Crossan reads these scenes as overtures to a narrative about someone executed for sedition, who purported to be the Jewish messiah or was considered as such by his followers.[26] Religion professor Bart D. Ehrman argues that Jesus presented himself as the Jewish monarch who augured a coming messiah. The sign hanging on the cross with him bears the epitaph, "King of the Jews," at a time when such placards recorded criminal transgressions. Ehrman posits that "He thought he was a prophet predicting the end of the current evil age and the future king of Israel in an age to come."[27] In any case, the childhood episodes, with their folkloric embroidering and placement of Jesus in Bethlehem, stress his distinctness, implying that from infancy he was unique. Non-Christians can agree that Jesus is *sui generis* as the central figure of history's most popular religion. Another fact remains clear: Jesus of Nazareth never married.

The four canonical gospels mention a desert hermit named John, who was immersing penitents in the Jordan River. Mark, written around 70 CE (roughly forty years after the crucifixion) shows John baptizing Jesus. Some twenty years later, Matthew has John acknowledge Jesus as his successor. In Luke, composed between 80 and 110 CE, Jesus is baptized by someone unnamed, and the heavens open.[28] John, written thirty years after Mark, contains no water ritual. John the Baptist follows Jesus and proclaims, "He must increase, as I must decrease."[29] Increasingly the gospels foreground and apotheosize Jesus. As the Jesus of Nazareth cult grew, narratives kept pace.

The basic story occurs around 30 CE. A rabbi returns from the Jordan River to Nazareth, an obscure Lower Galilee village where he grew up and supported himself as a woodworker. (Most first-century rabbis worked as day-laborers.)[30] Locals urge Jesus's return to his mother and siblings. He responds, "Who are my mother and my brothers? Here are my mother and my brothers. Whoever does the will of God is my brother and sister and mother."[31] Jesus redefines family as universal rather than local, chosen rather than imposed, spiritual rather than marital. This may explain his relationship status at a time when "It would have been almost unthinkable for a thirty-year-old Jewish male . . . not to have a wife."[32] Indeed, first-century Palestine's Jewish community made wedlock mandatory. Sects like the Essenes, with their water purification rituals, practiced celibacy. But they segregated themselves from society as a whole. Jesus did not.

Jesus travels to the fishing village, Capernaum, where he attracts his first four apostles: Simon, Andrew, James, and John. Jesus's inner circle eventually expands to include seventy-two disciples. Among them are Joanna, spouse of the reigning King Herod's steward; Mary, wife of a man named Clopas; and Mary Magdalene, from whom Jesus exorcises seven demons.

First-century Judaism was sexually segregated, with women assigned second-class status that included exclusion from the priesthood. Jerusalem's Temple had a separate outer court where women congregated. Judaism's main judicial body, the Sanhedrin, consisted of male judges. According to the Hebrew Bible, God formed His covenant at Sinai with Israelite men. The community itself was thereby male, which naturalized excluding women from official temple roles.[33]

Jesus ignored these rules by traveling with a mixed-sex entourage. He was not the Galilee's only faith healer to do this.[34] But the gospels show him going unusually far to stress his bond with female acolytes. He cures a woman who has bled for twelve years, unconcerned that she might render him ritually impure with her touch.[35] Jesus seems to have no marital aspirations; he does not characterize women as wives or wives-to-be. Men do not appear in his teaching as potential spouses. People become humanized, shining with potential for life outside matrimony.

The mixed-sex nature of Jesus's ministry connects with one of his extraordinary statements: "If anyone comes to me and does not hate his father and mother and wife and children and brothers and sisters . . . he cannot be my disciple."[36] Clearly, this fiat is not literal. Jesus is not stirring animus or recommending fist fights. He is deflating a series of roles: parental, marital, and fraternal.

These parts facilitate flattery and feigned sentiment by requiring people to don social masks: obedient son, deferential daughter, devoted wife. Conversely, spouses become unnaturally fixated on each other, losing sight of God.

With his followers, Jesus heads toward Jerusalem, performing miracles en route. He feeds 5,000 people with five loaves of bread and two fish.[37] He restores a blind man's sight.[38] His feats differ from those of the average first-century magician. They are performed free of charge with the request that viewers not disclose his powers. Instead, he instructs them to share news about the Kingdom of God.

Exegetes who stress Jesus's radicalism describe the Kingdom of God as a new world order ruled by one deity, under whom long-standing hierarchies dissolve. Others accentuate paganism's elimination; in the Kingdom of God a sole divinity reclaims history; all gather under His standard. Jesus speaks cryptically; the Kingdom of God is a pearl nested inside a shell,[39] a buried mustard seed,[40] a meadow filled with wheat and weeds.[41] While the metaphors are ambiguous, Jesus clearly presents himself as an agent of change. The familiar world will soon end. Whether earthbound, celestial, or unimaginable, the new domain will not include marriage. This is fitting, since Jesus has challenged "civilization's eternal inclination to draw lines, invoke boundaries, establish hierarchies, and maintain discriminations," giving little credence to "Gentile and Jew, female and male, slave and free, poor and rich."[42]

Eventually Jesus and his followers reach Jerusalem's Temple, the epicenter of Israelite worship. In an open area known as the Court of Gentiles, he brings business to a halt, ejecting peddlers and knocking over money changers' tables. Afterwards, he remains and attracts pupils. A group of Sadducees tries to trip him on his words with a question about Hebrew remarriage after the Resurrection. "You are in error because you do not know the

Scriptures or the power of God," he replies. "At the Resurrection people will neither marry nor be given in marriage; they will be like the angels in heaven."[43]

Jesus may have had dual nonmarital status. The third verse of Mark's sixth chapter refers to him as "Mary's son." For a culture that uses patronymics this is unusual. Comparative Religion scholar Reza Aslan explains that "Calling a first-born Jewish male in Palestine by his mother's maiden name—that is, Jesus *bar Mary*, instead of Jesus *bar Joseph*—is not just unusual, it is egregious."[44] Joseph vanishes quickly from the narrative, dying before Jesus's baptism in 28/29 CE.[45] Joseph is not Mary's husband but her betrothed. He obeys an angelic command to take Mary into his household. Avatar or non-avatar, Jesus is technically the progeny of unwed people.

Bible scholar Jane Schaberg believes in an oral tradition of Jesus as "illegitimate." She sees this idea flickering in the gospel of Matthew. In his genealogy, a list of who begot whom is interrupted with the clause, "Of her [Mary] was begotten Jesus, called the Christ."[46] The passive voice, with its vagueness, leaves Jesus's paternity unclear. The Holy Spirit as Jesus's begetter appears rarely in early Christian literature. Only the gospels of Matthew and Luke mention it: "A tradition of the virginal conception of Jesus (in contrast to a tradition of his illegitimacy) was evidently not known to the other New Testament writers."[47] Schaberg reads gospel allusions to the Holy Spirit nonliterally, as a defense of Jesus, who is "begotten through the Holy Spirit in spite of— or better, because of—his human paternity." She explains that "Matt 1:18, 20 can be read to mean that the Holy Spirit empowers this birth as all births are divinely empowered, that this child's human existence is willed by God, and that God is the ultimate power of life in this as in all conceptions."[48] Schaberg believes that missionizing Christians attempted to suppress this illegitimacy narrative and succeeded by the third century.[49] Still, Matthew's Jesus commands, "Call no one your father on earth, for you have one father who is in heaven."[50] In this ethos no human being has the right to claim paternal power. The Jesus movement, Schaberg suggests, founded a new family in which God could protect an unwed pregnant woman.[51]

Anonymous opponents of the never-married Schaberg responded to this claim by setting her car on fire.[52]

Ultimately Jesus's fate falls to Pontius Pilate, a prefect sent from Rome some ten years earlier to oversee its occupation of Judea. This meant governing an unstable region during a time of religious and political unrest. Anti-Roman preachers and self-proclaimed prophets were legion. Pilate had little tolerance for them or their followers; he ordered thousands of Jews executed without trials. The standard method with non-Roman citizens was crucifixion. But Jesus's death is not permanent; on the Sunday following his execution, Mary Magdalene and another woman named Mary report seeing him risen from the dead.

Whether Jesus's original twelve apostles viewed him as God's progeny is unclear. Paul the Apostle, Christianity's chief early evangelizer, disseminated this belief. It met widespread yearnings for a personal God that characterized the Axial Age.[53] As Chapter 2 shows, Paul's view of marriage is tepid at best. He judges sexual desire negatively and prescribes marriage as a means of containing it. He names celibacy as the superior lifestyle, advising virgins to remain chaste and widowed people to eschew remarriage.

Like Buddha, Jesus traveled with a retinue of people who shared his vision; among these, the disciple James was his biological brother (or, according to apologists who insist on Mary's perpetual virginity, his cousin). But that blood tie dissolved into the collective of a traveling family in which discipleship replaced kinship. This group was a metonym for Jesus's universal family.

The early church that evolved from Jesus's teaching and Paul's evangelizing extolled chastity over marriage—and not just from a sense of eschatology. If Jesus was God's agent on earth—a being whose existence preceded time—he was an emulative role model. Living as he did entailed living nonmaritally. The image of Jesus's followers as an extended family took hold.[54] Between the subapostolic period and the fourth centuries, a time that included Roman persecution, Christians addressed each other as "brother" and "sister," expressing a philosophy that supported fraternal bonds between nonkin. The Roman Catholic Church would ultimately administer matrimony. But Jesus's relationship status and antimarriage statements have never been successfully buried. They remain essential to an egalitarian vision of a world that can be.

Opening Intergenerational Dialogue

In general, the never-married do not communicate across generations—another factor that obscures our disadvantaging and our achievements. Three nonmarital medical pioneers illustrate this problem.

Hildegard of Bingen (1098–1179) was born into a wealthy Bermersheim household that probably included ten children.[55] Like many gifted medievals, she found an outlet for her talents in the church. Hildegard began monastic life at age eight as a voluntary oblate, moving in with the pious noblewoman Jutta of Spanheim (1091–1136). After an indeterminate period, they relocated to the Benedictine monastery in Disibodenberg. There they became anchorites who lived in an isolated cell. They dedicated themselves to religious contemplation and repetition of Psalms. At age fifteen, Hildegard took the veil.[56] She and Jutta became known for their piety, which attracted female religious to Disibodenberg's monastery. It developed into a double facility that lodged monks and nuns. When Jutta died in 1136, Hildegard succeeded her as the convent's abbess.

Hildegard claimed that she had always received visions from God. In her early forties, she began recording them in a collection called *Scivias*. Finished in 1151 or 1152, it represents twenty-six revelations. In one, two pillars protrude from a building. One is "the true Trinity." The second pillar has something like a ladder on which beings move up and down. One wears a luminous tunic and holds a scepter; she praises chastity: "I am free and not fettered, for I have passed through the pure Fountain Who is the sweet and loving Son of God."[57]

Hildegard wrote two German tomes on medicine, the *Physica* (*Natural History*) and *Causae et curae* (*Causes and Cures*). In the latter she reconfigures conception, positing that it occurs when male and female "foam" mingles during intercourse. The woman's froth cools her partner's fluid. Though incorrect, Hildegard's thesis elevates the traditional role of women from passive recipients of semen to agents who affect procreation.[58] *Causae et curae* offers herbal remedies. Hildegard advises wrapping a sick baby in a cloth lined with aspen leaves.[59] Doctors Wighard Strehlow and Gottfried Herzka observe that many of her remedies align with Chinese medicine: "She uses syllium for constipation . . . and horehound for cough."[60] While Hildegard's standard twelfth-century understanding of illness as an imbalance between the four humors (fire, air, water, earth) is erroneous, her view of illness as spiritual, psychic, and physical prefigures much herbal medicine.[61]

The wealthy Englishwoman Florence Nightingale (1820–1910) had an admirer in journalist Monckton Milnes. To her relatives' chagrin, she rejected his proposal, likening marriage to suicide.[62] The extraordinary privilege in which she lived ended at age thirty-two, when Nightingale entered the then disreputable world of nursing. She began training at Kaiserwerth Institute on the Rhine, accepting its Spartan conditions and donning its standard issue blue uniform.[63]

Nightingale's star rose during the Crimean War (1853–1856), a confusing conflict, with Britain, France, and the Ottoman Empire pitted against Russia. She upgraded Turkey's Scutarri Barracks. Nightingale sanitized the facility, having carpets cleaned and bed linens deloused. Personally financing renovations, she had windows installed to allow ventilation, sewers put in, and a kitchen built, so fresh food could be prepared for patients. She purchased additional sheets, so every soldier had decent bedding.[64] Forbidding bloodletting with leeches, Nightingale erected screens to give men undergoing procedures privacy.[65]

Nightingale did double duty as an administrator and a caregiver who worked alongside thirty-eight nurses. She changed bandages and dressed wounds. Every night she patrolled the barracks, oil lamp in hand, and spoke with her patients.[66] British soldiers' mortality rates dropped from 42 to 2.2 percent. Nightingale returned to England famous but in poor health. Still, the iconic "Lady with the Lamp" lived for another fifty years, testifying on military hospital conditions and writing *Notes on Nursing: What it is and What it is Not* (1859). Nightingale insisted that nurses receive "rigorous scientific training and practical education."[67] Almost singlehandedly, she advanced nursing from disreputable labor into a profession.

With her never-married friend Elizabeth Blackwell (1821–1910), the first female American MD, Nightingale fantasized about transforming her family estate into a hospital. The two conversed "from two to three hours, twice a day."[68] They disagreed about women's calling to medicine; Nightingale thought it was nursing, Blackwell doctoring. But each felt bonded to someone never-married who believed in women's capacity to excel in medicine.

Hildegard cast herself as a prophet of God. Nightingale styled herself in opposition to her relatives, whom she thought wealth had anesthetized. She made nonmarriage the foundation of her career. As a young woman, defending this choice to her elders was no small feat. Had Nightingale known of her unwed antecedent, Hildegard, her fight might have been less arduous. A tradition would have backed her.

Nightingale posited that nurses "must be above all flirting or ever desiring to marry."[69] Blackwell thought this harshly consigned female medics to celibacy. The linkage of sex and marriage limited Blackwell's thinking. Not all never-married physicians had been celibate. John Locke (1632–1704), the philosopher discussed in Chapter 2, received a degree in medicine from Oxford. In 1668 Locke planned and oversaw a surgery on the Whig politician Anthony Ashley Cooper, Earl of Shaftesbury (1621–1683). The procedure implanted a tube into Shaftesbury's liver which drained an abscess, saving his life.[70] A member of two extended households, Locke lived for eight years in Shaftesbury's London home.[71] For the last fourteen years of his life he resided in Essex with his former companion, writer Damaris Masham, and her husband. Had she considered Locke and others like him as nonmarital role models, Blackwell's thinking might have been quite different.

Listening to Our History

History can only reveal what people are ready to hear. Today, scholars from across the disciplines are taking up the subject of "singleness." As their work progresses, nonmarital history should become clearer. This can create a new psychological environment.

We must remember that romantic love came late to wedlock. Nonmarital people should know this and understand that our position in early modernity worsened. One must be cautious about generalizing, but to derive meaning from the past some generalizations are necessary. I believe that between the Reformation, when clerical celibacy started to become disreputable, and the twenty-first century, when rejection of wedlock became rife, an expanse of time passed during which never-married people had no "place." The person living outside matrimony was presumed to be partial, inadequate. With no sanctioned identity other than "loser," such people had to create niches for themselves. Many did so with names they assigned partners and written critiques of marriage. Others did so in deeds: solitary questing, constructing nonstandard families, and community building. The stigmas—childishness, unattractiveness, misanthropy—stuck. They're still around. But as previous chapters have shown, a positive reality belies these stereotypes.

Matrimony differs from culture to culture and era to era. Classical Greece had established rituals for sex between men; its art depicts same-sex eroticism. Wedlock was arranged, with men in their thirties often marrying teenage girls. Postwar America pathologized sodomy; its experts prescribed betrothal between two people in their early twenties whose respective biology determined their roles. Can matrimony mean roughly the same thing in these two cultures?

With qualifications, yes. Transhistorically, wedlock tends to draw adherents with similar means: legal force, social pressure, religious dicta, economic rewards, status accorded those who conform, and punishments imposed on people who dissent or renege. Marriage ratifies artificial distinctions: women are respectable or nonrespectable, men responsible or irresponsible. Wherever the dominant template for love relationships is an exclusive husband/wife paradigm, other pair bonds are diminished.

Despite these reward and punishment modalities, marriage

has never held exclusive appeal. Contemporary Americans who "feel" unwed and stay that way forego privileges, forge nonstandard families, create penumbras of privacy, and build community. We challenge the belief that extramarital romance and Platonic friendship mean less than wedlock. We ignore the discouragement of life-structuring friendships between men and women. We discourage married couples from seeing themselves as grander than they are.

Nevertheless, America's tax code still enforces the married/ single binary by acknowledging no other definition for adults. Anyone visiting an urgent care center fills out paperwork that involves checking a "single," "married," or "divorced" box. These forms conceptualize us out of existence. Those who scribble our own self-definitions can expect stares of bewilderment or annoyance. These attitudes make it harder for young people to articulate dreams of nonmarital futures; such goals have been pushed to the territory of the unexplainable.

Politicians pledge to protect married families. Beneath their rhetoric lurk bachelorphobia, spinsterphobia, and disdain for nonmarital children.

Headlines usually obfuscate nonmarital Americans' few legal advances. In 2010, the Obama Administration issued new rules about hospital visitation rights. Facilities participating in Medicare or Medicaid would have to honor patients' preferences for visitors. Spouses would no longer get automatic top billing; the guest could be a live-in lover, nonbiological sibling, or mentor. It was a wonderful moment for nonmarital people, but the president's memorandum, which mentions race, religion, sex, and sexual orientation, left us out.[72] The document omits to mention relationship status— a glaring error, since spouses long wielded authority on hospital floors. No wonder nonmarital people have trouble identifying as a distinct group. The few laws that protect us don't mention us.

America's mainstream media relies on binaries: Democrat/ Republican, leftist/right-winger, laissez-fare capitalist/socialist . . . the list of either/ors goes on. Nonmarital people cannot be wedged into these categories because we exist everywhere. We share the same disadvantages but have not reached an inflection point—that galvanizing moment after which nothing is the same. Once the nonmarital Seneca Falls Convention or Stonewall Riot occurs, adults and children living outside marriage will be harder to ignore.

We can start redefining our relationship to history by arguing that our common challenges do not come from innate freakishness, misery, or childishness. Rather, they stem from judgments that matrimonially-obsessed societies press on us. These are often passively received from generations of habitual suppositions that make matrimony preeminent. Despite such prejudices, America's nonmarital population continues to swell. Nonmarital living is more accepted than it was even ten years ago. So, in twenty-first century America, nonmarriage is acceptable and unacceptable, tolerated and proscribed. This paradox invites scholarly investigation.

Nonmarital history shows myriad adults for whom wedlock was an option rejecting it in favor of other lifestyles. This has occurred on a person by person, family by family basis. When nonmarital people work together as a group something else can happen: an undoing of matrimonial privilege. Collaborating effectively requires overlooking our major differences. If nineteenth-century suffragettes had focused on their dissimilarities rather than one shared disadvantage, women would likely still lack the vote. Nonmarital people have yet to organize and create an agenda of demands. Until we do, journalists will characterize surges in nonmarriage as trends rather than initiatives.

How We Could Be

Shaping a theory that integrates the historical, psychological, and social dimensions of nonmarriage would take work, but it could be done. Is such a theory necessary? No: the relationship hierarchy atop which marriage sits is destructive. Replacing it with another hegemonic theory and a different hierarchy could be equally detrimental. If we concur that love takes various forms, families configure differently, and government should not intervene in such matters unless absolutely necessary, no single unifying conception is needed. It helps to remember that love is a non-zero-sum-game, which takes diverse shapes. Some of its modes of expression are sexual; most are not.

People who say they will never marry are often accused of desultoriness or cynicism. As I have tried to show, nothing could be less true. Many nonmarital people set up their families deliberately. Without necessarily rejecting romantic love, they see wedlock as detrimental or irrelevant to the good life. To reject the conjugal prototype is to devalue enforced normality—a breathtakingly optimistic act. Others follow the flow of their emotional and sexual feelings or lack thereof. Many see the world, not as it is but as it could be. In this spirit it is important to believe that a day can come when relationship status entails no ranking order, where each person is free to build a family by following individual beliefs and preferences.

What will this world look like? Grim, Marriage Movement spokespeople warn. It will resemble the postapocalyptic landscapes of many science fiction films, in which bands of survivors scavenge, and culture remains as a fractured shell. These alarmists seek to preserve matrimony as the means of regulating adult sex, legitimizing (and delegitimizing) children, and sometimes, reinstating a gender-based labor division. They castigate never-married adults as selfish failures and predict joyless futures for us. In so doing, they ignore the most reliable studies, which find wedlock irrelevant to contentment levels. Repeating identical captions and peddling corrupted data, they squelch analysis, as if really studying marriage would reveal truths better left untouched.

In general, marriage advocates assume that nonmarital people miss life's greatest joys. Meeting them head on, a marriage-free world will not be a world without love. Such a world is not possible. As philosopher Simon May argues, love-based relationships are the "ground of our being" and the basis of any meaningful life.[73] But emotions involved in loving another person suffuse any serious relationship. These relationships are judged with similar questions: do this person and I understand each other? Where do our beliefs converge and diverge? Is this someone I trust? As with lovers of whom one does not really approve, attraction to dubious friends can be overpowering. The focus on quality and significance of relationship, rather than mass-producing couples according to one formula, will make a marriage-free world shine. Relationships that emerge will enjoy a certain freedom from constraint—no guarantor of harmony, but a step forward.

Because wedlock has a hyper-inflated status, it receives more stringent evaluation than any other relationship. But the process of commencing a sexual love affair, proceeding with a serious friendship, and connecting with a mentor are strikingly similar. This likeness suggests that a marriage-free world will foster more than enough love. Much marital supremacism rests on the fact that wedlock is established. Disestablishing it will not eradicate erotic relationships, friendship, or family. It will liberate them. The seeker of love and companionship will begin with no preset convictions of how and where they will be found and what shape they must ultimately take.

A marriage-free world will not be obligation free. Interpersonal relationships always entail responsibilities. But a single hierarchy of obligations will not dominate. To what and whom we are obligated, and how those duties play out will not result from accidents of birth or legal requirements of an institution underinformed people enter, often by rote.

A marriage-free nation has numerous benefits for children. The state will remain obligated to protect minors from physical and emotional abuse. Its duty will warrant an interest in capable adult caretakers, not spouses. Kids will not grow up revering matrimony. No one will be made to feel second rate for being born out of wedlock. Without matrimony as the dividing line between family and nonfamily, nonmarital households will not be considered second rate. To quote Ted Olson and David Boies, "This badge of inferiority, separateness, and inequality must be extinguished." Understanding how pluralistic love has been and how diverse family can be, kids will face life with an expanded set of options: living in collective groups, living with a lover, enjoying fairly solitary lives, and everything in between. No single default model will dominate.

A society obsessed with wedlock does not merely generate punitive distinctions; it creates anxiety about finding one's ultimate "match": apprehension that manifests at a young age. A marriage-free society will not encourage such disquiet. There will be no marriage market. That is to say, spouse hunting as a competitive activity undertaken to meet familial expectations, elevate status, or secure financial gifts will end. Young people will be encouraged to acknowledge the future's unpredictability. No one will have to take vows of lifelong fidelity as a concession to policymakers who consider Americans worthy of health care on that condition. No man will have to convince himself of feelings he does not have for another adult to make his aging bioparents happy. No woman will marry a friend to get her a green card. In a world without marriage, laws and customs will accommodate individual tastes, preferences, and styles of living—not the other way around.

The seemingly insuperable bond between erotic fidelity and legal protection will be dissolved. This will require eschewing the jealousy that marriage culture encourages. There will be no trade-off: subsidized housing and spousal-immunity privileges for an agreement to have sex with one person; FSAs for holders of promise-to-love-you-forever licenses. Government agencies will not credential adult sex. Celibacy and the relinquishment of erotic ties will be respectable options; so will chosen monogamy and penalty-free sexual friendships. No one will have to worry that a truncated romance might drain them financially.

Americans can learn to respect privacy as the Na of China do. Accordingly, people can build families that do not rest on monogamous love affairs. Families can emerge incrementally rather than beginning when two people say "I Do." Such families need not end when two lovers terminate their relationship.

With marriage disestablished, the government will no longer bestow an entire set of rights and privileges on one style of relationship. Nonmarriage will no longer be matrimony's degraded other. The wedding industry, with its slick packaging of conjugality, will shut down. However, nothing will stop two people who wish to celebrate their romance ritually, from doing so. A religious ceremony will be one option. It will carry the legal weight of today's bar or bat mitzvah. Lovers who have such ceremonies will not get recognition that comes with being part of an esteemed majority. This in itself will be immensely beneficial. While the ceremony will not have governmental backing, the couple's household, like many others, will look pretty married. It will be headed by an amorous twosome who share a reciprocal identity and combine resources. But this will not be the standard toward which everyone is encouraged. So, those who choose a marriage-like setup, rather than having it thrust at them, will have exercised mindful choice. This should make such relationships better.

Other families will be bachelor focal or spinster focal; many households will be friend centered or singleton. Diverse family structures need not compete; they can support each other. Love and meeting life's challenges together encompass a variety of configurations that go under the name family. What unifies them is intention; a deliberate decision somewhere along the way that these are one's core people. This differs greatly from generational accident or adherence to a cultural script.

Optimally, a wide network of members, many of whom are not blood relatives, will shore up each family. Households will revolve around ideals of interdependence and community instead of exclusion: the married couple versus everyone else, blood that is thicker than water. People in fluid families will have rights and obligations toward each other far more nuanced than current family law allows. Living apart together and other forms of relationship that honor privacy, will be common. (Of course, they already are.) Lovers who have natal children will be expected to provide for them initially but won't necessarily raise the kids. In other the words, the sacrosanct bond between sexual intercourse and conventionally defined parenting will be broken. A child might have multiple legal parents rather than a duo mandated to provide everything. Some parents might be blood relatives; none might be.

Change Already Underway

Meaningful change happens when people look backward and move forward, reaching in ways that initially exceed their grasp. Proposing a marriage-free society, one often gets a knee-jerk,

"No!" The concept is disconcerting, even for those who don't want a spouse. But political discussions can no longer omit marital supremacism. Those who insist that relationship equity was achieved with *Obergefull v. Hodges* paste slogans over the marriage system. Like wallpaper on a fissuring wall, the mottos will fray, revealing conceptual gaps. Dialogues about immigration rights cannot be shut down when inconvenient facts appear. One cannot initiate a debate about equal pay for equal work, where marriage is a factor, and pretend that it is irrelevant.

Some concede that a marriage-free world sounds interesting—even preferable. But wedlock is too entrenched. Acknowledging all forms of pair bonding will have destabilizing effects.

This claim must be addressed. Matrimony is an institution especially prone to act as a vehicle for group egotism. Abolishing marital privilege won't eradicate that narcissism but will stop fostering it. Eliminating wedlock will certainly not ignite the French Revolution's worst excesses or cause subtler forms of chaos. The Canadian Province of Alberta now protects "adult interdependent relationships," allowing cohabiting life partners to share health care benefits. No sexual bond is required. The Canadian Census reports that just under 25 percent of Canadians live in nuclear families: "Single-parent households, opposite-sex couples deciding not to marry, singles living alone, same-sex couples, and couples without children are some of the forms families are taking off."[74] The American Federal Office on Personnel Management grants employees leave to care for people who are tantamount to family.

These policies are not upending Canada or the United States. Nonmarital life is becoming more popular; while law tends to move at a glacial pace, it is bound to ultimately respond. Professor Cass Sunstein of Harvard Law School has come out against legal marriage. Sunstein argues for a country in which "the word marriage would no longer appear in any laws, and marriage licenses would no longer be offered or recognized by any level of government."[75]

"What if Friendship, Not Marriage, Was the Center of Life?" a 2020 *Atlantic* headline queries. Analyzing the marital-supremacist ranking order, its author, Rhaina Cohen, asserts, "Our worlds are backwards."[76] Celebrities too are challenging matrimony. "I don't say I'm looking for a man who I want to have two or three kids with," singer Demi Lovato remarked recently. "I think it could be so much fun to share children with a woman."[77] Lovato did not say "wife" or "lover." In a decision that seems organic to gay history and culture, broadcast journalist Anderson Cooper is raising two boys born by surrogate with his ex-lover, nightclub owner Benjamin Maisani. Cooper's friend, talk show host Andy Cohen, is on board as well.[78] March 2021 saw the *New Yorker's* publication of Andrew Solomon's widely discussed article, "How Polyamorous and Polygamists Are Changing Family Norms." Solomon mentions paradigm-shifting legal reforms. In June 2020, Somerville, Massachusetts, passed an ordinance that lets groups of three or more people who "consider themselves family" register as domestic partners. The neighboring city of Cambridge quickly followed suit.[79]

Philosophers are positing intriguing suggestions. Samantha Brennan and Bill Cameron suggest that "we separate marriage contracts from parenting and think about children as a possible basis for family building outside the aegis of marriage or even romantic love."[80] They observe that children require homes, food, stability, love, and environments that best ensure future success, all of which could come in various setups.[81] Modern marriage, which is earmarked as a lifelong romance, meets none of childrearing's requirements.

Legal scholars suggest practical measures for a society that does not privilege marriage. Nancy D. Polikoff envisions computer archives: "States would keep records under a 'designated family relationship' registration system. People who register would be publicly declaring that their relationship should count as family under laws that now list family members defined only by marriage, biology, or adoption."[82] The registry would include various partnerships and families, according no special status to married heterosexuals and LGBTQ+ pairs who mirror straight marriage. For this registry, I imagine new terminology. Instead of "marriage, biology, and adoption," we might have "long-term partnership," "significant, resource-sharing relationship," "life-structuring friendship," and, "primarily responsible for child."

Some theorists favor relationship contracts.[83] Each contract would reflect the signatories' circumstances and goals. Participants could develop agreements that fall within the law, which requires contracting parties' consent and proscribes illegal compacts (e.g., promises to maim one another). Contracts allow individuation and let adults, rather than states, shape relationships. Instead of government validating one conception of the good life, Americans would endorse their own vision of what makes family meaningful. A domestic contract could enable lesser earning household members to establish authority in decision-making. In sexual relations, contracts could stipulate guidelines and consequences. One might state that a relationship is sexually open as long as partners use protection and keep their activities outside the home. Another compact might allow intimacy with others that falls short of sexual intercourse. Yet another could set monogamy as an ideal with a proviso that failure would not jeopardize the bond. Prepared by attorneys and notarized, such documents would legalize off-the-record agreements that people now make every day.

Contracts would prevent the government from setting sexual-relationship guidelines and intruding if a romance ends. They would let resource-sharing partners delineate exactly what is owed whom if a relationship ends and which adverse circumstances would cancel the debt. Nonromantic bonds would be covered. Several adults could agree to share a child's upbringing and sign a contract that divided responsibility for distinct areas, such as financial support, meal preparation, and help with school. The contract would reflect people's individual strengths. American courts are already set up to enforce contracts.

Clare Chambers cautions that contracts could activate pressures similar to those of contemporary marriage.[84] Certain agreements might accrue status. A man could hear from his girlfriend, "If you really loved me, you would sign a monogamy contract." Children might be taunted: "In our church, families have contracts between two adults. Why does yours have four?"

Like marriage proposals, personal relationship contracts would often occur "at a time of optimism, even a time of heady romance."[85] This would also be true of documents signed between platonic friends, friends with benefits, lovers, alloparents, and/ or blood kin. Charged feelings of infatuation can cloud people's perceptions, which is why the excitement stage is not an ideal time to make any binding commitment. Not every PME victim in Chapters 5 and 6 was infatuated when they married, but none saw their intended as a lethal adversary. So, like wedlock, personal relationship contracts demand rare foresight.

A more refined version of the personal contract approach could address this problem. It would involve clauses detailing rights and obligations of people in various kinds of relationships. Chambers describes these as "piecemeal in character, referring only to particular aspects of a relationship and with no assumption that multiple aspects should be located in one primary relationship."[86] As duties and privileges would not be amalgamated in a single bond, piecemeal directives would make it possible to combine or separate matters like property ownership, health insurance, and inheritance. A relationship could encompass co-owning and maintaining a property; another might entail shared health insurance. All relationships subject to directives would be significant: part of a signatory's core community. But neither coupledom nor any other relationship configuration would receive special status. This would enable movement from a historically tainted system of privilege to a culture in which individuals, regardless of their differing endowments, are considered equal in terms of love and family.

Marriage licenses will be eliminated. Until this happens, engaged couples will have to take a course. It will resemble driver's education classes required to obtain a license. The class will provide divorce statistics and explain criteria for spousal support, detailing recent alimony rulings in the state where a particular couple wishes to marry. Marriage education must stress a basic point: legal marriage surpasses any private agreement the principals make.

Once licensure is over, such classes will be unnecessary. Married couples can continue living as they have lived. They will simply avail themselves of their state's registry and enroll as family members and/or sign the appropriate contracts. Those who have been reluctant to leave bad situations, however, will surely feel freer to do so.

Eliminating licenses will make alimony a null concept. Garnishments, imprisonments for inability to pay . . . will become horrors of the past. Those serving alimony-related jail sentences will be released. An agency will be established to evaluate payers' situations and decide what *they* are owed. Like the Environmental Protection Agency and the Food and Drug Administration, this entity will be separate from the courts. It decisionmakers will consist of jurists, historians, ethicists, and representatives from other relevant disciplines. They will assess each erstwhile couple, factoring in the health, education, earning potential, and financial assets (including monies and properties inherited) of both parties. If officials find that significant financial damage has been done to the payer, and/or health problems developed as a result, they will draft a schedule of monetary compensation. Recipients will be mandated to make financial reparations for a period to be determined.

These reforms are a beginning. They combine optimism with the desire to strip marriage of superstatus. They will be rejected as absurd by people who see wedlock as benign and unique. But they pave the way for a world in which some lovers might commit to each other privately, without governmental controls or exhibitionistic galas, and others might not. Pushing for a marriage-free society, we nonmarital Americans can celebrate our lives, savoring the joys of living alone; creating fluid, loving families; and giving our partnerships respect that the current marriage system withholds. This requires creativity combined with awareness that nonmarital people will never lose the justness of our cause.

(Endnotes)

1   Alexandra Schwartz, *Vogue*, August 2020, 68–9, 89.

2   Edmund S. Morgan, *The Puritan Family: Religion and Domestic Relations in Seventeenth-Century New England* (New York: Harper & Row, 1944), 82.

3   *Mansfield Park*, ed. John Wiltshire (Cambridge: Cambridge University Press, 2005), 53.

4   "It is Not Good That [Wo]man Should Be Alone: Elite Responses to Singlewomen in High Medieval Paris," *Singlewomen in the European Past: 1250–1800*, ed. Judith M. Bennett and Amy M. Froide (Philadelphia: University of Pennsylvania Press, 1999), 82–3.

5   *Wayward Lives, Beautiful Experiments: Intimate Histories of Riotous Black Girls, Troublesome Women, and Queer Radicals* (New York: W. W. Norton & Company, 2019), 254–6.

6   Christopher N. L. Brooke, *The Medieval Idea of Marriage* (Oxford: Clarendon, 1989), X.

7   Jack Wasserman, *Leonardo Da Vinci* (New York: Harry N Abrams Inc., Publishers, 1984), 7.

8   Leo Damrosch, *The Club: Johnson, Boswell, and the Friends Who Shaped an Age* (New Haven: Yale University Press, 2019), 26–7.

9   Turner, *The Ritual Process*, 196.

10   The Dalai Lama and Thutben Chodron, *Buddhism* (Somerville, Massachusetts: Wisdom Publications, 2014), 1.

11   Karen Armstrong, *Buddha* (New York: Penguin, 2001), 9–10.

12   Ibid., 46–61.

13   Ibid., 62–3.

14   Ibid., 67–71.

15   Ibid, 82–3.

16   The *Digha Nikaya* provides an account of Buddha's final days. The *Majjhima Nikaya* has stories that detail his efforts toward enlightenment and early teaching. These are among Buddhist texts probably composed between 500 BCE and the first century.

17   Armstrong, *Buddha*, 118–19.

18   Bhadda Kapilani, "Red Hair," *The First Women: Poems of the Early Buddhist Nuns*, trans. Matty Weingast (Boulder: Shambhala, 2020),46. This collection of seventy-three poems may be the oldest extant volume of women's literature.

19   Wendy Garling, *Stars at Dawn: Forgotten Stories of Women in the Buddha's Life* (Boulder: Shambhala, 2016), 235–6.

20 *Buddhism*, 25–6.
21 Mircea Eliade, *The Sacred and the Profane: The Nature of Religion* (New York: Harcourt, Brace, Jovanovich, 1957), 199.
22 Armstrong, *Buddha*, 186–7.
23 Michael Cook, *A Brief History of the Human Race* (New York: Norton, 2003), 158.
24 "Buddhists," http://www.pewforum.org/2012/12/18/global-religious-landscape-buddhist.
25 Elizabeth Abbot, *A History of Celibacy* (Cambridge: Da Capo Press, 2011), 175–6.
26 *Jesus: A Revolutionary Biography* (New York: HarperOne, 1994), 5.
27 *How Jesus Became God: The Exaltation of a Jewish Preacher from Galilee* (New York: HarperOne, 2015), 86–128.
28 Luke 3:21.
29 John 3:28–-30.
30 Paul Johnson, *A History of the Jews* (New York: Harper, 1987), 150.
31 Mark 3:31-4.
32 Reza Aslan, *Zealot: The Life and Times of Jesus of Nazareth* (New York: Random House, 2014), 37.
33 Lerner, *The Creation*, 177–8.
34 Karen Armstrong, *A History of God* (New York: Ballantine Books, 1993), 81.
35 Luke 8:48.
36 Luke 14:26.
37 Mark 6:30–40.
38 Mark 8:22–6.
39 Matthew 13:45.
40 Matthew 13:31–2.
41 Matthew 13:24–30.
42 Crossan, *Jesus*, 219.
43 Matthew 22:29–30.
44 *Zealot*, 37.
45 Johnson, *A History*, 126.
46 Matthew 1:16.
47 *The Illegitimacy of Jesus: A Feminist Theological Interpretation of the Infancy Narratives* (Sheffield, United Kingdom: Sheffield Phoenix Press, 2006), 67.
48 Ibid., 68–9.
49 Ibid., 169.
50 Matthew 23:9.
51 Schaberg, *The Illegitimacy*, 76–7.

52 Jennifer Green, "Pondering a Sexual Jesus," *Ottowa Citizen*, April 3, 2007, https://www.pressreader.com/canada/ottawa-citizen.

53 Armstrong, *Buddha*, 20–2, *The Battle for God* (New York: Ballantine Books, 2000), 169.

54 Rader, *Breaking Boundaries*, 37.

55 Sabina Flanagan, *Hildegard of Bingen: A Visionary Life* (New York: Barnes and Noble Books, 1989), 25.

56 Ibid., 37.

57 Hildegard of Bingen, *Scivias*, trans. Mother Columbha Hart and Jane Bishop (New York: Paulist Press, 1990), 428.

58 Lerner, *The Creation*, 59–61.

59 Flanagan, *Hildegard*, 86.

60 *Hildegard of Bingen's Medicine*, trans. Karen Anderson Strehlow (Rochester, Vermont: Bear & Bear Company, 1988), xi.

61 Ibid., x.

62 Judith Lissauer Cromwell, *Florence Nightingale, Feminist* (Jefferson, North Carolina: McFarland & Company, Inc., 2013), 64–5.

63 Ibid., 82.

64 Lynn M. Hamilton, *Florence Nightingale: A Life Inspired* (Wyatt North Publishing, 2016), 43–7.

65 Cromwell, *Florence Nightingale*, 121.

66 Ibid., 123.

67 Ibid., 7.

68 Janice P. Nimura, *The Doctors Blackwell: How Two Pioneering Sisters Brought Medicine to Women and Women to Medicine* (New York: W. W. Norton & Company, 1921), 216.

69 Ibid., 201.

70 J. R. Milton, "Locke's Life and Times," *The Cambridge Companion to Locke*, ed. Vere Chappell (Cambridge: Cambridge University Press, 1994), 9.

71 Ibid., 8–9.

72 President Barack Obama, "Presidential Memorandum—Hospital Visitation," April 15, 2010, https://obamawhitehouse.archives.gov/the-press-office/presidential-memorandum-hospital-visitation.

73 *Love: A History* (New Haven: Yale University Press, 2011), 255–6.

74 Samantha Brennan and Bill Cameron, "Is Marriage Bad for Children? Rethinking the Connection Between Having Children, Romantic Love, and Marriage," *After Marriage*, Ed. Elizabeth Brake, 85.

75 Richard Thaler and Cass Sunstein, *Nudge: Improving Decisions About Health, Wealth, and Happiness* (New Haven: Yale University Press, 2008), 7.

76 *The Atlantic*, October 20, 2020, https://www.theatlantic.com/family/archive/2020/10/people-who-prioritize-friendship-over-romance.

77 Josh Duboff, "Demi Lovato Finally Feels Free." *Bazaar*, May, 2020, 140–4.

78 Rachel Paula Abrahamson, "Anderson Cooper Announces Birth of Second Child," NBC News, February 10, 2022, https://www.nbcnews.com/news/us-news/anderson-cooper-announces-birth-second-child.

79 Andrew Solomon, "How Polyamorists and Polygamists Are Changing Family Norms," *New Yorker*, March, 2021, https://www.newyorker.com/magazine/2021/03/22/how-polyamorists-and-polygamists-are-challenging-family-norms.

80 "Is Marriage Bad?", After Marriage, 86.

81 Ibid., 87.

82 *Beyond (Straight and Gay)*, 131.

83 See Elizabeth A. Kingdom, "Cohabitation Contracts: A Socialist-Feminist Issue," *Journal of Law and Society* 15:1 (1988): 77–89.

84 The Limits of Contract: Regulating Personal Relationships in a Marriage-Free State," *After Marriage*, 57.

85 Ibid., 58.

86 Ibid., 77.

Glossary: Definitions

agapetae: In the fourth through the sixth centuries, Christian virgins who took vows of chastity and cohabited with celibate men, sharing prayer, study, and household duties. This word can be revived.

alloparent: A nonrelative who assumes a parental role. Biologist Edward Wilson coined word in 1975.[1] In alloparenting arrangements, childcare duties are shared. Alloparent-based families do not require marriage.

alternatives to marriage: Elizabeth Brake lists as viable replacements for wedlock "close dyadic friendships, small group family units, or networks of multiple, significant, nonexclusive relationships that provide emotional support, caretaking and intimacy." Philosopher Jeremy Garrett adds "living singly, cohabiting, and other forms of nonrecognized partnering."[2]

amatonormativity: Brake uses this term for the belief that "romantic love is the normal or ideal condition for a human life—so lives that don't include it are imperfect or abnormal."[3] She combines two Latin words: *amare* (to love) and *norma* (a yardstick by which things are measured).

asexual: A modifier describing people who lack erotic feelings or the urge to act on them. To the extent that they are unified, asexual people see themselves as having an orientation that involves attraction rather than compelling physiological response. Like others whose relationships do not follow connubial prescriptions, asexuals should have access to socioeconomic benefits that now hinge on wedlock.[4]

bachelor: In Roman times, a youth of either sex employed by a farmer. In the Middle Ages "*bas chevalier*" denoted an attendant knight who did not yet have his own banner. In Geoffrey Chaucer's *The Canterbury Tales* "bachelor" means an unmarried man.[5] This may be the word's first use as such. Modernity added implications of callowness.

bachelor focal: Homes occupied by never-married people are often seen as makeshift, transitory, or aberrant. I suggest using this modifier to honor households run by bachelors, with bachelorhood as a formative principle.

bachelor-phobia: A term for groundless disapproval of bachelors. Common in modern self-help literature, bachelor-phobia stems from a belief that any man who resists marriage is irresponsible, shallow, and/or emotionally delayed.

biomom/biodad: Poet Adrienne Rich (1929–2012) argued against classifying women as "mothers" or "childless women," since "many of the greatest mothers have not been biological."[6] The same can be said of "the childless man" and the "father." The terms "biomom" and "biodad," remind us that motherhood and fatherhood can expand beyond the procreative. The designations come from Ashton Applewhite.[7]

community: Christopher Ryan and Cacilda Jethá elegantly define this word as "the all-important web of meaning we spin around each other—the inescapable context within which anything truly *human* has taken place."[8]

consensual nonmonogamy: The practice of honestly conducting nonmonogamous sexual relationships, with the assumption that such behavior is neither criminal nor socially disruptive. The designation's original source is unclear.

continuum of singleness: Medievalist Cordelia Beattie posits that instead of considering unmarried people as a homogenous mass, historians should conceptualize a variety of lifestyles and philosophies occurring along a spectrum. She suggests a continuum of nonmarital people, from the totally marriage averse to the marriage supportive.[9]

deeply invested: Marriage often serves as a metaphor for seriousness, as when someone is said to be "married" to a career, job, or cause. "Deeply invested," as in, "he is deeply invested in his company," is less biased.

egalitarianist: This adjective refers to people who believe in both gender and relationship-status equality.

embracing nonmarital life: Encyclopedia entries, multivolume monographs, and biographies of nonmarital people generally state that these individuals "did not marry." Often, saying that someone embraced (i.e., chose) nonmarital life is more accurate.

ever-married: The status conferred on widowed and/or divorced people, which comes from the belief that being temporarily married makes them permanently better. Today ever-married privileges include citizenship rights, Social Security benefits, and access to a former spouse's income.

family: Two or more people united by beliefs and attachments, whose definitive feature is the totality of relationship(s) as evidenced by the principals' dedication, caring, and self-sacrifice over time. With some tweaking, this definition comes from the New York State Court of Appeals decision, *Braschi v. Stahl Associates Co.* (1989).

Flinstonization: Ryan and Jethá invented this term for anachronistic narratives about prehistoric human beings. As television's animated Flintstones were a "modern stone-age family," ancestors who lived 40,000 years ago often resemble modern western households in social scientists' accounts: "The generally accepted myth of the origins and nature of human sexuality is not merely factually flawed but destructive . . . This false narrative distorts our sense of our capacities and needs. It amounts to false advertising for a garment that fits almost no one."[10]

fragile-family advocacy: Social anthropologist Anna Gavanas uses this term for individuals and groups who assert that breadwinning is the centerpiece of masculinity, masculinity is vital to marriageability, marriage evinces self-esteem, and self-esteem is transmitted from biological fathers to sons within a nuclear family.[11]

friend/friendship: David Konstan defines friendship as "a mutually intimate, loyal, and loving bond between two or a few persons that is understood not to derive primarily from membership in a group normally marked by native solidarity."[12] This fine anthropological denotation fails to isolate friendship's essential features. Philosopher Laurence Thomas does so, placing intimacy stemming from mutual self-disclosure at the heart of friendship.[13]

the Geller Test: This is a way to classify films. A movie passes the Geller Test if it lacks any plotline involving a proposal, engagement, or prewedding event (e.g., a bridal shower, bachelor party, or rehearsal dinner). There must also be at least two never-married characters with names, who talk to each other without referring to matrimony.

glad-to-be-married propaganda: Married authors' self-congratulatory writing that exudes and demands enthusiasm for wedlock.

interdependent: The Canadian province of Alberta's 2002 Adult Interdependent Relationship Act applies this modifier to two people sharing a hopefully permanent bond, who cohabit and participate in each other's lives. Interdependence qualifies such partners for legal benefits, including health-care coverage. Neither amorous feelings nor sex are required. While it began as a designation for one partnership, "interdependent" can refer to anyone who is seriously, protractedly bonded with one or more individuals.[14]

lifespace pioneers: Bella DePaulo invented this term for adults who build neighborhoods and homes to fit their temperaments rather than the other way around. DePaulo's research reveals many successful experiments: cohabiting groups of friends, relatives who live as neighbors, and collectives of farm-like properties with separate dwellings.[15]

living apart together (LAT): Of uncertain origin, this designation refers to unmarried lovers who maintain separate residences.

living together part-time (LTP): This modifier applies to unwed lovers who balance cohabitation with separate living.

marital evangelism: The practice of agitating on marriage's behalf. This involves publicizing wedlock as a sacrosanct institution and proselytizing for marriage-based families at the individual and legal levels. Marital evangelism traffics in the belief that wedlock is an indispensable relationship supportive of culture everywhere, in the same way. That this is false, that marriage contains variances and contradictions inevitable in a 5,000-year-old institution, does not faze wedlock's missionaries.

marital exceptionalism: The belief that matrimonial relationships are utterly unique, and marriage provides positives that no other relationship can.

marital fallacy: The misconception that amorous love between adults and wedlock are the same thing or are inextricably connected.

marital supremacism: An ideology infused with the belief that married people are better than those who do not wed, that this superiority entitles licensed couples to special privileges, and that nonmarital children are damaged. Like most supremacist ideologies, this one generates publicity that claims a commitment to healthy self-affirmation.

marriage-centric: A view of the past or present that renders matrimony the *sine qua none* of life and the central, stabilizing institution of culture.

marriage dissident: Someone aware of the marriage principle who rejects and/or works against it.

marriage free: This modifier appears on the website, Unmarried Equality, which social worker Sarah Wright and Gordon Morris, CEO of the Toye Corporation, maintain. Unmarried Equality uses the term for "people who have made a conscious decision not to get married or are actively opposed to marriage."[16]

marriage-free state: A nation that does not have legal marriage. Clare Chambers uses the term in her argument for eliminating government-accredited matrimony, "since when the state recognizes marriage it endorses a particular and deeply controversial conception of the good."[17]

marriage fundamentalism: This term comes from the Washington, DC think tank Family Story, which was founded by social entrepreneur Nicole Sussner Rodgers. Family Story defines marriage fundamentalism as:

> a set of beliefs and values that view the "traditional" married family—a man and woman in their first marriage—as the most fundamental unit of society. Marriage fundamentalists believe that: these families are "the best" type of family, particularly for children, but also for adults and society; poverty and other economic risks are largely avoidable today if people stop making "bad choices," particularly the supposed bad choice to become a parent without being married.[18]

marriage mystique: The excessive sentimentalization of matrimony accompanied by the belief that it is fulfilling in ways that defy comprehension, articulation, or proof.

marriage opportunist: An individual who does not believe in matrimony but weds for access to legal benefits, increased financial opportunities, status, and accolades.

marriage principle: The belief that most people should, will, and do marry. The notion is threefold: first, human beings are amenable to functioning in couples, so the romantic twosome is an optimal worldwide lifestyle. Second, matrimony rightly endows couples with honor. Third, those who don't gravitate toward marriage should.

marriage proponent: Gavanas uses this term for people who "construct the monogamous, heterosexual, and married lifestyle as the hallmark of gendered normality, maturity, and morality."[19] Marriage proponents do not necessarily march or fundraise on behalf of wedlock. They simply insist that unwed adults are aberrant and unsatisfied.

marriage refugee: Someone in a marriage-centric community who leaves to avoid coerced unions or the social compulsion to wed. The term includes adults who flee marriages where they are physically unsafe or where coupledom's norms feel intolerably repressive as well as those ending marriages who leave to avoid financial coercion.[20]

marriage renegade: A spouse who relinquishes marriage's conventions and privileges in pursuit of something that connubial life seems to preclude.

marriage system: The institutionalized practice of allotting resources to married people. These include but are not limited to citizenship, employment, household necessities, legal dispensations, tax breaks, health benefits, and social prestige. The marriage system has proffered different rewards at various points in history. But it continuously differentiates between married and unmarried individuals, between once-wed and never-wed people, and between children born in or out of wedlock.

marriagesplain: The explanation of something by a married person or persons, typically to an unmarried individual or individuals, in a condescending, patronizing manner.

matrimania: DePaulo invented this word for the excessive celebration of wedded coupling and the accompanying sense that life outside marriage is empty and meaningless.[21]

matrimonial territory/space: Sociologist Fatima Mernissi uses "sexual territoriality" to denote the gendering of space as a means to safeguard masculine privilege.[22] Similarly, matrimonial spaces secure conjugal privilege. Matrimonial spaces include bridal registries, wedding chapels, and neighborhoods designed to accommodate marrieds.

nonmarital: Without a collective designation, people distanced from wedlock are defined by what we are not. We are not spouses, though we frequently have long-term amorous partnerships. We are single, though we often nurture close friendships, including kinship bonds. We are divorced rather than evolving into a different family configuration. Common descriptors convey deficiency, fragmentation, or passivity. The adjective "nonmarital" describes people born without wedded bioparents, individuals who do not aspire to matrimony or view themselves in matrimonial terms, bachelors, spinsters, singletons, marriage renegades, and marriage refugees.

nonmarital child: Of unclear origin, this term refers to children born outside of wedlock. It replaces the condemnatory "illegitimate," which stems from longstanding legal definitions of such children as *fillius nullius* ("child of no one").

nonmarital consciousness: This is nonmarital people's awareness that we belong to a group that has endured injustice—a condition not natural but culturally enforced.

nonstandard households: These are homes occupied by nonmarital constellations of people. I do not know if Michael Warner coined it, but I first encountered the term in his writing.[23]

normalization movements: Social crusades that encourage people to adapt behaviors of those in the numerical majority. They assume that something statistically dominant is good and desirable. Actually, numbers indicate nothing about the intrinsic worth of a particular choice, relationship, or way of living.

pair bond: Anthropologist Agustín Fuentes observes that "Unfortunately, in our society we often confuse 'pair bond' with 'marriage.' They are not the same thing." He perceives "two types of pair bonds: the social pair bond and the sexual pair bond."[24] The first is a relationship between two people that differs from most friendships in its intensity and mutual investment. The second contains erotic intimacy.

parenting partners: Attorney Darren Spedale uses this denotation for uncoupled people bringing up children together. They are not linked to each other, or, necessarily, the children by marriage, blood, or formal adoption. What unifies them is shared concern for the kids in their lives.[25]

politics of shame: With this phrase Warner refers to a host of governmental policies and cultural practices that regulate sexuality, encouraging one identity (the marital), and setup (lifelong coupledom). Extolling this standard denigrates those who don't share it. Warner posits, "It does not seem to be possible to think of oneself as normal without thinking that some other kind of person is pathological."[26] Shame politics thereby encourage feelings of disgrace in nonmarital people.

postmarital extortion: This is the process of obtaining money from an ex-spouse through legal coercion. It rests on the premise that once-wed people deserve economic support for having been temporarily married.

promiscuous: Ryan and Jethá use this word to describe adults who conduct a few simultaneous sexual relationships. They note that the Latin root of promiscuous is *miscere*, which means, "to mix." Since it was a feature of prehistoric cultures, promiscuity is traditional. It need not and usually has not involved sex between strangers.[27] Promiscuous people then, are those with mixed tastes, rather than wanton, sex-addicted miscreants. The more fashionable modifier for maintaining a few erotic relationships is "polyamory."

right not to marry: Kaiponanea T. Matsumura asserts that this is a crucial, albeit ignored freedom. When corporations incentivize marriage by making it a prerequisite for health insurance, and the Internal Revenue Service excuses spouses from paying estate taxes, they trounce this right.

SALA: Sociologist Kris Marsh created this acronym for those who are "single and living alone—that is, without a 'significant other' or romantic partner."[28]

self-partnered: Writer Eva Victor uses this term in lieu of "single" to evoke the richness of life outside a romantic partnership. What sets her definition apart from similar modifiers is that the self-partnered person directs erotic, psychic, and material resources that would typically go toward a romantic partner toward themself.[29]

sex-and-everything-else-partner (SEEP): Modern marriage entails the assumption of a reciprocal identity that demands living life as a team. People who see their spouses as "Sex-and-everything-else-partners" accept this arrangement.[30]

single man's/single woman's family: Historian Naomi Tadmor uses this term to denote any nonconjugal family unit. She contends that both the term and family configuration are traditional.[31]

singleton: Eric Klinenberg uses this noun for anyone who lives alone. He distinguishes between singletons and singles, who are unwed but may reside with housemates, children, or other cohabiters.[32]

singlism: This is DePaulo's word for the underrating and undervaluing of adults who are not in romantic partnerships (marital or nonmarital).[33]

spinster: Originally used for never-wed women, among whom spinning textiles was a vital source of income, this word lost its occupational meaning between 1550 and 1750. By the late sixteenth century, it neutrally denoted any never-married post-adolescent woman. In the eighteenth century, it became disparaging. As Carrie Jenkins observes, "spinster" continues to connote a "dull, sexless woman who is probably deeply weird in some way."[34] I use "spinster" for any productive woman who perceives herself apart from the marriage system, finding self-realization outside of nuptial roles. Reclaiming this term is one way to weaken the dominant cultural narrative that naturalizes marriage.

spinster-focal: This is an adjective for households in which spinsters are influential and respected. In such homes, spinsterhood is an organizing principle and a set of values transmitted to the younger generation.

spinster-phobia: The noun denotes a range of irrationally negative feelings about spinsters. Spinster-phobia can take the form of pity, fear, contempt, and various combinations of these emotions. It can be overt or subtle and find expression in offhand remarks or institutionalized biases.

spousal imprinting: This socialization process shows children and adolescents how to be married. Modes of spousal imprinting include speaking in the plural, doing an hourly telephonic check-in, and consulting one's husband or wife before scheduling plans.

therapeutic marriage-centrism: A philosophy that generates maritally focused self-help regimens, which ignore wedlock's historical, legal, and social dimensions. Instead, such programs stress how people in married couples feel and express those emotions to each other. I derive the term from Ruth Rosen's "therapeutic feminism."[35]

unmarriages: Ruth Mazo Karras coined this word for medieval nonmarital sexual relationships. These included men of means supporting concubines; erotic relationships between employers and servants; and males and females who "frequented" each other: "probably the best translation in early twenty-first century parlance is hanging out with."[36] Unmarriages also include erotic relationships between priests and male or female companions; cohabiting lovers, and, in late medieval Norway, adults who lived together as what today might be called domestic partners. While Mazo Karras refers only to the Middle Ages, her noun can be appropriated by today's nonmarital lovers.

(Endnotes)

1   *Sociobiology: The New Synthesis* (Cambridge: Belknap Press of the Harvard University Press, 1975).

2   Quoted in Simon Cābulea May, "Liberal Neutrality and Civil Marriage," *After Marriage,* Ed. Elizabeth Brake, 11.

3   Quoted in Jenkins, *What Love Is,* 65.

4   Julie Sondra Decker, *The Invisible Orientation: An Introduction to Asexuality* (New York: Skyhorse Publishing, 2014), 28, 60, 150.

5   "Where as thise bacheleris synge 'allas,'/Whan that they fynden any adversitee/In love, which nys childyssh vanytee." "The Merchant's Tale," 1274–6, *The Riverside Chaucer,* ed. Larry D. Benson.

6   *Of Woman Born: Motherhood as Experience and Institution* (New York: W. W. Norton & Company, 1986), 252.

7   *Cutting Loose,* 175.

8   *Sex at Dawn,* 167.

9   "Living as a Single Person: Marital Status, Performance, and the Law in Late Medieval England," *Women's History Review* 17 (2008): 327–40.

10   *Sex at Dawn,* 33.

11   *Fatherhood Politics in the United States: Masculinity, Sexuality, Race, and Marriage* (Urbana: University of Illinois Press, 2004), 77–8.

12   *Friendship in the Classical World* (Cambridge: Cambridge University Press, 1997), 1.

13   "Friendship," *Synthese,* 72 (1987): 217–36.

14   Polikoff, *Beyond (Straight and Gay),* 112–14.

15   *How We Live Now: Redefining Home and Family in the 21st Century* (New York: Atria Books).

16   "Marriage Free," Unmarried Equality, http://www.unmarried.org.

17   "The Limits of Contract: Regulating Personal Relationships in a Marriage-Free State," *After Marriage,* ed. Elizabeth Brake, 51.

18   Family Story, https://familystoryproject.org.

19   *Fatherhood Politics,* 44.

20   See "Refugee Facts: What is a Refugee?", The United Nations Refugee Agency, https://www.unrefugees.org/refugee-facts/what-is-a-refugee.

21   See blogs such as "The Perverse Effects of Matrimania" and "Matrimania Mars the Olympics" at www.BellaDePaulo.com.

22   *Beyond the Veil: Male-Female Dynamics in a Modern Muslim Society* (Cambridge, Massachusetts: Schenkman, 1975).

23   *The Trouble with Normal,* 54.

24   "On Marriage and Pair Bonds: Humans Bond, Love, and Marry Heterosexually and Socially," *Psychology Today*, May 9, 2012, https://www.psychologytoday.com/us/blog/busting-myths-about-human-nature/201205/marriage-and-pair-bonds.

25   Alex Davidson, "Q&A: Darren Spedale, Co-Parenting Pioneer, Talks About His Latest Venture," *The Advocate*, December 5, 2013, https://www.advocate.com.

26   *The Trouble with Normal*, 60.

27   *Sex at Dawn*, 44–5.

28   *The Love Jones Cohort: Single and Living Alone in the Black Middle Class* (Cambridge: Cambridge University Press, 2023), xiii.

29   "Self-Partnered: Spoil Self," *In Style*, February 2020, 66–8.

30   DePaulo, Singled Out, 4.

31   *Family and Friends in Eighteenth-Century England: Household, Kinship, and Patronage* (Cambridge: Cambridge University Press, 2007), 37.

32   Klinenberg uses the word throughout his monograph, *Going Solo*, presuming that readers understand its meaning.

33   "Introducing Singlism," *Singlism*, 14–18.

34   *What Love Is*, 141.

35   *The World Split Open: How the Modern Women's Movement Changed America* (New York: Penguin Books, 2000), 315.

36   *Unmarriages*, 157.

Acknowledgments

I am grateful to Leora Tanenbaum for convincing me to write this book and helping to conceptualize the proposal, which Rob Dowling skillfully edited. Mary Collins offered excellent advice at an early stage. Other colleagues at Central Connecticut State University gave their time. My sister, Heidi Hartwig, my soulmate, Katherine Sugg, and my guide, Candace Barrington, read every draft and gave superb feedback. These brilliant women are a font of good will from which flowed recommendations for books and articles, links, quotes, newspaper-clippings, revisions, revised revisions, and late-night texts. They showed me their works in progress, as did Burlin Barr, whose quiet encouragement was invaluable. Eric Leonidas was a source of warmth, intelligence, and hospitality. Bill Doolittle provided crucial technical support on several occasions. I appreciate Stephen Cohen and Dean Robert Wolff, who arranged for me a semester of unpaid leave. The university subsequently granted me a year-long sabbatical, making the manuscript's completion possible.

I am indebted to John Farrell, a loving friend who shows me how it's done. Edward Currie explained some fine points about early medieval literature while sharing with me his exciting scholarship (and his devotion to a certain professor). Even an author of non-fiction needs a muse; apparently Blanford Parker is mine. He helped with the subtler Catholic concepts and gave me unwavering encouragement. Jeffrey Stern and Frances Rodriguez gave me everything—most importantly, Elias, Eva, and Eden, who superintend the education of my heart.

James O'Connor understood that I came with this crew. He tolerated my strange hours and shared with me his honed ability to differentiate between authentic and spurious science. He also taught me Newton's laws of motion while connecting my computer and printer with the right cable. We might now have dinner without discussing forced spousal reconciliation or England's 1650 Commonwealth Adultery Act, but I make no promises.

Amy Schilling's yoga classes helped me to remain physically and mentally intact during long writing stints. And I cannot thank Dayanne Lopes Libório enough for taking care of my house while showing me how a serious businesswoman works.

I appreciatively recall an anonymous *Publisher's Weekly* reviewer who suggested that I detail the benefits of non-marital life. Today, thinkers from across the disciplines do this in their work on non-marital families, non-standard households, and legal disparities between marital and non-marital Americans. I'm grateful to those cited here, several of whom have communicated with me. Of the scholars mentioned, Bella DePaulo stands alone. For thirty years she has been the voice of our nation's uncoupled population, bringing clarity, humor, and insight to the issue of relationship-status discrimination. It seems that wherever I went during my mental travels, she had been there first. I appreciate the opportunity to share my conclusions with her. I'm sorry I cannot do this with the late Barbara Seaman, whose influence on me keeps deepening, or the late Joan Goldstein, who placed a premium on information, even when it proved inconvenient.

Before embarking on this project, I had lost my bearings as a writer. John Coulter helped me find them. I will always owe him a debt of gratitude. I am thankful for Jarred Weisfeld's openness to my ideas and his stabilizing presence behind the scenes.

Hannah Bennett did a masterful job with the behemoth I handed her; when she stepped away, Rene Sears picked up the editing process without missing a beat. In the book's late stages Ashley Calvino calmly, graciously handled a plethora of details. To this team I am especially grateful.

As I write this, Alvin Geller and Marcia Geller are probably sitting in a Westchester diner, gossiping thoughtfully and reminiscing about the old neighborhood. After an unpleasant marital stint that produced me, they segued from coupledom into a long, close friendship. They exemplify the truth that married is not best. During the writing process I received valuable support from each of them. I dedicate the book to both of them.